AN INTERNATIONAL CIRCUS AFFAIR

Modern Vaudeville Press
113 E Mayland St
Philadelphia, PA 19144
United States of America
www.ModernVaudevillePress.com

info@modernvaudevillepress.com

Print ISBN: 978-1-958604-24-3

EBook ISBN: 978-1-958604-25-0

Library of Congress: 2024917416

By Jeff Raz, with Stephanie Greenspan, Ori Quesada, and Devin Holt.

Edited by Kim Campbell with Benjamin Domask-Ruh and Thom Wall.

AN INTERNATIONAL CIRCUS AFFAIR

How a Nanjing Acrobat in San Francisco Changed American Circus Forever

By Jeff Raz
with Stephanie Greenspan, Ori Quesada, and Devin Holt

Modern Vaudeville Press

This book is dedicated to the people from all over the world who have created a thriving, fifty-year-old circus community in the San Francisco Bay Area.

CONTENTS

Act One: Before the Journey to the West

Act Two: East meets West

Act Three: Stars of the Future

Act Four: From Sunshine to Stage Lights

Act Five: Each One, Teach One

Act Six: Journey to the East

FOREWORD

I sometimes tell people that I have done four things in my life.

First, I improved circus in Nanjing.

Next, I took Chinese circus to Australia.

Third, I brought Chinese circus to America.

Lastly, I took American circus to China.

Those are the four things I have done. They were not all easy. Some took a great amount of effort.[1]

---

1   Lu, Yi., Holt, D. (2023). *Training is Bitter*. Periodgraph Press.

AUTHOR'S NOTE

The City by the Bay meets the City on the Yangtze

This is a tale of two cities. Two cities separated by 6,200 miles, by language, by culture, by history—but connected through a shared love for a particular art-form: acrobatics. Or, in the American parlance, *the circus arts*. This book tells the story of a 20-year acrobatic affair between two very different cities, Nanjing and San Francisco, and how that relationship profoundly changed circus in the United States and in China.

Sitting in a comfortable chair in a nice tent or theater, watching a circus show by companies like Cirque du Soleil or The 7 Fingers, this relationship might not be visible to you… but without the circus affair between San Francisco and Nanjing, those shows would look very different. And much of that difference is rooted in one man's arrival in San Francisco—the Nanjing Acrobatic Troupe's master trainer, Lu Yi, on the invitation of Judy Finelli of the Pickle Family Circus.

Judy Finelli, master juggler turned circus director, saw that if the new wave of American circuses were going to thrive, they needed great acrobatic trainers. She dreamed of bringing master teachers from Russia and China—two countries with rich circus traditions that she deeply respected—to the USA. In San Francisco, these masters would give American acrobats the best of both worlds.

Lu Yi, child acrobat turned trainer and director, saw that Chinese circus was losing its audience and that Chinese acrobats were losing their drive.

He dreamt of starting over by training an exuberant, passionate troupe of American circus performers and taking them back to China. There, they would attract bigger and younger circus audiences while fostering a new generation of young Chinese athletes excited about becoming professional acrobats.

Neither of these dreams materialized as planned. Cross-cultural communication is fraught, even for people who share a passion. "East meets West" is a convenient way of describing this story, one that I will use occasionally in this book, but these simple words are loaded with ignorance and stereotypes. Paradoxically, some of the stereotypes we had of one another—the wise and inscrutable Chinese teachers and the creative, impressionable Americans—have facilitated the circus affair that Judy Finelli and Lu Yi started, a relationship that changed the circus arts.

. . .

The history that this book explores is ongoing and far reaching, but it was not supposed to be this way. *An International Circus Affair* started life as *Lu Yi's Acrobatic Training Techniques*.

In late 2022, Lu Yi's autobiography, *Training is Bitter*, written with Devin Holt,[2] was released. Devin and I took some signed copies to the Berkeley bungalow that Lu Yi shared with his wife, Wang Hong Zhu. After admiring the books for a few minutes, Lu Yi, a man more interested in the future than the past, said, "There needs to be another book, a training manual."

---

2   Devin Holt worked with Lu Yi as an acrobatic student and then as co-author of his autobiography *Training is Bitter*. Devin shared his knowledge of Lu Yi's history and, using his MA in journalism, was our in-house writing guru.

Devin and I set to work, enlisting Dr. Stephanie Greenspan,[3] an aerialist, physical therapist, and researcher who studies circus injuries and prevention internationally; and Ori Doria-Quesada,[4] who started acrobatic training at age seven and now holds Lu Yi's old job training the Youth Circus at San Francisco Circus Center. I agreed to be the head writer, leveraging my experience with Lu Yi as my trainer with the Pickle Circus in the 1990s, and then as my colleague at San Francisco Circus Center. We asked Chad Benjamin Potter,[5] my former student at The Clown Conservatory who currently works as an events producer, to help fundraise for the project.

Chad's questions about widening the scope of the book gained traction when we realized that Lu Yi, who was in his 80s and managing the effects of Parkinson's disease, often struggled to communicate in our interviews. We started interviewing people influenced by Lu Yi—a list that kept expanding as we found more and more lives that the Nanjing/San Francisco affair has profoundly affected. We had a new book.

Thom Wall at Modern Vaudeville Press liked an early draft and joined the team as our publisher and editor, a perfect match as Thom is a world-class juggler as well as a writer and historian. Lu Yi's daughters, Lu Yue and Lu Na, helped translate during our interviews with their father.

---

3   Dr. Stephanie Greenspan also helps some of Lu Yi's former students stay healthy as a performing arts physical therapist in San Francisco. She did many of the interviews and shares her knowledge of what happens to bones, muscles, and tendons during circus training and performance in this book.
4   Ori Quesada started training with Lu Yi as a child and now performs nationally while holding Lu Yi's old job as Head Trainer of the San Francisco Youth Circus. He did some of the interviews and brought his deep knowledge as a student, performer, and teacher of Chinese acrobatics to this story.
5   Chad Benjamin Potter is an events producer who trained in clowning and acrobatics with Lu Yi's student Xiaohong Weng at San Francisco Circus Center. He broadened the scope of this book and helped with the business of creating it.

I will be your ringmaster, introducing fascinating people and letting them tell you their stories. I'll share my own thoughts and opinions, as well as some of my experiences when I become part of this history halfway through the book.

. . .

An International Circus Affair is divided into six acts, and between these acts, we will shine a spotlight on some of the most interesting people in this tale of two cities.

Act I – I will introduce two of our protagonists, Judy Finelli and Lu Yi, and give you a sense of the circus world in their respective countries before their fateful first conversation.

Act Two – You will meet the 1990 cast of the Pickle Family Circus, Lu Yi's first American students, and follow them through rehearsal and onto the road.

Act Three – Students of the original San Francisco Youth Circus now take center stage. They were Lu Yi's hope for the future, the performers for his American version of the Nanjing Acrobatic Troupe.

Act Four – A new creative partner for Lu Yi, choreographer Tandy Beal, takes a bow, along with a new cast of Pickle Circus performers, including "Pino & Razz."

Act Five – We will send in the clowns and...

Act Six – ...we will follow those clowns to China.

. . .

This book is not the last word, the full story, or the complete history of the circus affair between Nanjing and San Francisco. While writing and researching, we came to the conclusion that none of those lofty goals are possible—each person we interviewed had different opinions, and different "facts," about the same history. To quote the great San Francisco DJ and musician Sly Stone "[Historians are] trying to set the record straight. But a record's not straight, especially when you're not. It's a circle with a spiral inside it. Every time a story is told it's a test of memory and motive… It isn't evil but it isn't good. It's the name of the game but a shame just the same."[6]

Although the record of this history may not be straight, we have researched it in detail and given you footnotes so you can dig even deeper, circling and spiraling at your pleasure.

We all see with our own unique eyes, hear with our unique ears, and interpret with our individual hearts and minds. We all have our blind spots and biases; we have all lived a different history of the same events. Memory—even recent memory—is anything but objective. The joy of writing this book, and I hope the joy of reading it, is in the moments of love and the moments of conflict, which are sometimes one and the same.

Jeff Raz

Alameda, CA | November 2023

---

6   Light A. (2023, November 3). Rock'n'Soul: The amazing story of Sly & the Family Stone. *The New York Times*. A review of "Thank You (Falettinme Be Mice Elf Agin): A memoir." (Read that title out loud, phonetically, to get the name of one of Sly and the Family Stone's big hits.)

OVERTURE

A Journey to the West

Nanjing was a powerhouse in Chinese acrobatics by the early 1980s, led by the star performer turned innovative trainer and director: Lu Yi. Lu Yi had toured the world as a young acrobat, one of the few Chinese citizens allowed to travel abroad in the 50s and 60s. When he retired from performing, Lu Yi became the director of the Nanjing Acrobatic Troupe—and later, the youngest ever vice-president of acrobatics for all of China. These promotions were based largely on the strength of the surprising new acts he created alongside his skill in training world-class performers.

During this same time, 10,000 kilometers away, San Francisco's Pickle Family Circus was performing in city parks up and down the West Coast. The small non-profit circus was founded by members of an iconic political theater, the San Francisco Mime Troupe, so the Pickles combined some of the Troupe's worldview with traditional circus acts, putting clowns at the center of their shows. The Pickles operated under the philosophy that each member should make the same wage and that everyone should both perform and participate in running the business. They were socially conscious, partnering with local non-profit sponsors who received a portion of the revenue by selling advance tickets and running the game and food booths that dotted the midway—the bustling thoroughfare that leads the public to the performance arena.

In 1983, Lu Yi took some members of his Nanjing troupe to coach Australia's Circus Oz and the Flying Fruit Fly Circus. This was the first time Chinese acrobats had trained students in the West. This visit super-charged a vibrant

Australian circus culture; years later, Lu Yi received an award from the Australian government for his work there. In 1988, he brought his troupe to perform with the Big Apple Circus in New York.

It was after a Big Apple Circus performance in Stony Brook, New York that Lu Yi first met Judy Finelli, then director of the Pickle Family Circus. This book looks at the history that led to this important meeting, the relationship between circus artists from Nanjing and San Francisco that flourished from 1990 to 2010, and the continuing legacy of that relationship.

The artists Lu Yi encountered when he moved to San Francisco in 1990, including me, were only a generation away from the "flower power" days of the 1960s; the artists he brought with him from Nanjing were circus superstars. This was an unlikely pairing, one group had been raised in a circus system tightly controlled by the Chinese Communist Party, the other raised in the guerilla theater streets of San Francisco. Even with these challenges, and the fact that the collaboration began in an era of painful globalization, this affair continues today in a time of open hostility between the two countries. This is a rare long-term East-West cross-cultural success story, albeit one that is tempered by broken dreams.

...

Lu Yi's journey to America's west coast echoes the plot of *Journey to the West*,[7] a 16th century epic that is still immensely popular in China (but almost unknown in the U.S.). *Journey to the West* tells the saga of a monk, Tang Sanzang, who is sent on a trek west across China to get the holy Buddhist scriptures from India. Monkey King (*Sun Wukong*), a wild, wily, and creative monkey endowed with extraordinary powers, is coerced into journeying with

---

7   Wu, C. Jenner, W.J.F. (2005). *Journey to the West*. (C. Fair, Ed.). Disruptive Pub.

Sanzang as his bodyguard, along with Friar Sand (*Sha Wujing*) and Pigsy (*Zhu Bajië*). The monk Sanzang struggles to exert control over his bodyguards and at the same time teach them mastery over themselves.

In their 14 years of travel, the quartet forms a bond that gives Monkey King, Friar Sand, and Pigsy the discipline they need. Sanzang develops the spontaneity and wildness he lacks. This allows them to successfully finish their journey, get the Buddhist scriptures from India, and change China forever.

If Lu Yi is the Sanzang of our story, he is an orthodox priest of the 2,000-year-old discipline of Chinese acrobatics. Like Sanzang, Lu Yi gives his fellow travelers—the American circus performers he trained—the discipline they need to achieve their greatest powers. At the same time, these Americans encourage the flowering of Lu Yi's creativity, humor, and spontaneity. In our story, Lu Yi's students use his training to create new forms of American circus and join their teacher on a journey to the East that profoundly affects Chinese circus.

In *Journey to the West*, Sanzang travels west with his acrobatically adept trio of bodyguards in search of enlightenment. They face being ambushed by "tigers and wolves running in packs; thousand-foot dragons and ten-thousand fathom snakes breathing monstrous winds."

In our story, Lu Yi travels west with the acrobatic trio of Huang Zhen, Zhou Yue, and Xia Ke Min in search of a new style of circus. They face gyms full of American children and adults at retirement age who are still ignorant of acrobatic basics. They see the reality that hides behind American movies and learn the meaning of bankruptcy.

Both Sanzang and Lu Yi adapted to strange, sometimes dangerous environments. Both taught discipline and focus. Both honed their powers of creativity and wildness.

All circus acts, even the most outlandish clown routines, take dozens of hours of technical work to create and hundreds of repetitions to perfect. The creativity and art of circus is built on this training, on the orthodoxy of technique.

Our story is about a time when two different circus traditions from two different cities came together to blend a 2,000-year-old Chinese discipline with Californian creativity, mixing tradition with innovation.

ACT ONE:

BEFORE THE JOURNEY TO THE WEST

1. SHANGHAI AND NANJING

1947 - 1989

At the beginning of creation, a magic stone was formed at the top of the Mountain of Flowers and Fruit. The stone had a magic womb, which burst open one day to produce a stone egg. When the wind blew on this egg, it turned into a stone monkey, a stone monkey who could run, jump, eat, drink, and play with the other monkeys on the Mountain of Flowers and Fruit. One day, he discovered a wonderful cave for all the monkeys to live in and they named him Handsome Monkey King![8]

Eight-year-old Lu Yi, then called Lu Shun Yin, loved pretending he was the Chinese opera characters he saw on stage at *Dashijie* (The Big World), a large Shanghai entertainment center. Monkey King and the monk Sanzang were the most famous of them all.

It was 1947 and Lu Yi's family had recently left the war-torn Jiangsu Province for the relative safety of Shanghai. He and his brother joined the family business, selling hand-rolled cigarettes filled with tobacco from discarded butts. They spent their days at "The Big World" collecting raw materials for their father, watching the shows whenever they could get away with it.

Lu Yi tried to imitate the opera actors' martial arts and acrobatic moves. When he was 13, he was apprenticed to the Pan Family Acrobatic Group,

---

8   Wu, C. Jenner, W.J.F. (2005). *Journey to the West*. (C. Fair, Ed.). Disruptive Pub.

who performed at "The Big World." It wasn't Chinese Opera, his first love, but the acrobatic skills were his favorite part of an opera actor's repertoire. Lu Yi got his basic acrobatic training in a system that he later called "the three bitters"—bitterly long days (often 16 hours), bitterly hard concrete floors (without mats), and bitter beatings every day.

This is the root of Lu Yi's famous saying: "Training is bitter." However, when he became a trainer in Nanjing and eventually in San Francisco, his definition of "bitter" softened to include shorter days, more mats, and no beatings. He came to feel that training someone in acrobatics is "...projecting love onto that person—you are hard on them, and you love them, both at the same time."

In 1956, Lu Yi was chosen to join a large acrobatic troupe that represented China on a trip to the Soviet Bloc, performing for a month in each country, and later an eight-month tour to Africa.[9]

Using acrobatics as a diplomatic tool has a long history in China; in the first century B.C.E., the Chinese emperor sent an envoy, Zhang Qian, to "...promote economic and cultural exchange between the East and the West, and use acrobatics as a form of diplomacy to meet the needs of certain political conditions."[10] Circus skills were apparently also used in warfare—

---

9   "[Acrobat and historian Jingjing Xue] said that in October 1950, Chairman Mao Zedong, Premier Zhou Enlai and other leaders viewed performances by the best acrobats in China and, based on that night's performance, Premier Zhou proposed that a national acrobatic troupe be founded. The name-change from 'trick players' to 'acrobats' was a first sign of improved status. The government saw a political use for us: this troupe, the first of its kind in China, had visited the Soviet Union and set a precedent for artistic groups to travel abroad to perform and spread the message of the new China and become an avenue for cultural exchange with the outside world." Ala-Rashi, M. (2022). *China's Bending Bodies*. (T. Wall, N. Castro, Eds.) Modern Vaudeville Press.
10   Qifeng, F. (1985) *Chinese Acrobatics Through the Ages (Traditional Chinese arts and culture)*. China Books and Periodicals.

during a battle in 603 BCE, Xiong Yiliao is said to have juggled nine balls, which caused the opposing army to flee.[11]

After Lu Yi got home from the first international tour, the Pan acrobats, now called the Red Acrobatic Troupe, moved 300 kilometers up the Yangtze River to Nanjing, a city considered one of the Four Great Ancient Capitals of China. Inspired by the performers he'd met in Eastern Europe, Lu Yi began inventing new tricks for himself and his colleagues, such as kicking bowls and catching them on his head while riding a high unicycle balanced on a large ball. His most famous innovation, *Picking Flowers on top of a Head*, involved one acrobat bending back to pick up flowers with her teeth while standing on a bench balanced atop another acrobat's head.

Nanjing changed the young acrobat's life and Lu Shun Yin changed his name in Nanjing. "My parents gave me a name related to wealth and riches, but I wanted something… that spoke to my determination to be the best possible acrobat… That seemed more relevant, more honest. More like myself. So that's how I became Lu Yi. It means, roughly, persistence, or perseverance. Having a goal."[12]

In 1974, Lu Yi was put in charge of what was now officially called the Nanjing Municipal Acrobatic Troupe. He planned training programs for the students and, as Artistic Director, oversaw the choreography, costume design, and music for the performing company. Under his leadership, the Troupe thrived in China and on tours around the world. Soon, Lu Yi was getting invited to join powerful associations, to publish papers, and to judge national and international circus festivals.

---

11   Wall, T. (2019). *Juggling - From Antiquity to the Middle Ages: the forgotten history of throwing and catching.* Modern Vaudeville Press.

12   Lu, Yi., Holt, D. (2023). *Training is Bitter.* Periodgraph Press.

In 1983, Lu Yi and his colleagues from Pan circus days, Xia Ke Min and Lu Guang Rong, led workshops for 70 students in Australia, the first Chinese acrobats ever to provide training overseas. It was so successful that Australia's Prime Minister attended the final recital. In 1988, Lu Guang Rong moved to Australia and created the Flying Fruit Fly Circus training program, consummating a Nanjing/Melbourne circus affair that continues to this day, in parallel with the affair Lu Yi started two years later, half a world away in San Francisco.

In 1989, Lu Yi was 50 years old and, along with his job as the director of the Nanjing Acrobatic Troupe, he was also President, Artistic Director and Chairman of the Artist Jury in Nanjing, Vice-Chairman of the All-China Acrobatic Artists Association, a member of the China Cultural Union Committee and Chairman of the Jiangsu Acrobatic Artists Association. He was an important person in China, but he had to leave. He had to journey to the West.

2. NEW YORK AND MOSCOW

1953 to 1988

"I started juggling when I was six-years old. It became a secret thing I did because, in those days, it wasn't proper for a girl to juggle. I had learned to braid yarn in kindergarten; then, that summer, my brother and I played baseball and he had me play catch and bat on either side, so I became quasi-ambidextrous. One day I thought about braiding, and I realized that juggling was the same thing, only with balls instead of yarn. Years later, when I was at New York University taking a circus techniques course, I remembered how to juggle, and this gave me a leg up in class."

- Judy Finelli

Judy Finelli's juggling skills were prodigious—she became the first woman to compete at the International Jugglers' Association (IJA) stage competitions and became the IJA's first female president. She also married her New York University circus teacher, Hovey Burgess, and became his performing partner. Together they created Circo dell'Arte, a circus troupe that made money passing the hat in New York's Central Park. I vividly remember watching in awe as Judy and Hovey passed clubs at an IJA convention. They were the queen and king of juggling.

One day back in the late 1960's, Judy Burgess (Finelli) and Hovey Burgess were walking through New York's Chinatown when they saw an advertisement for the Lee Tang Wa Acrobatic Troupe from Taiwan. Hovey and Judy were circus fanatics. They had read books about Chinese acrobatics but had never seen this style of circus performed live. They bought tickets, went into the theater, quickly realizing that they were the only people in the audience who weren't Chinese. The house lights dimmed, the stage lights came up, and what they saw on that stage were circus skills beyond anything they had ever seen—or even heard about—in the United States.

Even though Chinese acrobatic companies, Chinese theater troupes, and Chinese opera groups had been performing in the U.S. for over a century, their audiences were mostly Chinese. This was not unusual then nor is it now: Universoul Circus plays to mostly Black audiences, partly because they advertise with Black-owned media and do group sales to Black organizations. Most of the people who go to Circo Hermanos Caballeros' shows are Latin as the majority of their publicity is in Spanish. There have also been painful reasons for these segregated audiences—even back in the days of the Gold Rush, San Francisco critics' reviews of Chinese musical accompaniment helped keep people who weren't Chinese away: "...the incessant noise... was so discordant and deafening, that a few minutes at a time was as long as anyone could stay in the place... The wailings of a thousand lovelorn cats, the screams, gobblings, brayings, and barkings of as many peacocks, turkeys, donkeys, and dogs, would not make a more discordant and agonizing concert than these Chinese musical performers [who] severely torture the white man to listen."[13]

Judy and Hovey, who many of us credit with being the godparents of the New Circus movement, watched the Lee Tang Wa Acrobatic Troupe's show in that Chinatown theater many times. They got to know the Chang Family Acrobats—one of the featured acts—becoming close with Eu Chang Ching, the principal acrobat.

---

13   Soule, F. Gihon, J. Nisbet, J. Garcia H.E. (1998) *The Annals of San Francisco.* Berkeley Hills Books.

Hovey and Judy also saw the Moscow Circus in the old Madison Square Garden and were "...blown away by both the clowning and acrobatics. Top of the line all the way." In 1970, as soon as travel to the Soviet Union was permitted, the couple went to Moscow and spent two weeks visiting the Moscow Circus School.

According to Judy Finelli, they didn't arrange anything beforehand: "I got the address, we just appeared at the school, and we were immediately welcomed. I spoke a little Russian and someone there spoke English, so we got along well. Because of the language connection, I felt more at home with the circus folks in Moscow than with the Chinese performers we'd met in New York. The Russians were very inventive with their use of circus, and it was like being in another world. I remember watching an amazing acrobatic class with a legendary teacher, Mr. Baumann—all he did was pull or push shoulders or hips in the middle of triple somersaults or double-doubles and suddenly the tricks would come out perfectly."

After visiting Moscow and getting to know the Lee Tang Wa Acrobatic Troupe, Judy had an idea: Circus in the U.S. needed a school and that school needed both Chinese and Russian trainers. She knew that even the wildest creativity in circus grows out of solid technique, and a combination of Chinese and Russian techniques would give creative American circus performers a base to work from.

It would be 14 years before Judy Finelli's dream of an American circus school would take the next step forward, and that step would be 3,000 miles from New York, in San Francisco.

3. BAGHDAD BY THE BAY AND THE BIG APPLE

California became the 31st state of the Union just two years after flecks of gold were found in the South Fork American River, 90 miles east of San Francisco. The Compromise of 1850 made California a free state, but "African Americans toiled as slaves in the [gold] mines… even though the state constitution banned slavery [and] laws were passed to force Native people into servitude, while authorities actively encouraged the slaughter of tribes."[14]

Even with these conditions and contradictions, the promise of gold attracted immigrant "49'ers" from all over the globe, including from China—and with these immigrants came their circus and theater. The 1850s saw the beginning of a long, deep, and turbulent history of Chinese performers who toured and emigrated to the Bay Area. The Chinese acrobats and actors who worked in California survived segregation, bigotry and eventually exclusion, setting the stage for Lu Yi's arrival 135 years later.

One of the earliest recorded performances was in October 1852, when a Chinese troupe offering "Magic, Necromancy, Juggling and Legerdemain" played at the American Theatre on Sansome Street in San Francisco. A week later, the 123 actors of the Tong Hook Tong Dramatic Company performed

---

14   *Gold Chains: the hidden history of slavery in California*. Retrieved February 6, 2024, from https://www.aclunc.org/sites/goldchains/

in the same theater, offering "The Defeated Revenge," "The Eight Genii," and other short plays.[15]

One San Francisco critic wrote: "The performance went on day and night, without intermission, and consisted principally of juggling, feats of dexterity and an exciting knife-throwing act... They [had short] dramatic performances, which were quite unintelligible to outside barbarians."[16]

A Cantonese opera from Guangdong province, where most of the early Chinese immigrants originated, was praised for "some very agile and dexterous ground and lofty tumbling, which seemed to be a portion of the plot... a great novelty... well worth seeing."[17]

In 1854, back in China, Cantonese opera star Li Wenmao, who specialized in acrobatic martial roles, organized his fellow actors in a revolt aimed at restoring the Ming dynasty. As a result, the Manchu government banned Cantonese opera for more than a decade. The combination of this ban and the promise of foreign wages lured many Cantonese opera players, as well as Chinese circus performers, to California.

A decade later, in 1864, the Central Pacific Railroad began hiring Chinese workers after facing a labor shortage that jeopardized the Transcontinental Railroad's construction. The Chinese population in California grew, but then the Civil War, dwindling sources of gold, and finally a labor surplus after the completion of the Transcontinental Railroad in 1869, made Chinese immigrants increasingly less welcome. In 1870, San Francisco passed some

---

15   Lei, D. (2003). The Production and Consumption of Chinese Theatre in Nineteenth-Century California. *Theatre Research International*. 28(3); 289-302. https://doi.org/10.1017/S0307883303001147
16   *ibid.*
17   *ibid.*

bizarre-sounding laws—the Cubic Air and the Stick ordinances—that targeted Chinese residents with precision. The first required lodging houses to have at least 500 cubic feet of air within its walls for each inhabitant. City officials only enforced this law in the crowded boarding houses of Chinatown. The second ordinance prohibited delivery of goods suspended from the ends of a pole, a method commonly used by Chinese merchants.[18]

Anti-Chinese sentiments were also reflected in American drama, including a Chinese character, Ah Sin, introduced by Bret Harte and Mark Twain in 1877. Ah Sin was a "moral cancer" and an "unsolvable political problem." Another character, from Henry Grimm's *The Chinese Must Go* (1879), embodied the stereotype of a cunning Chinese man competing for jobs against "honest Americans."[19] These characters are, of course, not actually Chinese—they were created by white writers based on a framework of economic and cultural fears rather than on actual observation. And they were almost certainly played by white actors, an issue that was still hot a century later when David Carradine got cast in *Kung Fu* instead of Bruce Lee. Representation and cultural appropriation are now, at long last, actively grappled with by theater, circus and other performing artists.

In the spring of 1882, the Chinese Exclusion Act was passed, creating an absolute 10-year ban on Chinese laborers immigrating to the United States. When the exclusion act expired in 1892, Congress decided to extend it for another 10 years. This extension was made permanent in 1902, with added restrictions requiring every Chinese person to obtain a certificate of residence.[20] This resulted in a nearly all-male Chinese community in the Bay

18   Huang, Y. (2023) *Daughter of the Dragon. Anna May Wong's Rendezvous with American History*. Liveright.
19   Lei, D. (2003). The Production and Consumption of Chinese Theatre in Nineteenth-Century California. *Theatre Research International*. 28(3); 289-302. https://doi.org/10.1017/S0307883303001147
20   National Archives. *The Chinese Exclusion Act (1882)*. https://www.archives.gov/

Area. In the words of an elderly Chinatown denizen: "America didn't have to kill any Chinese. The Exclusion Act assured that none would be born."[21]

The Chinese community had some victories, too. In 1885, the Chinese Exclusion Act was used to deny San Francisco-born chef Wong Kim Ark re-entry to the United States after a trip to visit his family in China. Wong challenged the government and, in 1898, the Supreme Court ruled in his favor. United States v. Wong Kim Ark established that the Constitution's 14th Amendment granted "birthright citizenship."

Through all this, troupes from China, and some from the U.S., continued to do shows in Chinatowns from California to New York and many in between. Chinese operas and plays—as well as circuses, films, and vaudeville shows—were vehicles for Chinese performers in San Francisco. In 1925, Los Angeles-born Anna May Wong, already a star of the silent screen, debuted as a "speaking actress" in a Vaudeville show in San Francisco's Orpheum Theater, singing a Chinese lullaby and a popular ditty called "Sally."[22]

Although the Chinese Exclusion act was repealed in 1943, anti-Chinese laws didn't disappear. For example, Mae Ngai recently wrote in *The New York Times* "...in the late 1950s, my parents tried to buy land in northern New Jersey on which to build a home. But no one would sell to them. A real estate agent said it was because they were Chinese... Now new laws are targeting Chinese people from owning property again."[23]

---

milestone-documents/chinese-exclusion-act

21   Chu, L. (2020) *Eat a Bowl of Tea*. University of Washington Press.

22   Huang, Y. (2023) *Daughter of the Dragon. Anna May Wong's Rendezvous with American History*. Liveright.

23   Ngai M. (2023, December 11). Anti-Chinese Laws are on the Rise. We've Been Through This Before. *The New York Times*. (Editor's note: In 2023 the ACLU and others filed a lawsuit, Shen v. Simpson, challenging Florida's SB 264 for violating the Fair Housing Act and the Constitution's equal protection guarantee.)

The United States recognized the People's Republic of China in 1979, after Chinese Communist Party chairman Deng Xiaoping increased foreign trade. The two countries started planning cultural exchanges, including the "Theater Bridge Project" between San Francisco and Shanghai, funded by the U.S. State Department.

In 1982, exactly one century after the Chinese Exclusion Act, San Francisco's American Conservatory Theater (A.C.T), led by William Ball (who will make a tragic cameo appearance later in our story) sent two teachers to Shanghai's Drama Institute. These San Francisco artists traded places with two Shanghai theater professionals. Five years later, A.C.T. sent Joy Carlin to direct *You Can't Take It with You* in Chinese with the Shanghai Youth Drama Troupe. A year after that, the renowned Chinese actor Sun Dao Lin came to San Francisco to play Kublai Khan in A.C.T.'s staging of Eugene O'Neill's *Marco Millions*.

During this project, three artists from the National Theater of Shanghai visited Ken Sonkin's "Personal Clown" class at the A.C.T. Conservatory. They were excited by Ken's approach to teaching Stanislavski's acting techniques, paired with tumbling and clowning; they appreciated the discipline of the acting work and the physical tricks combined with the wildness of clown characters Sonkin's students created. The Shanghai actors told the A.C.T. students about being trained in circus, ballet, singing, and martial arts before they were allowed on stage. At the farewell party in William Ball's penthouse, the Chinese contingent fell in love with miniature peanut butter and jelly sandwiches.

Two powerful countries, one capitalist and the other communist, were finding ways to bridge the divide between them through theater and circus, and PBJs.

. . .

Around this same time, in the early '80s, circuses in Europe and North America started exploring the possibility of hiring Chinese acrobats to perform with their companies. The circuses liked the skill level of Chinese acrobats but were concerned about communicating with them, dealing with Chinese government agencies, and introducing Chinese-style circus to their audiences. In 1984, Switzerland's Circus Knie was the first Western circus to bring in a Chinese company: Lu Yi's Nanjing Acrobatic Troupe.

Dominique Jando is a French clown and circus historian who was then traveling the world booking acts for The Big Apple Circus, a New York City-based company. He remembers this time well:

> In those days, a lot of the people running circuses in Europe and North America knew each other—Big Apple, Circus Knie, Roncali, Gruss. We kept in touch about performers, what each of us thought of this artist or other. We had a lot of performers in common. Circus Knie was the first to bring in a Chinese troupe, so we asked Freddie Knie how it went, and he said, 'no problems.' So, after that, Alexis Gruss staged his *Paris/ Beijing*, done in the way that Alexis always did shows, which is to say spectacularly. The Alexis Gruss show started with his company taking a 'trip around the world' doing Western style acts. Toward the end of the first half, the company climbed all over the rigging of a full-scale ship that had been brought into the ring. On cue, they pointed to the back of the tent, the lights went out on the ship and Monkey King appeared behind the audience. Blackout. Intermission. The second half was the Chinese acrobats. We loved it.

Dominique Jando and Ringmaster/Director Paul Binder, who started Big Apple Circus with his old juggling partner, San Francisco Mime Troupe veteran Michael Christensen, wanted to bring a Chinese troupe to New York. They contacted the Chinese Performing Arts Agency (CPAA). The CPAA played a key role in representing Chinese troupes to different foreign companies. York University professor Tracy Ying Zhang writes, "The assumption was that state-run acrobatic troupes were not commercial enterprises; therefore, they did not have authority to sign business contracts with foreign agencies… Under this arrangement, a significant percentage of the profits from the contract would go to both the troupe and the CPAA. Individuals were not allowed to receive salaries from foreign employers."[24]

The Chinese Performing Arts Agency invited the Big Apple Circus team to visit four companies: two different troupes in Guangdong province, Beijing's New China Acrobatic Troupe, the biggest in China, and the Nanjing Acrobatic Troupe. After negotiating to book one of the Guangdong Troupes, and getting nowhere, the Big Apple team asked the CPAA, "What do you suggest?" The answer was "Nanjing."

Dominique Jando: "Lu Yi ran the Nanjing Acrobatic Troupe, and he was a very good politician—he got that first contract with Circus Knie and he sold the Chinese Performing Arts Agency on his troupe for the Big Apple Circus. When we went to Nanjing, we were greeted by a banner that read, 'Welcome Big Apple Circus' and a band playing 'Yankee Doodle Dandy' on Chinese instruments. A bit much, but he was a good entrepreneur."

The New Yorkers agreed to book the Nanjing Acrobatic Troupe but, because Dominique felt that the company wasn't strong enough on juggling,

24   Zhang, T. (2016) From China to the Big Top: Chinese acrobats and the politics of aesthetic labor, 1950 - 2010. *International Labor and Working-Class History*. (89), 40-63. https://doi.org/10.1017/S0147547915000332

they insisted on also booking the Qian Brothers, a juggling trio that had won gold in the Paris Circus Festival two years before:

"We wanted the Qian Brothers because they were the most original act, and the best for American audiences. But in those days you could only book a whole Chinese troupe, not a single act. That was the tradition. In addition, Lu Yi didn't like the jugglers because they were from an old traveling circus family, not brought up in the troupe system like everyone else. And the fact that the Qian brothers got gold in Paris didn't make them any easier to work with."

When the New York team spoke with Lu Yi about coming to New York, he said the jugglers were not part of the deal—later the CPAA accepted the full package, jugglers and all, "but the agency might not have asked Lu Yi."

The juggling Qian Brothers would soon play a large, but unintended, role in Lu Yi moving to San Francisco to work with the Pickle Family Circus.

4. THE PICKLE FAMILY CIRCUS

Where did the name Pickle Family Circus come from? The following are possible answers:

(a) Cleveland

(b) the old vaudeville notion that 'p' and 'k' are the funniest letters

(c) an imprecise but noticeable similarity between the words 'Pisoni' and 'Pickle'...[25]

Larry Pisoni's grandfather had been an Italian vaudeville performer and Larry was a juggler in Judy Finelli and Hovey Burgess' New York troupe, Circo dell'Arte. When Larry Pisoni traveled westward to join the San Francisco Mime Troupe, he and his juggling partner Peggy Snider had a dream of starting their own circus. The San Francisco Mime Troupe offered them rehearsal space, a costume shop, and the use of their band to start a new kind of circus.

Peggy Snider, Pickle Family Circus co-founder, juggler, and office manager: "There was no Cirque du Soleil [in the early 70s], only what the public thought of as seedy circus companies that would roll through town and rip you off. We devised a different system, a collective who worked together and made sure the audience saw how we worked together. Didn't matter your background or skill, we were in this together to help our local community. Our philosophy, from the beginning, was that, as a community of friends, we would try to give back to the world more than what we took. After all, we grew up in the 60s. We would be non-profit, and act as a fund-raiser for

---

25   Lorant, T. Carroll, J. (1986). *The Pickle Family Circus*. The Pickle Press.

other needy organizations. An alternative to the Big Business approach of `stab 'em in the back and stomp on 'em.'"[26]

John Gilkey, a tall, lean juggler, acrobat, and clown says that "...everything at the Pickles was built around a circle. The circus ring is, of course, a circle. We had meetings sitting in a circle, which is a way for you to see everybody and for everyone to be heard. We're all putting up the show, we're all tearing it down, we're eating together and all sleeping outdoors in a circle—in tents and a couple of vans. You can't help but kind of fall into each other."

Peggy Snider: "We had a big circle with a little fence around it, the 'kiddy corral,' and that is where my son was parked.[27] I'd say, 'I have to go to an act with your father' and plop him there. We set all the props in the corral and performers would step in and play with him. Like Hillary Clinton, I thought it takes a circus to raise a child."[28]

With all these circles, Peggy Snider, Larry Pisoni, and the third member of the Pickle Family Jugglers, Cecil MacKinnon, created The Pickle Family Circus. It was both old and new—a classic American one-ring circus going

26   Lanter, O. (1987) Fun Getting Pickled: The Pickle Family Circus offers as much to its performers as it does to its audience. There are no prima donnas. *Juggler's World*, 39 (1). http://www.juggling.org/jw/87/1/pickle.html

27   "For decades, children traveled with the show [a circus in the '50s], and the community raised them. [Aerialist La Norma Fox]: 'I had more babysitters, I could never find my baby. Every time I look around, somebody had him.' [Aerialist Marjorie Cordell Geiger]: 'Here is this wonderful working woman—she's performing in the show plus she has this group to look after her children, and they raise talented children.'" Samels, M. (Executive Producer). (2018) *American Experience: The Circus*. [TV mini-series] A Winter Pink Films Production; PBS. https://www.pbs.org/wgbh/americanexperience/films/circus/

28   Peggy Snider is riffing on the title of Hillary Clinton's book *It Takes a Village,* and her famous quote, "It takes a village to raise a child," which is said to come from an Igbo and Yoruba proverb.

from small town to small town, but also a "clown-centered cooperative performing without a tent and without animals."[29]

The centrality of clowns has been a hallmark of San Francisco circus ever since and, as this story unfolds, clowns will play major roles in the Nanjing/San Francisco circus affair.

Peggy Snider: "We utilized the best of vaudeville, theater, American jazz, and modern dance and the 'slap schtick' of silent screen comedy. No live animals locked up in cages and dragged around the country, but plenty of the two-legged variety that, in costume, could transform into happy hippos, prancing ponies and dancing gorillas. We even had a band whose members wrote original music for the acts."[30]

The Pickle's faux animals usually danced. Dancing was an important element of the Pickles from their first show, when Bill Irwin played the trainer of dancer/choreographer Kimi Okada's Ramona La Mona the Tap-Dancing Gorilla. Kimi would choreograph many numbers for the Pickles over the years, including a full-cast gorilla number. Tandy Beal would later create dances for acrobats, gender swapping clowns, trash cans, and giant sandwiches.

The Pickle band played for these dancers, and all the other acts. They were a tight, swinging jazz quintet that did a set before every show and sometimes took outside gigs on tour. The band's skill at shaping the circus acts, adjusting

---

29   Schechter, J. (2001) *The Pickle Clowns: New American Circus Comedy*. Southern Illinois University Press.
30   Lanter, O. (1987) Fun getting pickled: The Pickle Family Circus offers as much to its performers as it does to its audience. There are no prima donnas. *Juggler's World*, 39 (1). http://www.juggling.org/jw/87/1/pickle.html

for mistakes in the ring, and accenting the comedy was one of the company's "secret sauces."[31]

Bill Belasco, the Pickle drummer for fifteen years, remembers learning from Nick Saume and Keith Terry, the drummers before him. "They told me to play with the rest of the band on the bass drum and high hat, that is, with my feet, and use my hands to accent the performers in the ring. This created polyrhythms. For the Big Juggle I had a Brazilian samba going with my feet, leaving my hands free to improvise with the jugglers. And when Lorenzo Pickle threw the giant weather balloon into the audience, I'd go into free jazz and the crowd would go ballistic. I loved working with the Pickles."

Bill Belasco remembers the Pickles playing in Nagoya, Japan in the mid-90s: "They had the best equipment and best technicians. We sounded great." The Japanese audiences loved the opening band set so much that Bill and the other musicians jokingly accused the rest of us performers of messing up a good jazz concert.[32]

Looking closely at the Pickle's business model, Peggy Snider says, "We had a core of four or five people in the office, and we worked with local not-for-profits that had enough volunteer-power to sell tickets in their town and put on midways (nursery schools, senior centers, community organizations).

---

31   Between 1990 and 2000, members of the Pickle band included Jeffrey Gaeto, Harvey Robb, Dale Gutridge, Bill Belasco, Marty Allen, Dave Udulf, Rocky Clemenoff, Sherie Chooljian, Peter Drescher and Helena Jack.

32   Circus bands have a long history of playing jazz. In the American Experience documentary *The Circus*, historian Sakina Hughes talks about the sideshow bands in the early 20th century: "...the circus doesn't get enough credit for the amazing work the African-American musicians did in spreading jazz and ragtime music. We think about the Harlem Renaissance, but the circus musicians were coming a generation before. One African-American newspaper said, '...and all the white people get wobbly, too.'" Samels, M. (Executive Producer). (2018) *American Experience: The Circus*. [TV mini-series] A Winter Pink Films Production; PBS. https://www.pbs.org/wgbh/americanexperience/films/circus/

They got a percentage of the ticket sales and all the money from the auctions, food, and games on the midway. Most of the people in the office were also in the show, so they had to practice juggling. At first there were just a few shows outside of San Francisco, but eventually we went north up the coast including to Alaska, and still later to the East Coast, Italy, England, and Japan."

The Pickle model became known as "New Circus," in contrast to the "Traditional Circus" exemplified by Ringling Brothers and Barnum & Bailey. The genre *New Circus* focuses on humans in a single ring (or on stage) performing within a unified story or theme, with music to support that theme, and often with unified designs for costumes, makeup, props, and set pieces. New Circus encompasses organizations as varied as Make*A*Circus, which added workshops and a second show featuring the whole audience,[33] as well as the Big Apple Circus and Circus Flora, both of which present animal acts and play "under canvas" (in a tent). It also includes Circus Bella, Flynn Creek Circus, Bindlestiff Family Cirkus and many other smaller shows, as well as the behemoth, Cirque du Soleil, which performs in tents, arenas, casinos and on cruise ships. These shows have live bands and use theatrical techniques, including lighting, stage sets, props and scripts with dialogue. Most of the directors and designers come from theater and/or dance, and many of the performers, especially clowns, also work in theater as actors, directors and sometimes writers.[34]

---

33   Make*A*Circus (M*A*C) came to San Francisco from England in 1974, led by Peter Frankham. The company created free day-long outdoor events where 400 to 1,000 children and adults enjoyed a professional circus performance, then took workshops in circus skills, and finally performed their own circus. The parks where M*A*C worked were primarily in underserved neighborhoods around the San Francisco Bay and Los Angeles. Many Pickle performers also worked in Make*A*Circus, including Peter Frankham's fellow Brit Geoff Hoyle. In the 90's, the organization shared the gym on Frederick Street, now called S.F. Circus Center, with the New Pickle Circus and the S.F. School of Circus Arts.

34   Theater and dance artists working in circuses is not new, nor is it a practice exclusive to New Circus. In the early 40s, George Balanchine choreographed 50 Ringling

New Circus has become a world-wide model, even spawning the newer genre *Contemporary Circus.*[35] The family tree of New and Contemporary Circus includes many branches in addition to the Pickles and Make*A*Circus. One branch started with Melbourne's Flying Fruit Fly Circus in 1983. With help from Lu Yi and his colleague Lu Guang Rong, this Australian circus was also rebelling against the traditional way of presenting circus shows.

Lu Guang Rong, interviewed from his home in Australia: "Circus was act by act, introducing each act like, 'Here is this beautiful woman from New York.' But in Australia, we cut all this out. Our team from Nanjing and the Flying Fruit Fly group wanted to set the mood or intention but not tell the whole story, keep it vague. Guy Laliberté, co-founder of Cirque du Soleil, visited us in Melbourne. Later he and many other New and Contemporary Circuses took this on. This is how Lu Yi had a big influence on the beginning of contemporary circus. We created a new platform for all the contemporary artists, no longer like traditional European or Chinese presentation of circus. People forget who did it first. Lu Yi did it first in 1983."

While many of the ideas and ideals of the Pickles have taken root and continue today, neither the original Pickle business model nor their physical layout have become widespread. While some New Circus organizations

---

elephants and 50 ballerinas to a score composed by Igor Stravinsky. Even earlier, in 1903, the Ringling brothers "...decided to hire a theater director to produce their opening pageant... rather than doing it themselves... They put on *Jerusalem and the Crusades*... A full scale drama playing out in two acts, it included a ballet, an 'oriental procession' and a battle on the ramparts of Jerusalem... The brothers claimed it involved a cast of 1200 including 300 dancing girls and more than 2000 costumes." Samels, M. (Executive Producer). (2018) *American Experience: The Circus.* [TV mini-series] A Winter Pink Films Production; PBS. https://www.pbs.org/wgbh/americanexperience/films/circus/

35   Contemporary Circus, which was pioneered by ex-Pickles Shana Carroll and Gypsy Snider, requires performers who have a variety of high-level skills, who work well in an ensemble and who bring creativity to their circus work.

are non-profits, there are few if any U.S.-based circuses that operate on the philosophy that everyone is paid equally and should work both on stage and in the office. Some circuses are sponsored by community organizations, but none have the model, first used by the Pickles in the 1970s, of working in-depth with local non-profit service organizations.[36]

Some New Circus organizations use elements of, but not the complete, site-plan that the early Pickles created: A circus set up outdoors in the daylight with a midway full of games and food that leads to an opening in the canvas sidewall. Walking through that opening and into a ring of sidewall—a big-top without its top—the audience sat on bleachers or in a mote of grass, a children-only mosh pit, that stopped at the performing zone, defined by a semi-circle of ring curb. A painted ground cover and backdrop, aluminum aerial rigging and a wooden bandstand completed the look.

Joel Schechter, in his book *The Pickle Clowns*, writes about this aesthetic: "Much like the S.F. Mime Troupe… the original Pickle Family Circus featured California sunlight as one of its special effects. The blues, reds and yellows of the costumes and canvas drops were heighted by the beautifully lit greenery of the surrounding parks …French circus historian Pascal Jacob has noted that New Circus… initially developed in the street and open spaces… where a larger sector of the public might converge."[37]

36   Part of the Pickle model included using a federal law, CETA (Comprehensive Employment and Training Act), to help balance their budget. In 1974, just as the Pickles were getting started, the San Francisco Neighborhood Arts Program began hiring artists, with CETA money, to create and present work in neighborhoods citywide, giving many artists, including Pickle performers, jobs, and giving tens of thousands of San Franciscans access to classes and shows. When CETA was repealed in 1982, the Pickle model became less attractive. Chen, K.B., Cortez, J. *Legacy of the Neighborhood Arts Program*. FoundSF. https://www.foundsf.org/index.php?title=Legacy_of_the_Neighborhood_Arts_Program
37   Schechter J. (2001) *The Pickle Clowns: New American Circus Comedy*. Southern Illinois University Press.

Unlike the Mime Troupe, the Pickles were not overtly political, although their internal structure and business model were created along egalitarian, politically progressive lines—equal distribution of wealth within the company and working with other non-profit organizations "so that much of the money generated would remain in the community to support the people who needed it most."[38] Pickle performances included a literal and metaphoric display of this egalitarian ethos.

Peggy Snider: "The political statement of the circus was the Big Juggle at the end of each performance. Everyone stood in a giant semi-circle, juggling and passing clubs. The message was that we are all equal, working together, making this happen."

Bill Irwin, part of the famous Pickle clown trio with Larry Pisoni and Geoff Hoyle, had a twist on their political message. "I was looking for a way to reflect a political outlook but at the same time trying to make fun of the self-serious 'leftier than thou' attitude of our subculture." When asked about a joke Bill made in a clown routine about being a "wage slave," he responded, "It's an old Marxist joke—Groucho's, I think."[39]

The political subculture that Bill Irwin is referring to was based, in part, on the ideas of Mao Zedong, the founder of the People's Republic of China. Director Jael Weisman,[40] who won an Obie award for his work with the San Francisco Mime Troupe, remembers that "...in the late 60s and early 70s, study sessions discussing parts of Mao's 'Little Red Book' occupied a lot of our time at the Mime Troupe." Joan Mankin worked with both the Mime Troupe and the Pickles (you will get to know her as this story unfolds). She

---

38   *ibid.*

39   *ibid.*

40   Jael Weisman was the director of the S.F. Mime Troupe's Obie award winning "Dragon Lady's Revenge" before becoming the director of the Dell'Arte Players Company.

helped introduce the San Francisco circus community to "Chairman Mao's Four-Minute Exercise," a physical warm-up that included some of the kicks and stretches that we would do a decade later under Lu Yi's watchful eye. In those early days, we did Mao's Four-Minute Exercise before rehearsals, performances, and even meetings.

Mao Zedong led China from 1949, before Lu Yi started training in acrobatics, until 1976, when Lu Yi was already a major figure nationally. The exercises and ideas that shaped the Pickles—operating as a collective, supporting local communities and being "an alternative to the Big Business approach of `stab 'em in the back and stomp on 'em"—came from the world of Lu Yi's formative years.

This political connection between San Francisco and Nanjing wasn't often a subject of conversation among Chinese and American performers (except between Xiaohong Weng and Jennings McCown, who you will meet soon). I once asked Lu Yi about his relationship with Deng Xiaoping, the Chinese leader who took power after Mao. Lu Yi thought for a moment and said, "He's short." When I pushed, Lu Yi added, "...But his head is big." That was the end of the conversation. Clearly, sharing details about Chinese leaders with Americans—especially in the aftermath of the Tiananmen Square massacre—wasn't something Lu Yi was going to risk.

. . .

In their first 15 years, the Pickle Family Circus attracted a large and deeply loyal audience in towns from Washington state down to southern California. Even today, people talk about bringing their children to Pickle shows every year at a park near their home. The circus was as big an event for these families as it was for farm families across the country in the days when small tent shows still criss-crossed the country.

Working with the Pickles was also a big event in many performers' lives. Derique McGee, who started taking clown classes when he was 15, the same year he won a hambone contest in his hometown of Berkeley,[41] remembers "...seeing administrators writing grants, watching folks make posters, doing the marketing part—I learned about the business part of circus."

He also learned the technical part of circus from Michael Ohta, the Pickle production manager, a man Derique calls "...the protector of everything and all of us." Michael taught the performers to set up bleachers, do the rigging and tie ropes. "He'd make games out of learning technical skills, 'Pretend you fell in a hole and only had one hand—how would you tie this knot?'" When Bill Irwin was moving to New York, Derique helped him put his clown props in storage. "Bill pulled out clown shoes from when he was in Ringling Brothers Clown College. Black leather, traditional clown shoes. 'Would you want these?' 'YEAH!' Sometimes I hang them in my dressing room."

John Gilkey: "I came into the Pickle Family Circus as a juggler, one skill. With the Pickles I got a general education. I broadened my performing abilities to include acrobatics and clowning, and I learned a circus life. I pounded stakes, I learned hard work and different forms of work, I learned community, communication skills, how to be more conscious of the environment, of my health, of what I eat. *[he laughs]* My first day I brought a salami sandwich for lunch; everyone else was eating steamed vegetables. I haven't had a salami sandwich since."

Larry Pisoni, Peggy Snider and Cecil MacKinnon were The Pickle Family Jugglers before they grew their trio act into a full circus. With the Big Juggle

---

41   *Hambone* is a type of body percussion originally developed by enslaved Africans.

and performers such as Judy Finelli, John Gilkey, Derique McGee, Wendy Parkman, Mark Jondall and Billy Kessler, juggling remained a key part of the circus's identity.

An updated version of the Big Juggle is now a hallmark of Circus Bella, a San Francisco company that explicitly follows the path laid out by the Pickle Family Circus and Make*A*Circus. Like their predecessors, Bella performs in Bay Area parks, with sunshine lighting up a ring full of jugglers, pole climbers, contortionists, aerialists, and clowns—all performing to a live band. At the end of every show, the full Circus Bella cast does an intricate club passing routine, an extension of the Pickle's Big Juggle semi-circle.[42] "We have to be in sync, all juggling at the same tempo," says Abigail Munn, Circus Bella's Co-Founder and current Artistic Director. "And the only way is to look at each other, then do the 'slow start' that Judy Finelli taught us, like a drummer counting off before the band kicks in."

The Pickles started as a juggling trio and, ironically, it would be a trio of Chinese jugglers who set off a chain of events that shifted the center of the Pickle's identity from juggling to Chinese acrobatics.

---

42   In recent years, Circus Bella has also pitched a tent for their winter season.

5. CALIFORNIA CALLING

1983 - 1989

Judy Finelli's friend Wendy Parkman was relieved to come down from the trapeze and take a bow. It was the final performance of a long, successful run for a "New Vaudeville" interpretation of Shakespeare's *Comedy of Errors*.[43] In her costume, a colorful leotard, Wendy couldn't hide her pregnant belly much longer. A few hours later, the former Pickle Family Circus aerialist was asleep in a cab, racing to Chicago's O'Hare airport. A few months after that, she was home in San Francisco holding a healthy baby girl. This is when Wendy Parkman started looking for a circus challenge that wouldn't take her away from her family.

Judy Finelli moved west after her marriage to Hovey Burgess ended. By1983 she and her new husband, Gary Thomsen, were expecting a baby. Since Judy and Wendy were both 'off the road,' they decided it was a good time to start a circus school in San Francisco—the first of its kind. This decision, timed for their family life and designed to meet their professional aspirations, would eventually spawn three generations of performers who continue to thrill circus audiences around the world.

---

43   The *Comedy of Errors* is one of William Shakespeare's earliest plays. A "New Vaudeville" adaptation was a hit at the Goodman Theatre in Chicago ('82), the Olympic Arts Festival in L.A. ('84) (where Cirque du Soleil made its first big splash in the U.S.) and then at Lincoln Center in NYC ('87). The production was broadcast on "Live from Lincoln Center." Three Pickle Family Circus performers were in the cast of *Comedy of Errors*: Wendy Parkman, Derique McGee and me.

The two women talked to Larry Pisoni about opening a small training program for kids. Larry, who was now the Artistic Director of the Pickles, had known Judy from their days with Circo dell'Arte in New York. He liked the idea of children's classes and in 1984, the Pickle Family Circus School opened at 400 Missouri Street in San Francisco's Potrero Hill neighborhood, the former church that had served as the circus's office and rehearsal space since the mid-70s. The school offered classes for five and six-year-olds, seven and eight-year-olds, and nine through 12-year-olds.

Three years later, in 1987, Judy Finelli took over the role of Pickle Family Circus' Artistic Director from Larry Pisoni. She was excited about expanding the school to finally realize her dream of raising a generation of American circus performers trained by masters from Russia and China. She also needed to upgrade the Pickle performers' skill level.

Peggy Snider: "Pickle acts were performed by people like Wendy Parkman and me, who started circus training in our late 20's. 'We are just like you, the audience, but we are up there in the ring.' Cirque du Soleil blew all that out of the water. They came to the U.S. in 1984 for a big event in LA. The arts council in Montreal granted Guy Laliberté, the owner, four million dollars; we started the Pickles with a four thousand dollar loan. Guy Laliberté said at that point that he modeled Cirque after the Pickles—we were the first to put a show together like this that wasn't corny, that had an aesthetic to it. Cirque du Soleil tickets were expensive, but just to look at their set-up was mind blowing. We needed a way to compete with them."

Judy Finelli started searching for world-class teachers ready to relocate to the Bay Area and willing to adjust their training techniques to fit the local norms and culture. When the Pickle Family Circus was on tour in Stony Brook, Long Island in 1989, Judy took a day off to see *The Big Apple Circus Meets the Monkey King*.

The Monkey King in the title *The Big Apple Circus Meets the Monkey King* was played by Lu Yi's deputy director Yang Xiao Di. Monkey King and stories from *Journey to the West* have now appeared in hundreds of movies, TV shows, comic books, cartoons and many Chinese operas, but in 1987 the character had never been part of a circus in China. Lu Yi had imitated Monkey King and the monk Sanzang back in his days collecting cigarette butts at "The Big World," even before he started his acrobatic training, so he was happy to be the first director to put Monkey King in a circus ring.

Paul Binder, founder and director of the Big Apple Circus: "When I told the Chinese I wanted a [circus] troupe and a Monkey King, there was a sort of shock and surprise. Then Xu Shu Er, the Minister of Culture and an actress herself, said, 'I don't see why not.' [She understood] I wanted to do a collaborative show, one in which we could question differences between two cultures."[44]

The Big Apple Circus Meets the Monkey King played in the Big Apple Circus's "Trump Tent," which some of the local press noted was "...named for Donald You-Know-Who." [45][46]

Unlike the show at Circus Knie, both halves of *The Big Apple Circus Meets the Monkey King* featured acts by the Big Apple Circus' regular company and the Nanjing troupe, which included Lu Yi's former performing partner and future Pickle school trainer Xie Ke Min. The Big Apple clowns and Monkey

---

44   Shepard, R.F. (1998, December 18). Monkey King Under the Big Top. *The New York Times.*

45   Winship, F.M. (1988, October 31). Big Apple Circus goes Oriental. *UPI.*

46   Dominique Jando says that Donald Trump agreed to pay for a new tent, "...and it had to be called 'Trump Tent' for one season; he even had a new façade designed with just 'Trump' on it, not 'Big Apple Circus.' Eventually, he paid the first 50% of it, and stuck us with the rest."

King, played by Yang Xiao Di, who also grew up in the Pan troupe, were the thread that tied the show together.

In the second half of *The Big Apple Circus Meets the Monkey King,* the Nanjing acrobats did a plate-spinning act with seven women spinning "...four plates on four sticks in each hand, doing somersaults, headstands, handstands, and multi-level formations without ever dropping the crockery," as well as a classic act with acrobatic lions who "...dance, tumble with acrobats, roll giant red lacquer balls onto a springboard, and make themselves altogether lovable by fluttering their pink eyelids." There were also "...cycling acrobats... devils on wheels, stacking as many as 10 persons on a bike," and a dragon dance "...colorfully snaking like runaways from a Chinese New Year celebration." The Qian Brothers were also there, "...a trio of jugglers who won a gold medal at the Paris Circus Festival [doing] the impossible with rings and squash rackets."[47] [48]

After the show in Stony Brook, Judy Finelli met Lu Yi for the first time. "We talked for three hours even though I spoke no Chinese and he didn't speak any English. We did mime and I remember because it was so terrific; he understood my admiration for his troupe and my enthusiasm for him to come teach at the Pickle Family School. At the time, he was too busy."

Peggy Snider: "A Chinese trainer named Lu Yi had worked with Circus Oz from Australia, a like-minded group who did mind blowing things. That was the first I knew that there was this guy out there who could jump from one culture to another. Judy took the lead and I remember filling out paperwork to get him into the country."

---

47   Gussow M. (1988, November 4). Big Apple is Back with Daredevils and Slippery Stars. *The New York Times.*
48   Winship, F.M. (1988, October 31). Big Apple Circus goes Oriental. *UPI.*

When the Big Apple Circus' season ended, the juggling Qian Brothers defected to the U.S. instead of returning to China. Lu Yi's distrust of the Qians, which had started because they were from a family circus and worked outside of the official troupe system, intensified. When some members of the Nanjing Acrobatic Troupe defected right after them, it became an international incident.[49]

As the leader of the company, Lu Yi returned to Nanjing under a cloud. After the Tiananmen Square protests and massacre, Lu Yi realized that his position in China was becoming untenable. The same government that sent him around the world as a young acrobat and supported his work as a trainer and director, even steering organizations like the Big Apple Circus to Nanjing, was now turning against him—and Lu Yi knew what it meant to be on the wrong side of the Chinese government. During the Cultural Revolution, he was held in house arrest, in a museum near his office, for many months and was eventually forced to confess to imaginary anti-government activities. His sister committed suicide when her son was also targeted.

It was time to leave China. San Francisco looked like a good place to go.

International politics also played a role in getting the Russian teeterboard artist, Sergey Zenov, to San Francisco. The collapse of the Soviet Union, along with the collapse of its circus infrastructure, made leaving his home country and relocating to the U.S. enticing.

---

49   "Four members of a Chinese acrobatic troupe that has performed with a New York circus since last fall disappeared in Vermont Sunday night after the circus's last show of the season and days before the acrobats were to return to China... after the Big Apple Circus caravan returned to New York City... a fifth member-the group's interpreter-turned herself over to United States National Park Service Police at Floyd Bennett Field in Brooklyn and asked for asylum." Wolff, C. (1989, August 9). 4 Chinese Acrobats Vanish as Interpreter Seeks Asylum. *The New York Times*.

Judy Finelli had found her teachers.

"I knew that the training Lu Yi and Sergey Zenov could offer was a vast improvement over the guesswork that American acrobats were then using. With no tried-and-true system, we were going nowhere. With this Russian and Chinese team, American circus performers could finally arrive!"

SPOTLIGHT ON...

XIAOHONG WENG AND JENNINGS MCCOWN

Jennings McCown is an American acrobat who "finally arrived" after working with a partner from Nanjing. Jennings started his "typical haphazard American circus training at a Midwest university in a corn field." The school had the oldest collegiate circus club in the country, which he joined. Coaches and fellow club members taught Jennings some juggling, trampoline, wire walking and partner acrobatics in mixed pairs.

Xiaohong Weng started his typical strictly organized Chinese circus training when he was an 11-year-old student selected by Lu Yi to join the incoming class at the Nanjing Acrobatic Troupe. He trained six days a week, eight hours a day for 17 years—first as a student and then as a performer—doing classic Chinese acts and flying trapeze.

One summer, Jennings McCown worked at a circus camp where he learned the rudiments of catching on the flying trapeze. After graduating, he and a friend from the college circus club drove an old van to Florida to do three seasons with small circuses, passing juggling clubs, doing a wire walking act, and performing on the aerial cradle as two men—an oddity at the time.

Jennings McCown: "Those three years touring with small shows from Florida to Maine, and then to the Midwest, was oldschool U.S. circus—move every other day, everyone does everything. I was on the stake crew, setting up the midway, putting up the big top."

When Xiaohong Weng was 28, Lu Yi got him work on a Princess Cruise Line ship. After two years at sea, Lu Yi got Xiaohong a job with a Chinese troupe performing in Branson, Missouri, an "entertainment mecca." Xiaohong joined a cast that included three former or future Pickle acrobats. At the end of 1996, Xiaohong left for Las Vegas, along with all the other performers. Xiaohong's wife and small son soon joined him.

Xiaohong Weng: "In Vegas, I worked mostly in Chinese restaurants, but Lu Yi got me a few performing contracts. I brought my son with me on those jobs, and we lived in the dressing rooms because the other acrobats were smoking and drinking in the hotel rooms. The dressing rooms were fancy, and we got free food, so it was OK. But when Johnny had to start kindergarten, I called Lu Yi."

Xiaohong packed his family into their car and drove to San Francisco to be Lu Yi's assistant at Circus Center.

After his third circus tour, Jennings got a job teaching trapeze at Club Med, and eventually landed in San Francisco.

The two acrobats met at San Francisco Circus Center and, after getting to know each other, Xiaohong suggested they do some hand-to-hand, just for fun.

Jennings McCown: "I had never done hand balancing, but I had watched Xiaohong coaching and immediately recognized that he was legit, that he had real skill, way beyond mine."

Xiaohong Weng: "Before I started practicing with Jennings, I never thought I could be a flyer; I was a base in Nanjing, basing Zhou Yue. And I was 34 years old, so in China I would have already been retired a long time. But I was a small size for Americans."

Jennings: "Xiaohong must have seen that San Francisco was not like China, that here we have adults learning—and enjoying—acrobatics. I wonder if that gave him a spark, 'Hey, I don't have to quit.'"

The two started with a simple Risley hand-to-hand—Jennings lying on his back, his elbows on the mat and his forearms at ninety-degree angles to the floor, Xiaohong putting his hands in Jennings', setting the grip and pressing into a handstand.

Jennings: "I trusted Xiaohong to guide me in learning to base hand-to-hand since he had been a base. I thought, 'If I'm going to do anything with anyone, I'm going to do it with this guy. He's state-trained; seriously, formally trained. A true pro. This is my only chance to work with someone like him.'"

Their first gig was less than one year after they started training together.

Xiaohong: "Jennings and I did a show at a friend's wedding, a tattoo guy, at Broadway Studios. Now this guy is divorced and doing teeterboard dressed as a bunny. This was before the dot-com crash, so we ended up doing a lot of gigs."

Jennings: "When Xiaohong and I started to have success, our partnership got steadier, stronger, better. Not all in one moment. When we attempted something and finally did it, he'd say, 'In China, kids do that,' but for me it was sort of a mountain. The toughest trick we did was when the base, me, starts on his back and rolls laterally while holding the top, Xiaohong, in a hand-to-hand. We could go two revolutions. Xiaohong would say, 'For working with a big dumb *yōuling*, this is pretty good.'"[50]

Xiaohong: "Gypsy Snider helped choreograph our act, but she was very artistic, even at that time—she had just started The 7 Fingers. Very slo-mo, beautiful, but not a lot of high technique. We accepted some ideas, but we didn't have that artistic technique. Imagine me and Jennings taking a ballet class, standing behind all the clowns, following them, looking in the mirror like two bodybuilders. This is when we learned how to become our own act, our own performers."

Jennings: "Xiaohong and I would train diligently, that's the only way he trains, but over time I began to look forward to just spending time with him. Eventually, we'd practice a trick, talk for 10 minutes, then do it again. He told me that in China, most acrobats are replaceable—a pole climber gets hurt, the next one takes his slot. Same with hoop diving. But not partner acrobatics. When two people are working directly with each other, skin to skin with no props in between them, this is when the individuality comes out. Xiaohong said that neither partner is replaceable, and I was surprised at how right he was. Working with other acrobats, I find I can't balance these people. Xiaohong is a unique person. He was the talent in our act."

---

50   *Yōuling* (ghost) is a Chinese slur for a white person, similar to the Japanese gaijin (translated as 'foreigner'). In this case, *yōuling* is not used maliciously.

Xiaohong: "Jennings is very important in my life. He's very knowledgeable, wild non-stop reading from the library, anything—European history, Chinese history, even learned some Chinese after he met me. He reads a lot and he's calm and humble. I learned from Jennings, always talking, arguing, sometimes arguing on purpose to see how he'd answer. Sometimes he said, 'Xiaohong, shut up, you're so annoying.' But he accepted a lot of my point of view. I'm from China, I was brainwashed growing up. But if you stand in my shoes, you might agree with me. He always tries to do that. He has an international view—he says, 'Here's the facts.' Not Chinese view or Russian view. He would ask me, 'What do *you* think?' Asking me to think for myself—politics, economics, stocks, history, geography. He's not all patriotism, 'I love America only,' but 'I'm learning this stuff. This person's opinion, that person's opinion.' I try to learn from him."

Jennings: "There was a Free Tibet demonstration in San Francisco. Xiaohong and I both went, but on opposite sides. He was taking the Chinese state line—'Tibet is part of China, it was a crap show there and China went in to help them out, build infrastructure, drag them out of poverty. Tibet should be part of China since we bent over backwards to help these people.' I went like other westerners, demonstrating against Chinese imperialism (well, the U.S. can't throw stones on that issue—glass house and all that). But in the West, we are unified about Tibet. The next day in the faculty lounge, Dominik Wyss, a coach from Switzerland, changed Xiaohong's screensaver to 'Save Tibet.' Xiaohong laughed."

Xiaohong: "I think about this for American people. Why don't Chinese people like American people? For centuries, the West always tries to get benefits from China, 'Oh, Shanghai is mine. I can make a railroad, run all the business in my territory, I can do what I want.' It's still going on. The G7[51]

---

51   The G7 (Group of Seven) is a political & economic forum consisting of Canada,

meeting just finished, 'Oh, China is getting stronger, we don't want them to get stronger than us or balance us. We always want to be the boss.' I think China is right now moving to Russia, even though they don't like Russia, otherwise the whole world is going to be tipping in one way. No one likes North Korea, but China is holding North Korea so when they negotiate, China can say, 'They have a crazy leader and nuclear weapons.'"

Jennings: "If someone were to have told me, when I was growing up in the sticks, that one day I would meet a Chinese acrobat who would not only become my partner but become the brother I never had, I would not have believed them. Life is strange. Xiaohong has been my brother through many adventures, through many years."

Xiaohong: "Maybe me and Jennings can balance out the whole world. We're training, we're chatting, we're arguing. I learn from him. He always listens to my stories."

France, Germany, Italy, Japan, the United Kingdom and the U.S., with the European Union (EU) as a "non-enumerated member."

ACT TWO:

EAST MEETS WEST

6. LANDING AT SFO

1990

> Danger haunted all living creatures on earth. Human beings needed to learn a better Way. The Bodhisattva Guanyin found Sanzang, a monk, and asked him to journey to the Western Heaven to get the scriptures, bring them to the East and save all living things. "But I warn you, Sanzang, there are many wild animals, fiends, and demons on the way." Although trepidatious, Sanzang agreed to go. The Bodhisattva Guanyin said, "I will send you with a disciple and bodyguard, Monkey King. He is an appalling criminal who threw heaven into chaos and is now imprisoned beneath the Five Elements Mountain. He will protect you on your journey to the West."[52]

On March 18, 1990, Lu Yi stepped off a plane from Nanjing at the San Francisco airport, followed the other passengers to the baggage claim and found his luggage. He had made this journey west alone. His family, his longtime performing partner and two of his students would join him later. For the time being, he was on his own in a strange new city that was now his home.

Political pressures had forced him to leave China. Now he needed to make a new life teaching the 2,000-year-old art of Chinese acrobatics to the jugglers,

---

52   Wu, C. Jenner, W.J.F. (2005). *Journey to the West*. (C. Fair, Ed.). Disruptive Pub.

clowns, and aerialists of the 15-year-old Pickle Family Circus—starting a "circus affair" between Nanjing and San Francisco.

The former Pickle and Cirque du Soleil performer Bill Forchion, who now goes by Djeli, sees Lu Yi's journey to the West differently: "Arriving in the U.S. was not running away from anything in China. Lu Yi had this bigger vision—San Francisco was a new opportunity for him to engage, to bring thousands of years of Chinese tradition to another culture, and not overtake that culture but mix with it."

Because of the political situation in China, Lu Yi knew that taking his whole family to the U.S. at once would raise eyebrows—or worse. His teenage daughters Lu Yue and Lu Na, along with two performers from the Nanjing Acrobatic Troupe—20-year-old contortionist Zhou Yue and 28-year-old pole climber and hoop diver Huang Zhe—arrived two months later. Lu Yi's performing and teaching partner, Xia Ke Min, would not make it to the U.S. for another two years. Lu Yi's wife, Wang Hong Zhu, wouldn't arrive for almost another year after that.[53]

Huang Zhen, a tall, dashingly handsome acrobat: "At that time, China was closed so the only American things we were allowed to see were the movies. We moved to America from China to help the Pickle Family Circus, but everything was different when we got here. It was really hard in the beginning."

---

53   Chinese names have the family name (or last name) first, and the given name (or first name) second. Some people choose to reverse their names when they move to the U.S. (e.g. Weng Xiaohong often went by Xiaohong Weng, or just Xiaohong, when he lived in San Francisco.)

Shana Carroll,[54] a young, elegant Pickle aerialist: "It was magical. My mother was really interested in Chinese art and culture, so I grew up surrounded by it. We used to go to dim sum in the 70s before it was a thing to do outside of Chinese culture. A month after the Nanjing group got here, it was one of the Pickle performer's[55] birthday in a backyard on Harrison Street in the Mission. She had a piñata. The Chinese group had never seen one. Lu Yi crushed that piñata on his first try. He had the force. I remember him walking up and down the stairs on his hands."

Lu Yi and his daughters, 19-year-old Lu Yue and Lu Na, who was two years younger, shared a one-bedroom Berkeley apartment with the two acrobats.

Huang Zhen: "The three girls lived inside one room; me and Lu Yi stayed in the living room. I didn't know how to cook but I had watched my parents, so I tried to cook for everyone. Lu Yi would make toast with eggs for breakfast, then we would take the BART subway, then bus to work. A long trip to work."

Lu Yue, Lu Yi's older daughter: "In China, we were much better off than average people—our father was an important person. Here in the U.S., we had nothing. My sister Lu Na and I felt we needed to work harder to have a better life here, to get to the level we had in China. In China, all the students,

---

54   Shana Carroll later created The 7 Fingers with Gypsy Snider, Peggy Snider's daughter and Larry Pisoni's step-daughter who grew up in the Pickles. The 7 Fingers, originally called "Les Sept Doigts de la Main," is a collective headquartered in Montreal founded in 2002 by seven performers who had worked together on Cirque du Soleil. They were early creators of "Contemporary Circus," and continue to be one of the most successful organizations in that genre. Many of Lu Yi's students have worked, and currently work, with The 7 Fingers, including their show *Dear San Francisco* in San Francisco's North Beach neighborhood. In 2023, Shana was inducted into the the *Ordre des arts et des lettres du Québec*, a prize for artistic excellence and was nominated for a Tony award.
55   It was Miriam de Sela's birthday. Miriam and her sisters Ayin and Lhasa all performed with the Pickles.

including us, were academically driven—no cooking, no recreation, no job, nothing but studying. In Berkeley, with our mother still back in Nanjing, our father helped us become more independent. We learned to shop, cook, register in school, get a job. Of course, we missed home. Our mom has six siblings, so we have a lot of relatives back in China. We were allowed to call home once a month, an expensive long-distance call. For 10 minutes. Everyone took turns saying something."

Lu Yue and Lu Na got to know the Pickle Circus performers, absorbing the new culture from them, and picking up English. They remember liking the family feel of both the Pickle school and the performing troupe. Shana Carroll, who was the same age as Lu Yue, became close to the sisters and the rest of the Nanjing group. She even taught Huang Zhen how to drive.

Shana Carroll "I would spend late nights playing Mahjong until four in the morning at their apartment. It was like being transported into China—the way the table was set, the towel placed on the pillow, the socks they wore. It was thrilling to be close with them at that moment, before they became more westernized, and to help be that link between the West and the East."

Huang Zhen: "Shana would take us to work then we would go eat together. She would come home with us and watch Chinese TV shows. She spoke Chinese way better than our English. She would help us a lot."

After getting to know them, Lu Yue saw a difference in her father's new Bay Area students. "The Americans had a lot of passion and were very receptive to learn about Chinese acrobatics. In China, the acrobats have no choice—it's a career and a way to make money. In the U.S., the students and performers loved circus and they wanted to be part of it."

Ori Quesada, who started training with Lu Yi at the age of seven says, "I think what Mr. Lu Yi saw in me was my passion. He would always tell me that even though I was not given the ideal body for acrobatics, I had the heart."

Shana Carroll: "[American circus in the late '80s] was a way more marginalized form than it is now. When I was a trapeze artist at the Pickles… there was no way of researching what was out there. I played around on the trapeze and every move I found, I thought I'd invented it! On one hand, this definitely pushes creativity and a great sort of ownership of your work. On the other hand, it was a much harder path… And there was a 'circus freak' stigma. I always had to put up an armor."[56]

Lu Yi's students Francisco Cruz and Will Underwood: "We never told anyone outside of circus that we did circus because they immediately thought of clowns and animals. But we would go around the city and do circus skills, kind of like parkour, but there wasn't YouTube yet, so we didn't know what that was."

For Lu Yi, this change in social status—going from being a national arts leader to being an American "circus freak"—was only one of the challenges he faced in his new home.

The Nanjing Acrobatic Troupe and the Pickle Family Circus could not have been more different: The acrobatic troupe, located in the old imperial capital of Nanjing, was created in 1957. It was a large, government-supported organization that trained young students to become professionals who would then join the troupe to perform on stages in many Chinese circus festivals

56   Honis, A (2023, July 6). An interview with Shana Carroll, member of the Order Arts and Letters of Quebec. *CircusTalk*. https://circustalk.com/news/shana-carroll-member-of-the-order-of-arts-and-letters-of-quebec

and tour extensively in Australia, Europe, Latin America, and Africa. The troupe's focus was on taking traditional Chinese acrobatic acts—such as pole climbing, hoop diving, plate spinning and contortion—to a high technical level, and sometimes combining these traditional skills in new ways.

On the other hand, San Francisco's Pickle Family Circus performed in city parks, mainly around Northern California and Oregon. They featured intimate, outdoor shows with a live band, clowning, juggling, dance, and acts on trampoline, trapeze, and slack rope. Clowning was at the center of every show, starting in the mid-70s when the Pickles featured a clown trio of Bill Irwin, Geoff Hoyle, and Larry Pisoni. The Pickles pioneered the New Circus movement, along with their sister company Make*A*Circus. In 1990, when Lu Yi arrived, they were a beloved, but still small, non-profit organization.

In addition to his duties working with the Pickle Family Circus School, Lu Yi became the Master Trainer for the Pickle's performing company. In this role, the differences between his work in China and his challenges in the U.S. became even more stark. In Nanjing, his troupe of 60 acrobats were hand-picked from auditions held in local school gyms.[57] Most of these students, some as young as six years old, lived on-site with the older performers and trained full time. In San Francisco, the dozen or so Pickle performers were adults—some were past retirement age in Nanjing—and they all had the independent, complicated work lives of San Francisco artists, piecing together a living from their Pickle work, other freelance performing, teaching gigs, and possibly a "straight" job or two.

Huang Zhen: "Lu Yi thought the level of skills at the Pickle Circus was really low. He had ideas for acts, but performers would come and go. In China,

---

57   Mariam Ala-Rashi points out that "nationally, some Chinese acrobatic students come from orphanages in rural areas where some poor peasant families submit children to acrobatic schools so that they will receive an education and three warm meals a day."

he had a permanent troupe and the power to do whatever he wanted—the government gave him the money and he could spend how he saw fit. At Pickle there was a board of directors that decided how the money was used."

These differences were a challenge, and they were also the basis of Lu Yi's dream, a 10-year plan to revitalize Chinese acrobatics. According to Lu Na, acrobatics wasn't very popular in China at that time. "The tickets were cheap, and most shows were just OK." Shana Carroll adds "...in China, acrobats would perform, and no one would applaud. They didn't care. The acrobats were still paid to train, but they were just smoking and not training." Lu Na says her father had "...always dreamed about sending American circus performers back to China to perform and interact with Chinese performers, to re-energize young Chinese acrobats and clowns."

Lu Yi's dream of transforming circus in China would take 20 years to achieve. First, he had to transform the Pickle Family Circus.

7. LA LA LUNA SEA

1990

Training is six steps, all sweat:
First sweat from skin.
Second sweat from muscles.
Third sweat from ligaments.
Fourth sweat from bones.
Fifth sweat from behind the knees.
Sixth sweat from blood.[58]

On his first day of work with the Pickle Family Circus, Lu Yi waited with his translator in the Pickle's converted church on Potrero Hill. San Francisco was now his home, this room was now his gym, and the Americans who would walk through the door in a few minutes were his first big challenge—nine inexperienced adults who needed to be flexible, strong, and knowledgeable enough to perform Chinese acrobatics in front of live audiences in less than four months. The Nanjing/San Francisco circus affair was about to begin.

Lu Yi looked around. This room was a lot smaller than his rehearsal hall back in China. The Nanjing Acrobatic Troupe worked in a gym with 30-foot ceilings, his troupe sometimes performed in the movie theater next door, and his office overlooked the whole space. Here, he didn't have an office. The main part of the Pickle church had been cleared of pews and

---

58   Lu Yi quoting a Chinese Opera star, from San Francisco's Pickle Family Circus. (1990, May). *La La Luna Sea*. [Program]. San Francisco, California.

the nave now housed a trampoline, mats, some large mirrors, and a vertical pole. Juggling clubs, stilts, gorilla costumes, bass drums, hats, hoops, and handstand benches all lay around the edges. Old Pickle Family Circus posters covered the walls.[59]

Tandy Beal, who had just been hired as the Pickle's choreographer (she will play a major role later in our story), remembers when Lu Yi arrived. "He was leaving his country and his family and coming into a gym that was cold and under-funded. We needed to say thank-you to him for making this journey."

The Pickle performers had tried to pick up some basic Chinese in advance of meeting their new trainer, although most of them didn't get very far in a language in which a word changes meaning depending on its tone. Language issues aside, they were excited.

John Gilkey: "We'd seen Circus Oz from Australia doing hoop diving and pole climbing acts that Lu Yi taught them. It was pretty exciting that we were getting the same guy that they got."

Xia Ke Min, who was on the first trip from Nanjing to Australia and later worked with Lu Yi in San Francisco says, "...Australian acrobats work harder than Americans. They wake up at seven o'clock. Americans at seven o'clock, they won't wake up."

The cast of *La La Luna Sea*[60] the Pickle Family Circus show of 1990-91, arrived at the church around 9am, hugged each other and then awkwardly

---

59   The office and rehearsal space for the Pickle Family Circus was an old church at 400 Missouri Street on Potrero Hill, often called The Church. It also housed the Pickle Family Circus School. In the early 1990's, the circus moved to a much larger space, a gymnasium/theater building at 755 Frederick Street that had been part of Polytechnic High School. In 2001 the name was changed to San Francisco Circus Center.
60   *La La Luna Sea* cast: Shana Carroll, John Gilkey, Huang Zhen, Zhou Yue, Diane

lined up in front of Lu Yi. Their new trainer greeted each of them in turn, feeling their hands and arms, looking at their bodies and asking, through the translator, about their parents' height and about their acrobatic specialties.

Lu Yi got to the last performer in line, Diane (Pino) Wasnak: "He looked me up and down quizzically—I was closing in on the old age of 29. 'What is your specialty?' he asked through the translator. I answered, 'I am a clown.' His demeanor changed and he spoke directly to me. 'Ahhhh! You clown! You special trick!'" Lu Yi's circus partner of 40 years, Xia Ke Min, had become a celebrated clown in China after he retired from acrobatics. Although this Pickle clown, Diane Wasnak, was the opposite of Xia—a short, trim American woman—Lu Yi was good to his word that one day he would teach her a special trick, an acrobatic clown act that would make her a star on four continents.

John Gilkey: "Lu Yi can be very quiet, he's inward with his energy and pulls you in. That was a wonderful focusing energy for us. He became a magnet. We experienced it in those first days, when there wasn't a community around him yet, just a dozen or so performers in the Church. He was already a magnet, a soft-spoken genius."

Introductions finished, the Pickles got down to training—stretching, a series of kicks across the floor, then splits, handstands, forward rolls, and cartwheels.

Shana Carroll: "The Pickles had never had a coach before. He probably thought we were hopeless; looking at what we could do, which was almost nothing, and we were adults."

Wasnak, Charlotte Bachman, Ayin and Miriam De Sela, Aaron Jessup, Mykal Lewis, Noah Chorny, and Joan Mankin; Directed by Peter Brosius and Judy Finelli; Choreographed by Tandy Beal; Written by Erin Cressida Wilson.

After this warm-up, they moved on to their first specialty acts—hoop diving and pole climbing. Hoops and poles were new disciplines for the Pickle performers and they needed to build both their strength and their flexibility, and balance these two traits. In acts such as hoop diving and teeterboard, the need for strength and power is obvious—bodies have to fly. But without flexible shoulders in a teeterboard jump, an acrobat can't land correctly, and good splits are necessary for some of the basic hoop diving vocabulary. Flexibility also allows for clean body lines and pointed toes. Lu Yi would often say, "If someone takes a picture of you in the middle of a trick, that picture should look pretty."

Before the cast could dive through hoops, they had to work on the fundamentals of forward and backward rolls. "Forward roll, stand up." "Again." "Three rolls, no stopping." Then they worked on handsprings, then dive rolls, then dive rolls through a hula hoop.

The work on the pole started with pull ups—facing the pole, reaching high to grab the pole then pulling themselves up with their feet dragging along the pole. "Do again." Then the monkey climb, using hands and feet. "Up, down, up, down, up, down." "Again." "Stay strong." Then the squat, or frog climb, which works the inside of the legs, and finally a straight climb—all arms, no legs.

John Gilkey: "When Lu Yi gives you a note about the way you're climbing the pole, there's no doubt, you just don't doubt the guy. He didn't lord over us, he's the kind of a master who doesn't have to ask for respect, it's just there."

Seven hours later, the cast finished their first day's work with some conditioning—push-up hops across the room. They had heard some of Lu

Yi's favorite English phrases that day—"Do again." "Stay strong!"—and they would hear them a lot more in the months to come.

Lu Yi: "Acrobatics is an art for which you're willing to lose your life. That is not an exaggeration. The Pickle performers needed a lot of conditioning. They needed the basics. Chinese acrobatics is in-depth; you have to train more on the basics in Chinese acrobatics than in other forms. A strong foundation in strength, flexibility, handstands, tumbling, and partner acrobatics is important for anything you do in circus. Once you gain skills in those areas, you can become a successful acrobat. This also helps prevent injuries and accidents."

John Gilkey: "We knew we were absolutely fortunate to be in the presence of a master, almost like an alien from another planet dropped down with this information that nobody knew. Nobody in North America was doing hoop diving or pole climbing at that time; no one in the West except [Australia's] Circus Oz, as far as we knew, was doing that stuff. It was a secret."

In a few weeks, Lu Yi added teeterboard to the *La La Luna Sea* cast's training schedule, while continuing to work with them on diving through hoops and the basic vocabulary of Chinese pole, first near the floor for conditioning and safety, and later farther up the pole for performance.

A teeterboard looks like a large seesaw. The flyer stands on one end with either a mat or a catcher behind the flyer. The power is supplied by one or two other acrobats jumping on the high end of the teeterboard to launch the flyer. Because there is a lot of power in the act, and that power is amplified by the teeterboard, Lu Yi regularly warned the Pickles about the danger. He taught discipline with teeterboard, working it in a strict progression: The flyer starts a new move with a lot of protection—aerial spotting with two lines attached to the flyer's spotting belt that run up through pulleys rigged above the height of the trick and back down into the spotter's gloved hands. Lu Yi almost always did the spotting, especially with aerial lines.

A crash mat would be set behind the flyer for a trick like a double lay out. If the trick involved catchers, like a back tuck to a three high, an acrobatic base with a second mount on the base's shoulders would stand behind the flyer. The porter(s) would hit the high end of the teeterboard, the flyer would launch into a back tuck while the base of a two-high would adjust to put the second mount in position to catch the flyer.

When Lu Yi felt that the flyer was ready, that their legs were strong enough and their timing good enough that they wouldn't blow out a knee when the porter(s) launched them, he would ask the flyer to take off the belt. This was always a tense moment. Lu Yi, and sometimes another spotter, would stand to the sides, ready to break the flyer's fall if anything went wrong; the base and second mount had to take care of themselves.

. . .

Having Lu Yi suddenly in the center of the Pickles' world was experienced differently by different performers.

Shana Carroll: "Lu Yi had favorites and it could be very, very difficult if you weren't a favorite. Judy never gave the feeling that there were favorites. It had always been a collective, but this was a different culture that encouraged people to be competitive."

John Gilkey: "It felt like a privilege to be in that relationship with Lu Yi and his humility. I remember little things like the way he would touch, one finger here and there, to give focus to that part of your body."

While they were getting a crash course in Chinese acrobatics, the cast was also rehearsing with a complex script. *La La Luna Sea* was the Pickle's first attempt to stage a full-length circus play.[61] Judy Finelli had carefully assembled a team to create this ambitious show, including writer Erin Cressida Wilson from New York, director Peter Brosius from Los Angeles, Santa Cruz choreographer Tandy Beal, Bay Area composer Jeffrey Gaeto and Lu Yi from Nanjing. She wanted the performers to play characters and have objectives just like actors, not to simply do acrobatic technical exercises. "Lu Yi immediately grasped what I was trying to do."

The wild creativity of *Luna Sea* would be built on the orthodoxy of Lu Yi's technique.

---

61   Judy Finelli had directed a short circus play *Café des Artistes* in 1989. The Pickles' sister circus, Make*A*Circus, had been experimenting with scripted circuses since1983, when I wrote a script for their show that featured the entire audience.

8. UNDER THE BURNING SUN

"Everyone in San Francisco knew the Pickle Family Circus. It was simple and really fun. But we performed in a tent without a top. Because there was no top, the handstand mat was really hot. The pole was really hot. When we did teeterboard, we had to keep moving it because the sun would be in our eyes, making the flips harder."

- Huang Zhen

Long-time Pickle drummer Bill Belasco remembers the Pickles as a hippy organization, "...and when Judy Finelli got the Chinese over here, everything went up a notch. Huang Zhen and Zhou Yue raised the bar. They were so much fun to percuss—so talented. It inspired the band."

La La Luna Sea was a huge undertaking and touring the show would be a first, very public, test of the Nanjing/San Francisco circus connection. This timeline from the 1990 *La La Luna Sea* program gives a sense of the challenge getting the show on the road:

Jan. 18 – Still no script or writer.

Jan. 25 – Pickle Family Circus School classes for Very Young People start.

Feb. 2 – Erin Cressida Wilson writes a new script, beloved by all.

Feb. 5 – Immigration problems delay arrival of Chinese performers and trainer.

Mar. 7 – Dance, improv, voice and acting lessons start.

Mar. 18 – Lu Yi arrives in San Francisco.

Mar. 29 – Chinese performers still caught in red tape.

Apr. 21 – Aerialist Shana Carroll works 20' high for the first time.

Apr. 23 – The agony of hoop diving begins in earnest.

May 14 – Zhou Yue and Huang Zhen finally set foot on American soil.

June 2 – Diane (Pino) Wasnak practices teeterboard for the first time.

July 2 – Final dress rehearsal in the gym.

The plot of *La La Luna Sea* was woven around a conflict between the two main clowns, Diane (Pino) Wasnak and Joan (Queenie Moon) Mankin.

> Queenie Moon took Pino's saxophone. That's how *La La Luna Sea* begins. Then… Pino goes on a journey, a journey to find her saxophone, but everywhere there are villains, odd men on poles, grumpy guys with agendas. A tightrope walking crone becomes a maiden; everything old is new again; things are not what they seem. There is music on the moon. In the end, music is important enough to risk everything. In the end, music is everything. It's as complicated as the universe itself and as simple as two saxophones.[62]

The summer of 1990 found the Pickle Family Circus performing *La La Luna Sea* in parks up and down the Pacific coast. This was a strange new world for Nanjing natives Zhou Yue and Huang Zhen.

Huang Zhen: "I had never performed outside. We had to do everything, we even had to set up the tent sidewalls—this is not a performer's job! When I was in the U.S. before, with the Big Apple Circus, we didn't have to do set-up. People explained that the Pickles were a family, so it was different from other circuses."

Diane (Pino) Wasnak: "Everyone set up except Zhou Yue and Huang Zhen, who sat and smoked cigs. When I was pounding stakes, Lu Yi said, 'Why?

---

62   Description of Erin Cressida Wilson's script from San Francisco's Pickle Family Circus (1990, May) *La La Luna Sea*. [Program]. San Francisco, California.

Why not a machine?' I said, 'We don't have the money,' and he said, 'China has a machine.' Then Zhou Yue asked, 'When do we go to the hotel?' Everyone laughed. One of the technicians got two small tents and said, 'Here's your hotel.' Zhou Yue yelled at Lu Yi; she just went off."

Huang Zhen: "At night, we slept on the ground in little tents and then had to wake up at 6 am because of the sun and the heat. None of the Pickles spoke Chinese and I didn't speak English, so I had a little translator book. They teased me, but with acrobatics, the physical body is your language."

Shana Carroll: "The Chinese philosophy was that there are no stars but that artists shouldn't have to do manual work. But for the Pickles, the culture went back to the whole hippy movement. The Chinese acrobats didn't want to work in the way the company worked."

Lu Na, Lu Yi's younger daughter: "There weren't separate changing rooms for men and women; Americans just took their clothes off in front of each other. This would never happen in China. Zhou Yue and Huang Zen had to go hide somewhere to change."

Shana Carroll: "We were a working-class company. We worked as a collective, we all worked other jobs outside, and it was holding us back from becoming a company like Cirque du Soleil. Lu Yi wanted us to have this dignity and prestige. He pushed us to start performing in more indoor theaters."

Some of the Pickle performers also wanted the prestige of Cirque du Soleil.

Huang Zhen: "When we were on tour in New York, we visited Montreal. Cirque du Soleil was working on their show *Saltimbanco*, and they wanted me to join. By that time, it was everyone's dream to work there, but I said I had a contract with Pickle."

Huang Zhen also had a new, and covert, relationship with Shana Carroll.

Shana Carroll: "I was falling in love with Huang Zhen, but it was a secret because he had a wife back in China. When we were in Alaska, where we got to stay in hotels, Huang Zhen and I each had a roommate, but I would end up in his room anyway. One night we had food delivered and I answered the door in just a shirt. Lu Yi was standing across the hallway, and he was like, 'Sorry, sorry, so sorry.' We were found out."

Huang Zhen: "When the Pickles came home from the New York tour, we had nowhere to perform but we all needed money for food and rent."

Shana Carroll: "Before Lu Yi and the others left China, they had applied for visas for their loved ones. One day a visa came through for Huang Zhen's wife. I didn't know what to do. I didn't want to break up a marriage, or be a mistress."

Shana got on a plane and cried all the way to Montreal.

Shana Carroll: "I loved studying trapeze at the school in Montreal. Things were falling apart with the Pickles and Huang Zhen and I realized we wanted to be together, so I helped him come to Montreal."

Huang Zhen: "I told Lu Yi I can't just stay home to wait, that I had an offer with Cirque. He said, 'Oh yeah, that's a good place to be,' but he thought I was making a joke. I was the first one to get into Cirque du Soleil from the Pickles."

Shana Carroll: "Lu Yi felt very betrayed when Huang Zhen left. We don't have that notion of lifelong loyalty to a company here, so it was all mysterious to me."

Shana Carroll and Huang Zhen got married in 1993. "Lu Yi came but was kind of grumpy."

Watching his first show with the Pickle Family Circus was also bittersweet for Lu Yi.

Circus historian Ernest Albrecht wrote in *Spectacle* magazine that working in the United State, Lu Yi was "...pulled in two directions: a longing for the artistic level of achievement he had been a part of in China and an appreciation for his new-found freedom and the openness of American performers. As a way of putting the two parts of his life together... [he has] wed the skill level of Chinese acrobats with the outgoing personality of western artists."[63]

East had met West with joy and sweat, pain and love.

At this moment, co-founder Peggy Snider wrote, "I cannot help but think that, with the next generation of 'new circus' artists already entering the ring, circus arts in this country will be in good hands."[64]

63   Albrecht E. (2009, Spring) Lu Yi. A tour of Chinese acrobatics. *Spectacle. A Quarterly Journal of the Circus Arts*. (12).
64   San Francisco's Pickle Family Circus (1990, May) *La La Luna Sea*. [Program]. San Francisco, California.

SPOTLIGHT ON...

AMERICAN CIRCUSES

If you were to watch circuses like a bird watcher stares at birds, you would need a guide book to tell you what each "species" of circus looks and sounds like, and how they behave in their natural habitat. Focusing on three species—*Traditional Circus*, *New Circus* and *Contemporary Circus*—your guide to American circuses might look something like this:

TRADITIONAL OR CLASSIC CIRCUS:

Plumage: Lots of sequins and feathers; clowns in full costume and makeup; ringmaster in top hat and tails.

Habitat: Tent or arena with one or three rings; aerial rigging; often "thrill acts" like the Wheel of Death.

Behavior: An opening parade with all the performers, human and animal; a series of acts, each one with its own performers, some that are "death defying." Every act has its own "ta-da" moment, its own type of flourish. Clowns do some big acts, called "entrées" and also take focus as the roustabouts set up rigging or an animal cage or bring in a big piece of equipment.

Song: Live band or recorded music, often loud; ringmaster speaks, may sing; clowns may speak.

Examples: Ringling Bros. and Barnum & Bailey Circus, Circus Vargas, Clyde Beatty Cole Brothers, Culpepper Meriwether, Zoppe Family Circus.

NEW CIRCUS:

Plumage: Colorful costumes, less sequins and feathers, all part of one unified design; clowns in simpler costumes and less makeup; might not have a ringmaster.

Habitat: Theater, tent, or park (with one ring) or casino (mainly Cirque du Soleil).

Behavior: Fewer performers and almost all are human; a series of acts, often with a theme or story, with most performers appearing in multiple acts; the company has its own type of flourish; clowns do some entrées and work in transitions, sometimes as roustabouts setting up rigging or props.

Song: Live band; sometimes the clowns, the bandleader and/or the ringmaster speak.

Examples: Cirque du Soleil, Circus Bella, Universoul, Big Apple Circus, Sweet Can, Flynn Creek Circus, Circus Flora, Midnight Circus, Bindlestiff Family Cirkus, Troupe Vertigo.

CONTEMPORARY CIRCUS:

Plumage: Streetwear; no clowns, no ringmaster.

Habitat: Theater or nightclub (stage, not a ring).

Behavior: Small cast, all human, mostly young; smoothly flowing from act to act with all performers doing multiple roles, including dancing, spotting, setting up rigging and props; no flourishes.

Song: Live and/or recorded music, sometimes circus performers play music, sing, and/or speak.

Examples: The 7 Fingers, Nouveau Sud Circus Project, Cirque Mechanics.

Unlike most birds, modern circuses do a lot of cross breeding, so you may find yourself looking at a show that has elements of two or even all three of these "species;" *Traditional, New* and *Contemporary.*

If you are lucky, you will spot circuses migrating through the U.S. from other countries and, since circus as an art-form is an international affair, you will almost always see performers from elsewhere when you sit down to watch an American circus.

Even if you miss the big ones, there are hundreds of small circuses, as well as individual circus artists performing in burlesque, drag, and variety shows, at theme parks and county fairs, on TV competitions like "America's Got Talent" and busking on streets all over the country. And you can catch fledgling circus stars in shows produced by some of the 150-or-so circus schools in the U.S.

Now that you are ready to go circus watching, we'll return to our story at the point when Pickle Family Circus School meets their new acrobatic trainer—and Lu Yi starts the San Francisco Youth Circus.

ACT THREE:

STARS OF THE FUTURE

9. YOUTH CIRCUS: GEN ONE

1990 - 1992

Sanzang had no interest in honor and glory, and his only joy was to cultivate Nirvana. Investigation revealed that his origins were good and his virtue great; of the thousand sutras and ten thousand holy books there was not even one that he did not know; he could sing every Buddhist chant and knew all the religious music.[65]

"Lu Yi was not very imposing in size, but he was incredibly focused. He wore glasses, always had a little smile and a twinkle in his eye. He was polite and respectful and did not speak much English. Since he had been working with the Pickle performers, there was a very different culture and training style in their rehearsals and these performers were now many notches above the previous Pickle acrobats."

- Wendy Parkman, Co-Founder, Pickle Family Circus School

The adult performers in La La Luna Sea were thriving under Lu Yi's tutelage, but it was the children he was about to audition for his acrobatic classes that were, to him, the future. They would be the first generation of his troupe, the San Francisco Youth Circus. Respecting the system of honorifics used in China, the Youth Circus acrobats would call him "Mr. Lu Yi" or "Master Lu Yi" (adult performers, including myself, called him simply "Lu Yi.") He would train these children the way he had trained young performers in his

---

65   Wu, C. Jenner, W.J.F. (2005). *Journey to the West.* (C. Fair, Ed.). Disruptive Pub.

Nanjing troupe, eventually creating a U.S. version of the disciplined and sustainable Chinese model, with the added creativity and wildness of young Americans.

Shana Carroll: "Lu Yi was brought over to be the Pickle company coach, but he quickly lost interest in us. He wanted to work with the children. We had a very recreational school at the time, just a few classes on Saturday. He wanted to redo that structure. He said the Pickles needed a professional circus school that started children training at a young age."

The transient nature of performing careers in the U.S., lack of government funding for the arts, and competition from powerful circus organizations in Montreal would eventually challenge Lu Yi's dream of recreating his Nanjing Troupe system in San Francisco.

Xia Ke Min, Lu Yi's long time performing and teaching partner: "It's not easy to train even one circus performer. It takes a long time and commitment. In China, students are trained by the government. In America, the kids have school and other activities, so the training is more relaxed. It's harder to train one kid in America."

Long time Pickle and Cirque du Soleil performer Aloysia Gavre[66] grew up on Potrero Hill, near the Pickle Church. As a child, she would go to all the Pickle Family Circus shows in the park near her house, and take Saturday circus class with Judy Finelli, Wendy Parkman, and Hannah Kahn. "When I was 14, my younger brother and I went to audition for Lu Yi. He said, 'I love your brother, but you are too old and you don't have the fire. If you bring your brother, you can come.' My brother stayed for a year and then

---

66   Aloysia Gavre later performed the Pickles and Cirque du Soleil before co-founding Cirque Mechanics. She later co-created Cirque School in L.A., which spawned Troupe Vertigo.

quit, but during that year, Lu Yi instilled in me the joy of working hard towards something for the fun and excitement, even if you don't feel the final success. He was playful and quirky; he was an actor."[67]

Pickle co-founder Peggy Snider: "There were a lot of cultural issues. For example, Lu Yi only wanted students who could come five days a week, but no parent was going to send their kid to the circus five days a week. And one day Lu Yi came to me and said, 'I have the best idea for the circus. We dress the children as two different teams, the Cowboys and the Indians.' I was like, 'Lu Yi, we can't do that!' and he was like, 'Why not?'"

Judy Finelli, as the director of the Pickle Family School, told Lu Yi that he wasn't going to be able to run auditions like he and other acrobatic trainers did in China—watching hundreds of prospects try acrobatic skills, examining the most promising children's bodies, asking questions about their parents, and only taking the best of the best. "At first, he was a bit disheartened but little by little, he became impressed by the effort the students put into their practice time with him, and away from him."

Judy Finelli, Wendy Parkman, and the other main teacher Hannah Kahn were leading classes for children from five to 12 years old on Saturdays, although Judy's deteriorating health due to multiple sclerosis meant that Wendy and Hannah were taking more and more of the teaching load. After making some adjustments in the audition methods he used in Nanjing, Lu Yi went to Wendy and Hannah's classes to hand-pick the kids he would teach.

---

67   Aloysia Gavre, Aidan O'Shea, and Beth Clark, all Wendy Parkman's circus students at Urban School, were the only teenagers in this first group of Youth Circus students. You will meet Aidan later in this book; Beth went on to a career as a slack rope artist and founder of Sweet Can Productions, a theatrical circus, working with her husband Matt White and many other Lu Yi-trained performers.

Wendy Parkman: "He came to meet the five, six, and 7-year-olds to see if anyone was ready for a more rigorous program. He looked each person in the eye. He looked at their arms, wrists, legs, spines. I'm sure there were giggles at this intense kind of observation; he was actually assessing their bone structure. The parents and children were curious and somewhat mystified by this 'performance' of assessment, as was I, but quite a few children and their parents were game to sign up for this program."

Lu Yi's assessment has some similarities to pre-participation physical exams often done in sports. In the U.S., these screenings are usually looking for anything that would increase the risk of an athlete getting injured—where do they have weakness? Do they have good muscle performance and coordination? Are they hypermobile? Because of U.S. HIPAA laws, these exams are usually done in private.

First generation Youth Circus student Francisco Cruz[68] says that Lu Yi didn't want to see any skills, "...he just checked our knees, elbows, back. He told me, 'You might be able to tumble but you have flat feet so we will see. You won't be able to do handstands because you aren't flexible.' I was accepted. As Lu Yi went down the line of other kids he said, 'yes, yes, no, no,' just like he did in China. He thought that if you can't be good at acrobatics, why waste your time."

What Lu Yi was doing is often referred to as "talent identification," and it is done across sports and performing arts—trying to identify who has physical characteristics that make them likely to become an elite performer. Lu Yi knew what body types could handle the stresses of each specific discipline and what might make performing that discipline difficult—flat feet are a

---

68   Francisco Cruz was in the first Youth Circus group; his brothers Raphael and Dominic joined, too. He was interviewed with Will Underwood, another first generation Youth Circus performer.

liability for a tumbler, elite hand-balancers can't have tight shoulders, flyers can't have floppy joints.

Back in China, Lu Yi's Nanjing Acrobatic Troupe was offering the equivalent of lifetime contracts to young children, so knowing as much about each prospective acrobat as possible—and about their parents—was necessary. One way to imagine the Chinese business model is to think of it as a professional basketball league, if the NBA drafted players out of grade schools and committed to employing each player for the rest of their career. Lu Yi was, in this analogy, the general manager and head coach of the Nanjing Acrobatic Basketball Team. He "drafted" new performers every two to five years, bringing in children with great potential while trying to fill the gaps on his current roster. For example, if one of his hand-to-hand bases retired, he would look for a big, strong kid. If a contortionist retires, he's looking for someone stretchy.

In San Francisco, Lu Yi still wanted to evaluate each student's body in order to select students who would likely become elite and then train them for success and safety. This book is testament to the number of Lu Yi's American students who have had success, stayed healthy and enjoyed a long career and a life-long relationship with Lu Yi, their *lǎoshī* (teacher).

Some of the training techniques Lu Yi used in Nanjing, which were much more humane than what he grew up with, were not going to work in San Francisco. His new students already had full lives—acrobatics would have to fit in with homework, soccer, and family vacations. Parents would have more influence over how Lu Yi worked than they had back in Nanjing. And he would have to learn how to manage a gym full of American children.

Francisco Cruz's friend and fellow Gen One Youth Circus student Brad Henderson:[69] "I was in fourth or fifth grade and wasn't hooked at first. I liked it but I was scared at the pace we were learning stuff. Lu Yi was strict. It was a little intimidating because it was almost militant. And we had to wear uniforms—black sweats with red tees for boys and the girls wore white tights with red leotards. The school needed money so everyone was welcome—but only some got to work with Lu Yi."

Francisco Cruz: "We didn't come from a background of gymnastics or any other discipline. If we didn't point our toes, he would hit our feet; if we needed to straighten our back, he'd hit our back. This created some conflict with parents, but this is how he explained it, 'I have to hit. The hit creates the instinct.'"

Given these challenges, Judy Finelli decided to find Lu Yi a teaching assistant. By her own assessment, Karen Quest was an odd choice. A former juggler with the Pickle Family Circus, Karen was not an acrobat, although she had been a gymnast in high school, and she didn't speak any Mandarin. She now says that "Judy can see things in people they can't see in themselves." Karen was performing in Japan and studying Japanese when Lu Yi first arrived in San Francisco, but she started assisting him soon after she got home.

In class, Karen's job was to line the children up, make sure they respected Lu Yi and try to intuit what was needed. "I wish I had known about Lu Yi's background then—he wouldn't have been an enigma. I would have known he had this hard life."

---

69   Brad Henderson was another first generation Youth Circus student and a lifelong friend of Francisco Cruz. We interviewed Brad and his sister Sadie together. Brad's three siblings, Sadie, Devin, and Marta also joined the Youth Circus.

After observing Lu Yi, Wendy Parkman, and Hannah Kahn, Karen was able to integrate American educational techniques with the training and spotting methods of Chinese acrobatics. This cross-pollination and integration of training techniques would become a hallmark of Bay Area circus. Here, for example, is the detailed approach that Karen Quest developed to teaching a child to do a basic forward roll:

> "I'd say, 'Stand with your arms straight over your head. Now bend at the waist and put your hands flat on the floor in front of you, but not too close. Now keep your bottom up in the air, bend your knees and tuck your chin. When you roll, your upper back will touch the mat, but your head never touches the ground.' With some kids, I put one hand on their belly and one on the back of their neck. 'Now bend your knees and push with your toes to get over. Propel yourself, you're a tight little ball. Now reach forward with your hands and don't touch the mat again! Try to end up standing with your arms straight over your head, the same position you started in.' If they couldn't stand up, I'd sometimes get in front of them as they rolled and say, 'Reach for me.'"

The challenges that Lu Yi faced in his new home were exacerbated by language. He was in his 50s when he started learning English. In China, he was known as an eloquent speaker and an innovative thinker. In his first year in the U.S. he had to rely on short English phrases like "Do again," "Stronger," and "Training is bitter." According to Karen Quest, early on, Lu Yi only used what little English he picked up from the kids—just the words he needed to convey the basic concepts of Chinese acrobatics.

Some veterans of the Youth Circus now talk about Lu Yi's struggles to teach in a second language as a positive. To them, he was an authority figure who could communicate even though he didn't speak English fluently, modeling a way to work in a foreign language.

First generation Youth circus members Maya Kesselman (Cruz) and Marta Henderson:[70] "He was so good at what he did that we didn't care if sounded silly when he explained things. Looking back, I realize this gave us confidence to learn new languages, to just try to communicate." Since circus is an international, multilingual field, this confidence with language has helped many of Lu Yi's students' careers.

Lu Yi's "otherness" in both language and style was an attraction to many students and parents—in the same way that "otherness" would help the performers Lu Yi sent to Nanjing two decades later. Lu Yi's focus on discipline and respect, along with his obvious skill and dedication to his students, won over the San Francisco parents.

Francis Cruz, father of three, including Francisco Cruz: "As I watched each of my three sons enter into a passion for acrobatics, I realized that Lu Yi was teaching them to love. It's not to learn a back handspring but to love doing a back handspring. Every time a student was successful, I'd see Lu Yi's face light up and I'd feel good. There was something that transpired between Lu Yi and my sons that was magic, and that was heaven for me."

---

70   We interviewed Marta Henderson, the youngest of four Youth Circus siblings, with her long-time friend and former Youth Circus partner Maya Kesselman (Cruz).

10. CIRCUS LOVE

"A lot of the training was not that fun. It was painful sometimes. We would come home and complain about knee and ankle pain, or how hard something was, but our parents trusted Lu Yi. They trusted him completely. Our dad told us, 'Lu Yi is like your second father. Listen to everything he says.' And Lu Yi learned over time to allow American kids a bit more leeway, more time to play, than the kids he trained in China."

- Brad Henderson

Changing his approach to auditions, however slightly, was only the first adjustment that Lu Yi had to make in his new position as head of the San Francisco Youth Circus. Once he had his chosen group of students, he needed to change many of the ways he taught. Lu Yi's own training was brutal, as he details in the book *Training is Bitter*. "Our teacher, Pan Yin, used to hit us every day, sometimes every hour. This is a very dangerous way to train. You get so nervous thinking about that stick that it's easy to mess up. If you ran a circus like that now, you would go to jail."[71]

Francisco Cruz and Will Underwood:[72] "Lu Yi told us that in China there are hand balancers who train by lighting a stick of incense, going up in their handstand and not coming down until the incense goes out. He also told us there was an acrobat who broke his leg and when it came out of the cast, it was crooked. He took a board, broke his leg again, and told the doctor, 'Make it straight this time. This leg is my life.'"

---

71   Lu, Yi., Holt, D. (2023). *Training is Bitter*. Periodgraph Press.
72   Will Underwood is another member of the first generation of the San Francisco Youth Circus.

Aloysia Gavre: "I was addicted to handstands. There was an enormous sense of satisfaction meeting your 10 seconds mark, then 20 seconds. Lu Yi's goal was 2 minutes. And you can do handstands anywhere, anytime and all his tidbits about technique gave you that meditative feeling. Quieting of the mind pre-show and post-show, that was Lu Yi's approach to teaching handstands."

Francis Cruz, father of three acrobats: "Acrobatics made our family more in touch with each other. The growth and development occurred from watching your children mature in an art-form. It could have been piano, guitar, something where the skill is honed not just because of the student's ability but because the person who is bringing them along loves them, loves that this talent is developing in their student."

Lu Yi's training methodology was new to Americans at the time, although many of the principles behind that methodology are now common practice here.

Francisco Cruz: "We would do basics, basics, basics. He wouldn't let us juggle. So many roundoffs, repetition, repetition. He would say, '250 roundoffs,' and I'd just have to put my head down and do it. Lots of v-ups. He was very basic and simple in the exercises we did. Not a lot of variety. High repetition."

Writer and former basketball star Kareem Abdul-Jabbar was coached at UCLA by John Wooden and later trained in martial arts with Bruce Lee: "... both [these teachers] emphasized practicing fundamentals over and over... In sports, we call this concept 'muscle memory.' By practicing the same movement over and over and over, your body will react without the brain telling it to."[73]

Francisco Cruz: "We didn't do stretching at the start of class; we'd do our kicks, cartwheels and roundoffs."

Dr. Stephanie Greenspan, who treats and studies circus injuries and prevention: "Movements like kicks, unlike static stretching, increase body temperature, getting muscles and the nervous system prepared for acrobatics. Muscle metabolism (how nutrients are used to generate energy for muscle contraction) and neural transmission (messages from brains to muscles) get more efficient. This leads to a more efficient muscle activation and better performance."

Francisco Cruz: "...then we'd jump back and forth on platforms, varying in height between two and three feet, for 2-minute increments or 50 jumps. Lu Yi told us, 'Do them as fast as you can.' His whole philosophy was 'air sense'—go in the air, do the flip, and land on the ground. No technique really. Go super high, and know where you are in the air. Don't give in to the landing. Land quietly."

Dr. Stephanie Greenspan: "Jumping on and off a platform with an emphasis on speed follows the principles of plyometrics.[74] Plyometrics is a form of training for more power—a quick stretch of the tendons, followed by a fast rebound, allows tendons to store and then release elastic energy. More power means higher and faster jumps. Lu Yi's emphasis on having a fast turn-

---

73   Abdul-Jabbar, K. Obstfeld, R. (2017). *Becoming Kareem: Growing up on and off the court.* Little, Brown Books for Young Readers.
74   Fred Wilt, a former U.S. Olympic runner, coined the term Plyometrics after watching the Russian team doing jumps before a meet while his colleagues were doing static stretches.

over—jump, land and go up again quickly—most likely helped his students become powerful in tumbling and acrobatics (his students are known for their ability to fly high in the air). Lu Yi helped young acrobats build power by training them for height and speed, and doing this without having to hit the ground harder on take-off or landing."

Francisco Cruz: "In the Chinese style, your body [needs] a good foundation to do the tricks. That's different from what I know of the Russian style. In the Russian style, they seem to get hurt all the time. I've never missed a show in my career. None of [Lu Yi's students] have Achilles problems. Many acrobats have Achilles problems because they trained on a sprung floor, and we trained on just a carpet."

Dr. Stephanie Greenspan: "An Achilles tear is often from the punch, the take off, not the landing. On a harder floor, the punch has to be softer and lighter; you can hit a sprung floor harder. Lu Yi figured out how to get the same height as you would from a sprung floor, but from a punch that is softer and lighter. Biomechanically, the effect of tumbling on hard floors could be compared to barefoot running. Running barefoot allows a runner's foot to feel when it hits the ground. This makes the runner naturally lighten the landing, decreasing the impact on joints. With sprung tumbling floors or cushioned running shoes, the athlete's feet don't feel the impact, so they don't make the natural adjustment to a lighter landing. Modern runners often hear the same thing as Lu Yi's students: 'Lightly, quietly.' "

Guang Rong Lu says that Lu Yi was heavily influenced by the Chinese philosophy of Yin Yang, two sides to everything. Hit the ground lightly to fly high; repeat the basics now so you can innovate later. "Lu Yi starts with the fundamental skills which are the building blocks. Just like with writing, you need a vocabulary and grammar, then you can develop a good book."

...

Francis Cruz: "When my son Raphael was healing from a broken arm, he would just sit in the gym and watch. Every time Raphael said, 'I'm ready,' Lu Yi would say, 'Not yet,' and go back to training the other students. Raphael was chomping at the bit—nothing motivated him more than seeing everyone else getting Lu Yi's attention. I thought that was genius. Lu Yi showed compassion, told Raphael that he needed to heal, while inspiring the need to train. By the time Lu Yi said 'OK, do handstands,' it was like a flood of 'finally you are looking at me and I'm training again!'"

Lu Yi eventually adopted that credo that "love is the only way to train children," but "love" in the setting of acrobatic training does not mean "without fear." There is always some fear because acrobatics is dangerous. When training a new trick, fear is multiplied the moment the safety belt comes off. Lu Yi chose that time carefully and would have spotters in place, including himself. If the trick went wrong, someone would catch them. Youth Circus veterans remember that "...sometimes you were so scared you'd go up and hide in the bathroom. Lu Yi would come up after five minutes. He knew you were trying to avoid doing a difficult trick."

Aloysia Gavre: "I wasn't fearless, I didn't have that fire—I never even got a back handspring without him spotting me—and I knew Lu Yi wished I was more fearless, but he kept me on and gave me so much love and support."

Will Underwood: "Lu Yi would always catch you. I remember one time doing monkey climbs, I slipped and fell, he reached out his arm and caught me. He put me down on the mat and told me to 'Do again.'"

Devin Henderson and Dominic Cruz, Francisco's youngest brother: "Lu Yi spent a lot of time spotting, which is part of why his coaching was so helpful. He would point, push, catch. You felt safe. The number of times his glasses got knocked off! Students would do a round off, land directly in front of him and he would lift you up so you would feel the suspension. He got hit a lot."

John Gilkey: "Spotting someone is a form of listening, of being open to other people and their needs. If you're spotting someone on pole or spotting an aerial act, that's a form of listening. It takes you outside yourself. You have to focus on them instead of on your ego. It's respect for circus."

Aloysia Gavre: "Lu Yi wanted me to bounce from the trampoline up to a three high, and then jump back down to the trampoline. I was too scared to go backwards when I couldn't see the trampoline, so for two weeks he had me crawl down the other two bodies. He was able to coddle me, and I was able to get over the fear."

Lu Yi: "For anyone you work with, you have to be responsible for them, make sure you don't cause injury with them. In a circus school or a professional show, you need to be a responsible trainer. The love and discipline have to go both ways, from the teacher to the students and from the students to the teacher."

Lu Yi's Chinese students loved him, and they certainly had discipline—but they weren't necessarily excited about acrobatics. Even the elite performers who came with him to the U.S. had a range of feelings about their un-chosen careers, from love for circus, to acceptance, to boredom.

Huang Zhen: "We were just acrobatic performers in China, no acting classes. In the U.S. we had to train as actors and be a part of the story. After I moved to Montreal, we had mask class, dance class, singing class. I started as just an acrobatic performer but putting it all together really made a big difference."

Putting circus together with dance, theater and music is thrilling to an audience. It inspires performers, whether they started with acrobatics as a child, like Huang Zhen, or they learned acrobatics later in life. "Putting it all together" has also helped create the vibrant, diverse Bay Area circus community. Before every show, every performer makes a choice, consciously or unconsciously, to be an artist or to just get through. If you have a complex, artistically dynamic challenge ahead of you—and you love what you're doing—it is easier to choose "artist." If a whole cast consistently choses "artist," the show gets better and better. If a whole community choses "artist," the art-form flourishes.

Lu Yi offered many things that his young San Francisco students loved. They were part of the community and they trusted Lu Yi because he had so much passion. Over time, his students became ambitious, they wanted to be in the gym, they wanted to be on stage, they wanted to be circus stars and they knew they needed Lu Yi's sense of discipline to get there. Some of the younger kids played around but when they saw the older kids learning tricks that were harder and more exciting, they got serious about training. All the students saw Chinese acrobats doing "crazy tricks" and they wanted to do what their Chinese counterparts were doing.

Francis Cruz, father of former Youth Circus students Francisco, Raphael and Dominic Cruz: "All three of my sons, at some point, said, 'I don't want to train today.' I said, 'My job is to drive. When we get there, you can either stay in the van and listen to me for two hours or you can go into the gym and train. But my job is to drive you. After that it is up to you.' They never stayed in the van."

When this first generation of Youth Circus acrobats had trained for a few years, Lu Yi sent them out to perform. They were guests in Pickle shows, similar to how his Nanjing students were slotted into acts with the professional troupe. They also went out on their own, American style.

Marta Henderson and Maya Kesselman Cruz: "We would go do gigs for Chinese people. Lu Yi had costumes sent over from China—orange flowing pants, green uniform top, and headpieces. But it wouldn't always be Chinese music; a cool mix of old traditional Chinese technique and adding our own style. Lu Yi was not there for all of them, but he would coordinate everything—who was driving, where we were staying. We were paid for these gigs and we performed as far away as Reno, and all the local festivals—Tenderloin Festival, opening of the de Young Museum, the Asian Art Museum, Yerba Buena Center."

Judy Finelli's two big projects were launched—high level acrobatic training for both the stars-to-be of the San Francisco Youth Circus and the Pickle Family Circus pros. The budding Nanjing/San Francisco relationship was reciprocal—the Chinese artists in San Francisco were learning creative new ways to be on stage, while the Americans finally had the structure to arrive as acrobats. Now that 2,000 years of Chinese acrobatic technique was available to Judy's students, she wanted to add the younger, more theatrical Russian style to the mix.

11. CENTURIES OF KNOWLEDGE

A "revolving ladder" sits horizontally in the air on a pivot. An acrobat stands on one end of the ladder, balancing another acrobat standing on the other end. At some point, the two acrobats flip the ladder around. John Gilkey was supposed to perform on a custom-made version created with two ladders—it was supposed to look like a biplane. John remembers a pep talk by one of the trainers before he climbed onto the apparatus for the first time; "Remember, someone died on this equipment. OK, go ahead and start playing." The biplane act never made it into the show.

In the 1970s and 1980s most American New Circus acrobats, unlike their Chinese and Russian counterparts, had no access to teachers who could keep them safe while they went about the hard work of daredevilry. Because circus in the U.S. was not yet considered an art-form, and training was still mostly family based, there were only a few circus schools.[75] This meant that, with the exception of Hovey Burgess at N.Y.U., there were very few teachers outside of circus families with deep experience and knowledge of circus skills, or circus equipment. No one was there to bring discipline and technique to the wild ideas (like the biplane) of the first generation of New Circus performers and directors.

Judy Finelli wanted Russian and Chinese trainers because they had that depth of knowledge—decades or even centuries of it.

---

75   Gamma Phi Circus at Illinois State University, founded in 1929 and Florida State University's Flying High Circus, founded in 1947, were the two biggest.

The roots of Chinese acrobatics go back nearly four millennia, but it blossomed during the Qin and Han dynasties (221 BCE - 220 CE). The acts evolved from peoples' everyday lives, often peasants' lives. Chinese farmers and village craftspeople could improve their societal standing by becoming acrobats, jugglers, rope dancers, and hand balancers. Performers exhibiting skills of strength and agility first appeared in the annual harvest celebrations of the Han Dynasty in a form known as *The Hundred Entertainments*. Within this set repertoire, generations of artists increased the level of difficulty of the tricks and improved their presentation.

In October 1949, six months after the Communists took Nanjing, the stronghold of Chiang Kai-shek's Nationalists, Mao Zedong announced the establishment of the People's Republic of China. This new Chinese government supported a renaissance of "Acrobatic Theater" even as it curtailed other arts, following the policy of "Let a hundred flowers blossom and weed through the old to bring forth the new [Baihua qifang tuichen chuxin]." As Mariam Ala-Rashi writes in *China's Bending Bodies*, "...utilizing the human body as an instrument to cater to a political agenda has been a tried and tested method for centuries... today's training methods [are] rooted in Mao Zedong's socialist China."[76]

This government support may have been because the agrarian roots of Chinese circus fit well with the government's lionization of farmers, as well as Mao Zedong's focus on strength and action: "Because man is an animal, movement is most important to him. And because he is a rational animal,

---

76   "In his memoir *Shanghai Acrobat - A True Story of Courage and Perseverance from Revolutionary China*, Jingjing Xue writes that he "...rubbed shoulders with key political leaders, while at other times endured countless threats and privation at the hands of the anti-intellectual and anti-artistic Maoist regime that included interrogation, forced labor, and detainment." Ala-Rashi, M. (2022). *China's Bending Bodies*. (T. Wall, Ed.) Modern Vaudeville Press.

his movement must have reason."[77] Mao may have also been influenced by his friendship with Xia Juhua, a famous acrobat who reintroduced the ancient *Pagoda of Bowls* balancing act. She became Lu Yi's boss at the Chinese Acrobatics Association and is now a member of the National People's Congress.

Acrobatic troupes were created in every major Chinese city with funding for their own theaters and schools. Much of the teaching was—and still is—done within the troupe. Older performers train the new generation.

Mariam Ala-Rashi refers to Jingjing Xue, who was recruited from a Chinese orphanage at the age of nine, for insight into the life of a student at the Shanghai Acrobatic Troupe. "Part of the curriculum were general subjects such as math, geography, Chinese, and history. Political education—including revolutionary ideology into the minds of future proletarians—was the objective in class across all curricula... Starting in 1956, a five-year acrobatic program was taught at the troupe. The program broke the thousand-year-old Chinese tradition in which one master single-handedly taught his students, and replaced it with an educational scheme based on the Soviet model. Staff included professional acrobats [troupe members], and cultural, dance and music teachers. We received training in all of these areas, laying the foundations for us to become skilled acrobats who would make our names throughout the world. All costs for education, food and board were covered by the government."[78]

77   Carter. J. (2021, July 21). *Power of Symbolism: The swim that changed Chinese history.* The China Project. quoted in Ala-Rashi, M. (2022). *China's Bending Bodies.* (T. Wall, Ed.) Modern Vaudeville Press.
78   *ibid.*

The Chinese government also paid for the troupe's facilities. Xiaohong Weng describes the original Nanjing Acrobatic Troupe's training space as "a ballroom dancing studio built in 1930, before the revolution, by Chiang Kai-shek who was then president of the Republic of China. The Troupe moved to another building in the early 1990s, after Lu Yi left. It was six stories tall, with the circus troupe on the fourth floor and parts of the fifth and sixth floors because the aerial acts needed the extra height. The first floor was a Chinese folk music group, second was Peking Opera, third was Shaoxing Opera, fourth was circus, half of fifth floor was a drama group and half of the sixth was a cultural library and offices. Ten years later, they built another space on top of the roof for acrobatic ground acts only."

According to Lu Yi, there were also specialized artisans who supplied acrobatic troupes with equipment. When he lived in Nanjing, all the circus equipment—umbrellas, hats, bowls, jars, etc.—complied with Chinese standards, which Lu Yi said were understood but not written down. "Only one person made the umbrellas, very special umbrellas, and there was a famous person in Hangzhou who made equipment for all the different Chinese troupes." Now there are more manufacturers, and some circus performers even buy their equipment from TaoBao (the Chinese version of Etsy or eBay).

. . .

Circuses didn't appear in Russia until the 18th century, although traveling performers entertained in the village fairs of ancient Rus. In the early 1790s, Catherine the Great, empress of Russia, fell in love with the circus when Charles Hughes arrived in St. Petersburg with his London's Royal Circus. Hughes had co-founded the Royal Circus in 1782 to compete with his former employer, the English circus pioneer Phillip Astley. The empress was so taken by the circus and its proprietor—Hughes may have been one of Catherine's lovers—that she ordered amphitheaters built for him in St. Petersburg and Moscow.

After the 1917 Bolshevik revolution, Vladimir Lenin recognized the popular appeal of the circus and, in 1919 signed a decree that, among other things, mandated the state appropriation of private circuses, "enterprises that are, on the one hand, profit-making and, on the other hand, democratic by virtue of the public that attends them." The Soviet Government established the Circus Section of the theater department of the "People's Commissariat of Enlightenment." In 1921, the Circus Section supervised the incorporation of all private circuses within the Russian Republic into local departments of public education. The speed with which the Bolsheviks incorporated circuses into their structures—two years before they did the same for cinema—was an indication of the prominent position the circus would enjoy in the Soviet Union.[79]

By 1939, 69 stationary circuses and fourteen traveling circuses operated in the Soviet Union, reportedly reaching nineteen million viewers annually. In 1964, Laurens van der Post, a South African, toured the Soviet Union and "...found the circuses even more significant than ballet, theater or opera, for the importance of the circus to the ordinary people themselves is evident." As he explained in his travelog, every major city featured a permanent circus, many housed in "buildings of unparalleled opulence."[80]

Before the Soviet Union was dissolved in 1991, Soviet circus schools offered four-year programs with classes in the full range of circus skills plus theater, dance, history, and more. Soviet circuses were known for their theatrical displays, wide variety of animal acts, high level acrobatics—both on the

79   Neirick, M. (2012) *When Pigs could Fly and Bears could Dance: A History of Soviet Circus.* The University of Wisconsin Press.
80   *ibid.*

ground and in the air—as well as great clowning (when the clown Yuri Nikulin died in 1997, the *Manchester Guardian Weekly* reported that he was beloved by 'tens of millions' across the former Soviet nations).[81]

...

What is considered American circus today started in England. Phillip Astley and his wife Patty Jones had found success presenting equestrian trick-riding displays in London; in 1768, they added a wooden fence, what is now called a sidewall, so that people had to pay before they could see the show.[82] After adding music, acrobats, and clowns between horse acts, they had a circus. This style of circus became popular in the U.S. when it arrived from England soon after.

Since many 18th and 19th century Americans never had the means to leave their small rural towns, a visit from the circus was a big deal—a must-go event.[83] With no television, radio or internet, the circus was their only chance to see exotic animals—not to mention people from all over the world doing amazing feats. The American Experience documentary *The Circus (Part 1)* suggests that circus helped create American culture: "In an age before radio,

---

81   *ibid.*

82   Whether an audience pays after they see the performance or beforehand makes a big difference for an art-form; if they pay after, like the early Astley shows or modern street performers, artists become very attuned to their audience—lunch depends on being able to adapt to each crowd and wow them. Unfortunately, when I was a street performer, the thought of missing lunch made us leery of trying new material and too tempted to 'borrow' someone else's best tricks. When the audience pays first, artists can often experiment more, but are in danger of losing their urgent connection with everyone in every crowd.

83   "America was an agrarian society. And it was a hard life that you had—you woke up early and you worked through the day. And then, all of a sudden, if you were so lucky, for one magical day you were transported from your work-a-day world into the spangles, into the spectacle that crisscrossed the country, the circus." Samels, M. (Executive Producer). (2018) *American Experience: The Circus*. [TV mini-series] A Winter Pink Films Production; PBS. https://www.pbs.org/wgbh/americanexperience/films/circus/

in an age before film, in an age before television, the circus offered audiences in vastly different geographical locations, a common cultural experience. It transforms America into a nation with a shared cultural identity."[84]

In the States, circuses grew up differently than their Chinese or Russian counterparts. Since 1825, when Joshuah Purdy Brown introduced a full canvas tent, most American circuses have been "under canvas," and almost always in a 42-foot diameter ring, the size Astley used because it works well for trick riding. Adding two more rings was the brainchild of John Ringling when his show started touring to big cities and county seats with a 10,000-capacity tent—even the cheap seats were relatively close to one of the rings. In contrast, Chinese circuses, both then and now, perform on theater stages, no horses, no ring. Permanent Russian circus buildings are custom designed around a ring, with lots of space to house animals of all kinds.[85]

The way circus shows are created also differs from country to country. In China, shows are staged by regional troupes, which can have up to 70 performers working for permanent, government-sponsored organizations that have their own theaters and training facilities. Students selected for their local troupe will usually spend their entire career there, graduating from student, to performer, to trainer—and possibly ending up as a technician or administrator.[86]

84   *ibid.*

85   Ward, S. (2023). *Opulence & Ostentation*. (T. Wall, Ed.) Modern Vaudeville Press.

86   In China, performing artists are categorized into four levels based on their theoretical, literary, and artistic knowledge, the level of their college degree, their artistic achievements, and performance skills, as well as the importance of their role within the troupe and the type of the venues where they have performed—provincial, national or international. Some mid-career performers who also work as technicians apply for their next level in a technical category. For example, Xiaohong Weng was a third level stage lighting designer while he was still performing with the Nanjing Acrobatic Troupe.

All Chinese troupes create acts from the same repertoire and put those acts together into full-length shows. To gain national recognition, Chinese acrobats must perform the existing canon with superior grace and artistry while also trying to invent harder tricks on traditional equipment (e.g. Xia Ke Min's quadruple somersault off a teeterboard in 1955). Innovations on the standard repertoire are rare, which is why Lu Yi holds a unique place in Chinese acrobatics. When a regional company does create something new—like the Guangdong troupe's 2002 double's acrobatics act performed as a ballet pas de deux—all the other troupes are expected to imitate and try to out-do the new "original." An annual calendar of circus festivals allows regional troupes to see what their competition is doing and show off their own work.

The Soviet Union also had regional schools dotted across the country's 11 time zones.[87] As in China, most circus students came from auditions, not from circus families. Unlike the Chinese system, students in Russia's regional circus schools created acts that they hoped would take them around the country, performing in shows with many different troupes and artists. An avid Soviet circus fan wouldn't need to leave their hometown to see a new show every month since their local circus building featured a wide variety of acts rotating in from around the country.

The basic unit of the Soviet system was the act, while the basic unit of the Chinese system is the troupe. In the U.S. today, the basic unit is often the individual performer. For most of America's circus history, however, acts were also the basic unit of circus—and most acts were family-based. An

---

87   According to the AYCO/ACE *Circus Census 2022* there are 148 circus schools in the U.S. but none of them match the scale and depth of the Chinese or Soviet programs. American Circus Educators. American Youth Circus Organization. (2022) *Circus Census 2022 Final Report*. https://www.americancircuseducators.org/wp-content/uploads/2022/10/ACE-AYCO-Survey-Final-Report.pdf

act would get hired onto a show for a season, bringing their own costumes, music, and style. Like in the Soviet Union, a good American circus director would need to bring in the right variety of acts from anywhere they could find them, then arrange these acts in a way that would thrill the audience—a big opening number, often called "spec," clown acts to cover the transitions, a big first-half closer and a "topper" act right before the finale. In China, a circus director needs to train and create each of those acts from within their company before they can program their show, a challenge that requires careful, long-term planning.

For the Pickle Family Circus, the troupe was the basic unit—although they did occasionally bring on an outside act. Even though the word "family" was in their name, it didn't refer to a biological family, rather a family of like-minded performers, technicians, and administrators. And most of the performers had little to no experience with other circuses, at least in the '70s and early '80s. Many of them came from theater, dance, music and/or street performing.

. . .

Judy Finelli: "Russians have been doing theater and circus in combination from the 1920s, when Lenin started the first circus school. They performed parts from history or movies or acts inspired by rock music, etc., whereas the Chinese are the technicians obsessed with perfection and not emotion."[88]

---

88   "The image of discipline and perfection was given great importance [by the Chinese Communist Party] and up until the early 1970s, most acrobatic troupes across the country still dressed their performers in army uniforms" Zhang, T.Y. (2016). Bending the Body for China: the uses of acrobatics in Sino-US diplomacy during the Cold War. *International Journal of Cultural Policy.* (22), 123-146.

Lu Guang Rong remembers a time when Chinese acrobatics was more like Russian circus: "Lu Yi was very good on the creative side because he was an artist. He was always looking to break boundaries. He was also influenced by the cultural revolution when we started producing revolutionary circus performances. We had a narrative for every show, adding theater and music. [But] when the U.S. and China started having a dialogue [in 1979], our leaders didn't think Americans would like to watch revolutionary circus, so we went back to traditional Chinese circus with big skills."

Zhou Liangtie, a magician and former acrobat from the Shanghai Acrobatic Troupe, talked about a different reaction to the "revolutionary circus performances" in his interview with Tracy Zhang. In this quote, Zhou is talking about the American magician Mark Wilson, who started staging magic shows around China in 1980. "After my colleagues and I saw Mark's magic, we thought 'Wow. Now we were allowed [by the government] to put on a show with disco music and young women dressed in miniskirts… People were tired of watching revolutionary operas and films; they wanted to see shows that featured attractive costumes and fun music. Meanwhile, performers, who had discontinued their careers due to 'bad class background,' could return to the stage [and were] eager to restore the repertoires previously considered 'bourgeois.'"[89]

Before coming to San Francisco, Judy (Finelli) Burgess and Hovey Burgess led a theatrical circus, Circo dell'Arte and the idea that circus performers can—and should—be skilled in theater as well as dance, mime, and music, was already part of the Bay Area culture. The founders of the Pickle Family Circus-Peggy Snider, Larry Pisoni and Cecil Mackinnon-came from the

89   Zhang, T. (2016) From China to the Big Top: Chinese acrobats and the politics of aesthetic labor, 1950 - 2010. *International Labor and Working-Class History*. (89), 40-63. https://doi.org/10.1017/S0147547915000332

San Francisco Mime Troupe,[90] a Tony Award® winning theater company. The style that the Pickle's pioneered, "New Circus," is a North American approach to combining circus, dance, theater and music. This addition of theatricality and a wide variety of emotions to circus fit perfectly with Lu Yi's dream of re-invigorating Chinese acrobatics.

Judy Finelli wanted to draw from all three of these rich circus traditions, Chinese, Russian and American. Since the Pickles were in San Francisco, she felt that the students could take advantage of American freedoms to learn both Chinese and Russian techniques, and acts, as well as ones from the United States. An American polyglot, multicultural, global approach to circus training. It was an ambitious plan.

---

90   The Mime Troupe still performs politically charged, physically bold musicals with a live band in parks around the Bay Area.

12. A DREAM TRANSMUTED

"This idea of combining Chinese and Russian teachers was in my head, but it would have needed more development. Mr. Lu Yi and Mr. Zenov were not thinking along those lines. I'm an American and I was overly optimistic."

- Judy Finelli

As Lu Yi was acclimatizing to life in the U.S., Russian acrobat Sergey Zenov was touring North America with the Moscow Circus, performing in Vladislav Chernievski's epic teeterboard act. Glenn Collins of *The New York Times* reviewed this act in 1988: "The control and technique of the Moscow Circus's gymnasts reveal their formal schooling in acrobatics and ballet, and 'are a product of the unique competitive environment of our training,' said Vladislav Chernievski, the leader of the show's teeterboard act... 'Other circuses have first-rate performers, but we do something special—each act creates a small vignette. These are playlets that give spectators not only the flavor of our life, but also reveal the soul of Soviet man.'"

Dominique Jando introduced Sergey Zenov to Judy Finelli, who traveled to Las Vegas to meet the Russian acrobat. Sergey met Judy after a show. "She invited me to lunch, with a translator. She said, 'We have a small company, the Pickle Family Circus, and we want to build a great circus school. I saw your act and I've seen the Moscow Circus School. Our school needs technical development and acrobatic training like you had.' I told her, 'I have a contract with Moscow Circus. It is not easy to replace me.' She said that was fine, that the Pickle show didn't start until December, and they needed time to work with my visa."

While Sergey was on the road finishing up his Moscow Circus contract, the Pickles were moving to a new, larger rehearsal space, a gym on the other side of San Francisco.

Peggy Snider: "We were in this little church on Missouri Street, which was too small to do the things we wanted to do. I knew about the two gyms over there on Frederick street, by Kezar Stadium, and thought maybe we could get one of them. Wendy and I went to the Soviet Union and did a tour of circus buildings with this in mind. I finally secured the building that the school is still in."

When Sergey Zenov's visa was in order, Judy Finelli brought him to San Francisco to work alongside Lu Yi in the new gym. Unfortunately, Judy's pair of international teachers didn't see eye-to-eye. Sergey was almost a generation younger than Lu Yi and he was still performing as a teeterboard base. He also did a lot of work fixing up the new gymnasium and used his technical degree in metal work to fabricate teeterboards, flying trapeze rigging, and a sprung floor made of 1,000 used skis.

Sergey Zenov: "Lu Yi was head coach and master teacher, and I was also master teacher. I knew every window and wall in the building—more than the rats knew. I cleaned and painted and got dead pigeons out of the walls of that old gym, but Lu Yi never even took a screwdriver in his hands."

Judy Finelli: "Neither Lu Yi nor Sergey Zenov thought that they could possibly be equals. It was a power struggle, one of them had to be on top."

Judy also misjudged the amount of hostility there was between the two largest communist countries—China had allied with the Soviet Union after its 1949 revolution, but the relationship soured a few years later and serious tensions continued into the late 1980s. This hostility traveled to San Francisco and almost short-circuited the Pickle Family Circus School's plans.

Judy Finelli: "Besides the political and cultural tensions, the acrobatic techniques in Russia and China are subtly different. Soon after Lu Yi and Sergey Zenov arrived, I had health issues that took me out of town so I couldn't run interference when arguments broke out. Of course, it might not have been politics or even technique; it might have simply been that their personalities clashed."

Russian and Chinese acrobats also have conflicting body aesthetics; Russians favor big buff bases, like Sergey, throwing around tiny flyers, while Chinese acrobats only need to do their tricks, they don't need to look buff.

First generation Youth Circus students Francisco Cruz and Will Underwood: "Anytime someone walked in looking 'gym buff' with a lot of muscle bulk, Lu Yi would say, 'Pretend muscle. Look at me, I don't look strong but I'm stronger.' He taught us that the muscle thing is quiet. Training is quiet."

Judy Finelli's dream of Americans learning acrobatic techniques from both China *and* Russia soon changed to Chinese *or* Russian. Sergey Zenov wasn't fitting in easily, but Judy still felt more connected with the Russian style of circus—especially its theatricality and emotion, which she felt Chinese acrobatics lacked. And she was still concerned about Lu Yi—he was used to working with perfect bodies in China... but in San Francisco, he had to work with adults and the children whose parents could pay for their training.

Judy Finelli: "I still didn't know how Lu Yi would adapt. He could see that it would take longer to get results here, but he also saw how grateful his students were and he was touched."

The fact that Judy herself had become a world-class juggler even though she suffered from scoliosis long before her multiple-sclerosis diagnosis, impressed Lu Yi.

Judy Finelli: "I had told Lu Yi that the Pickle Family Circus performers were capable of being good actors and funny, but they needed better technical skills. I wanted him to transform them into real acrobats. Lu Yi realized that the circus training might be bitter, but these Americans were doing it for love and if there is love behind the training, students will go far. He understood this challenge and that's why I wanted him to teach. It was different here, but he was completely capable of bridging the cultures to our benefit."

Sergey Zenov stayed in San Francisco and joined the Pickle Family Circus as a performer, along with his friend and colleague Youri Klaypotsky. These two Russians added flair and skill to the Pickle performances, especially in the teeterboard acts. On the road, Sergey and Youri would show us Americans some of their Russian techniques, like how a second mount can guide a base with his knees and how to prepare your shoulders to take weight just by using your imagination (it works). I used these techniques to base a three-high with Sergey on my shoulders and Huang Zhen flipping off the teeterboard onto his shoulders. Many of us in the Pickle cast integrated a few Russian techniques into our Chinese style, creating a do-it-yourself version of the "best of both worlds" approach that Judy had originally envisioned.

Judy Finelli: "Had I found the perfect Russian acrobatic teacher, maybe everyone would have come out with Russian technical skills. But I didn't. Lu Yi was the right person for the job."

13. CULTURE CLASH

> As they traveled west, Sanzang, Monkey King, Friar Sand, and Pigsy came to a river. Sanzang was thirsty and the water was clear. Pigsy scooped water in a bowl and gave it to the monk, who took a few sips and handed it back. Pigsy gulped down the rest. Soon, both Sanzang and Pigsy were in great pain. An Old Woman appeared at the riverbank and laughed when she heard that they had drunk from the river, "That is the Motherhood River. You are both going to have babies!" Pigsy squealed, "But I'm a man. Where will the child come out?" to which Monkey replied, "A melon falls when it is ripe. When the time comes, you will find a hole for it to be born through."[91]

In China, some acrobatic skills are considered for women—aerial, contortion, and diabolo—while others are considered for men—teeterboard, pole climbing and hoop diving. Female teachers teach the female students, male teachers teach the males. Paradoxically, this "gendering" of skills in China opened up training possibilities for people of all genders in San Francisco.

Since Chinese acrobatic teachers know the details of training their gender's assigned skills much better than other skills, Lu Yi arrived in San Francisco more proficient at teaching "male" acts. He found that some of the main performers in the Pickle Circus were women, and that girls would be important members of the Youth Circus. If he had still been in Nanjing, Lu Yi would have assigned a team of female teachers to train these women and

---

91   Wu, C. Jenner, W.J.F. (2005). *Journey to the West*. (C. Fair, Ed.). Disruptive Pub.

girls in aerial skills, contortion, and other "female" acts. But in the U.S. Lu Yi, Xia Ke Min, and later Xiaohong Weng, all men, were the only Chinese teachers.[92]

Lu Yi adjusted to this new reality by teaching women and girls the skills that he knew best and, as a result, many American women are experts at pole climbing, teeterboard and hoop diving. And it went the other way, too.

First generation Youth Circus student Brad Henderson: "In the early days, we were sometimes separated by gender to do different disciplines. We were also divided based on what people were naturally good at, which meant that Will Underwood, who was very flexible, ended up doing contortion even though this was usually only for females."

As Lu Yi and the other teachers from Nanjing focused on "male" acts, women such as aerialists Elena Panova from the Moscow Circus School and Hélène Turcotte from Montreal, as well as Mongolian contortionist Serchmaa Byamba, all built strong programs alongside the Chinese acrobatics training. This gave San Francisco students a chance to train in different styles of circus and get a good sense of the different cultures that embrace circus arts.

Trapeze artist and clown Felicity Hesed:[93] "Different people work well with different teachers and Lu Yi didn't work for me. I found it crushing when he'd say, 'Why are you doing acrobatics? You are too old, and you can't jump.' Elena Panova is also an intense, hard coach, and she really worked for me. Elena always wanted me to be better than I was, 'Of course you can do that,

---

92   Lu Yi was later joined by two other male teachers Xia Ke Min and Xiaohong Weng.

93   Felicity Hesed is a Clown Conservatory graduate, trapeze artist and circus director. Her solo show *Cara Vita* toured nationally and internationally, she was the Artistic Director of S.F. Circus Center and now runs People's Circus Theatre, working with many former and current Youth Circus performers.

why don't you just do it?' and she got me to a level on trapeze that I never thought I would attain."

Another area where Lu Yi struggled to adapt to the culture of his new home was the Chinese system of focusing on star students, grooming them for greatness, while giving little attention to others who seemed less promising as acrobats.

Brad Henderson: "He might put some kids with less potential to the side to do more basic training so he could focus his attention on the others. Or he would get the group all training together then pull certain individuals aside to work on higher-level skills."

When Xiaohong Weng arrived in San Francisco from Las Vegas in 1999, he wanted to change this star system. "Of the 15 to 20 kids in the Youth Circus, Lu Yi only focused on the top five or six. To me, it should be different. In China, students are paid to learn and perform circus skills, they are already circus professionals, but in the U.S. every student pays, so I tried to give attention evenly."

Like the issue with gendered circus skills, Lu Yi's focus on the top students—a technique he had employed with great success in Nanjing—created space for others. Xiaohong trained and influenced many Youth Circus performers, and a generation of American clowns.

Xiaohong Weng: "I think it is more in Western culture to treat everybody the same, whatever your talent—if you're good, OK; if not, that's still OK. But Lu Yi would ask me, 'Why do you want to spend time on those students? Physically, there is no hope that they will be great acrobats. It's impossible.' To me, the students looked sad. I'd say, 'Hey, Lu Yi, you're not even talking to these kids at all, for the whole two-hour class. They think you don't like them, that you think they have no hope of being an acrobat.' It reminded me of a Chinese saying that means something like, 'You think I am a tea cup that has a chip. You don't care anymore, so just break the cup.'"

Writer and Hall of Fame basketball player Kareem Abdul-Jabbar:[94] "When I salute someone of exceptional achievement, I'm not praising their talent, I'm honoring their discipline, their focus, their commitment, their passion—and mostly their hard work. In other words, 'talent' is earned. It is cultivated by desire and nurtured by sweat."

These culture clashes didn't derail the Nanjing/San Francisco circus affair; in fact, navigating them often made the relationship stronger. The addition of other circus cultures made for additional competition and misunderstandings—and growth for both students and teachers.

With Sergey Zenov, Youry Klaypotsky and Elena Panov, Russian circus culture has been well represented in San Francisco. Serchmaa Byamba, who settled at Circus Center in 1994 after performing throughout Asia, Europe and North America, single-handedly brought Mongolian contortion to the Bay Area. She has now trained a generation of young contortionists, as well as many adults. She, like Lu Yi, adapted and learned from her American students.

According to Serchmaa Byamba, "...almost every Mongolian young girl's dream is to be a contortionist, as wrestling is to the boys. I was one of those fortunate girls to train under the contortion legend Madam Tsend-Ayus. [After I became] a teacher, I had an older woman come to me to learn to do the splits, and she did it. I was so proud of her. It totally changed my mind about having to learn something in earlier childhood in order to become

---

94   Abdul-Jabbar, K.(2023, December 5). *Kareem Abdul-Jabbar Official Newsletter.*

professional. Contortion can physically benefit anyone and can be practiced safely."[95]

Serchmaa was not the only Mongolian circus performer in the West—according to Gerelbaatar Yunden, a former acrobat and circus director, there are currently about 1,300 Mongolian performers working in North America and Europe.[96] One of them, Yagaantsetseg "Rosa" Dashdendev, has taught contortion at Circus Harmony in St. Louis for the last 15 years.[97] While she has performed and taught many circus acts, including partner acrobatics on the back of a yak, her specialties are contortion and hand balancing. Acrobats who trained with Rosa and the rest of the Circus Harmony faculty are in sync with Youth Circus veterans because the two programs have a lot in common. Circus Harmony's mission could be describing the Pickle Family Circus: "...a non-profit social circus organization that uses circus arts to motivate social change ...help people defy gravity, soar with confidence, and leap over social barriers, all at the same time!"[98]

Maya Kesselman (Cruz): "When Dominic Cruz left Cirque du Soleil, Marta Henderson had never done her tricks with anyone else. Melvin Diggs and Sydney 'IKing" Bateman, who trained in St. Louis at Circus Harmony, came in and learned everything in a week. They had a similar background."

. . .

The Pickle Family Circus and School, now San Francisco Circus Center, is the Bay Area's epicenter of Chinese acrobatics, Russian aerial arts, and

95   Byamba, S. Serchmaa Byamba. Retrieved February 13, 2024 from https://www.mongoliancontortion.com/
96   Pierson, D. (2023, December 25). Mongolians Are Circus Stars All Over the World, Except at Home. *The New York Times*.
97   Circus Harmony. https://circusharmony.org/
98   *ibid.*

Mongolian contortion. Two other traditions, from yet another continent, were introduced by a circus that works out of an elementary school.

Aileen Moffit was a school teacher in 1989 when she visited Australia with her partner, aerial dance pioneer Terry Sendgraff. Aileen had started a circus program at Prescott Elementary in West Oakland a few years before, so she spent a day visiting Lu Yi's former colleague Lu Guang Rong and his Flying Fruit Fly Circus training program. "I saw school-age kids working on a bicycle act that built up to eight of them on the bike, fanned out in precise balance while circling the gym. Fruit Fly Circus had buses to shuttle the kids between school and the training site. The entire school was part of the circus, and the school curriculum reflected this in many of their lessons."

Since Aileen Moffit's Australia trip, Prescott Circus Theater[99] has integrated some of Lu Guang Rong's ideas. The company has hired many Lu Yi-trained teaching artists so "...Lu Yi's knowledge and skills inevitably translated into the acrobatic and work ethic training our students have received."

Prescott Circus Theater has also introduced two new circus disciplines to the Bay Area, both originally from Africa: stilt dancing and hambone.

Shaka Zulu, an NEA National Heritage Fellow, came to Oakland from New Orleans to teach a style of stilt dancing that made its way to the United States from West Africa.[100] Prescott's act "Higher Ground" puts the African

---

99   Prescott Circus Theater is a 40-year-old program based in a West Oakland elementary school founded by schoolteacher turned circus pioneer Aileen Moffett. https://www.prescottcircus.org/about-us/our-work/

100   Stilt dance, or *Mukudji*, is a form of West African cultural expression that maintains and affirms a community's values through rituals, festivals, and celebrations. You can see what it looks like in a video from *The New York Times*. Ryan, M., DeKornfeld, O., Yi, E. (2017, December 17). Dancing in the Air with 9-foot Stilts. https://www.nytimes.com/video/style/100000005271902/dancing-trinidad-stilts.html

roots of stilting front-and-center when they perform around the Bay Area. After an introduction, a half dozen young dancers, tweens and teens, enter to the rhythms of a djembe played by Pickle veteran and Prescott trainer Derique McGee or another faculty member. The dancers are on three to four foot tall stilts, dressed in colorful costumes festooned with long fringe that accentuates their movements, which include running in place with stilts flying high in the air and dancing while balanced on one stilt with the other stilt pointing straight up.

Derique McGee: "Shaka Zulu brought heart, the love of this skill, stilt dancing, that has deep roots. He brought the foundation of something that was painful but created joy."

Derique McGee also added "hambone," which was developed in the American South by enslaved Africans when their drumming tradition was suppressed by white enslavers out of fear that "talking drums" would be used to organize repellions.[101] Hambone artists create rhythms by slapping their hands on their chest and thighs. A Prescott hambone act starts with a group of young performers playing a basic rhythm on their bodies. After a few moments, the audience starts to hear and see variations and virtuosic solos weaving in and out of that basic rhythm. As with stilting, the audience is swept up in the movement, the skill, and the music; what every circus act hopes to achieve.

Derique McGee: "Hambone is a skill that can be presented in a circus and in historical context. The consciousness of circus is expanding to include

---

101   "...hambone persists in the United States as a response to dispossession. With the complete ban of drumming and literacy, enslaved Blacks turned to traditional and improvisational forms such as hambone..." Foley, A. (2021) *The Editor Function: Literary Publishing in Postwar America.* University of Minnesota Press.

things that aren't traditionally seen as circus—hambone and its cousins hip-hop dance, skateboarding, bike tricks, etc."

Many people see circus as an ossified entertainment, as something static. But if Western circus was truly static, it would still be just horses. Since the beginning, circus has been made up of the most interesting stuff from around the world, an ever growing list of acts, skills and styles of presentation. Giving these acts historical context, instead of exotifying them, is part of a newly expanded circus consciousness..

The San Francisco Circus Center continues to be home to master teachers from Russia, France, Switzerland, Mongolia, Canada, the Caribbean, and South America, as well as a couple of former Prescott artists from just over the Bay Bridge in Oakland. This makes Bay Area circus training look like an even more global version of Judy Finelli's original plan.

SPOTLIGHT ON...

DIANE WASNAK

"Diane Wasnak, once again, is the show's brightest light. Whether she's scampering up a pole, pedaling backward around the stage and flipping soup bowls onto her head or cross-dressing in white formal wear to court Razz's gigantic dowager, this remarkable physical comedian makes her amazing precision seem like something that just popped into her tiny head."

- Steven Winn, San Francisco Chronicle, *December 12, 1995.*

One day, clown Diane (Pino) Wasnak found herself listening to Lu Yi pitch a story idea for a new show to the Pickle Circus board of directors.

Diane Wasnak: "In the middle of his presentation, Lu Yi starts staring at me and saying something in Chinese. I look at Zhou Yue, who is translating for him, and she has a strange look on her face. She whispers, 'He wants to teach you his bicycle act. This is a big deal.' I think, 'Holy crap! Riding a bicycle?' I've hated bicycles since I was in a horrible accident—flipped over the handlebars and my face looked like hamburger. I swore I would never ride a bike again. A unicycle, yes; a bike, no."

After the initial shock, Diane realized that Lu Yi was offering to pass his tradition on to her, not just teach her a bike act. This was a gift that she had to take—even if it involved getting back on a bicycle-because the ritual of a master trainer passing his act on to a favorite student was much older than the act itself.

"Lu Yi was inviting me to join the 2,000-year-old legacy of Chinese acrobats. There is a big difference between Chinese students and students in America. In China, the teacher picks the student. In America, the student says, 'I'm going to pay this person to teach me this skill.' Now this amazing Chinese master was going to teach me his act. When I was a kid, I loved the movie 'Kung Fu,' It was my 'Kung Fu' moment."

Before they started, Lu Yi told Diane that she could not practice in front of other people and that she couldn't teach the act to anyone until she was ready to pass it on. "Zhou Yue told me he wasn't supposed to teach it to me at all because it was a solo act. In Lu Yi's agreement with the Chinese government, there were certain things he wasn't supposed to teach; Chinese treasures, like scotch to Scotland."

Diane was almost 30 when she started training acrobatics and she was 33 when Lu Yi offered to teach her his solo bike act. In the three years they'd worked together, she had become a teeterboard flyer, a hoop diver, one of the best women pole climbers in the world, an acrobatic clown... and her body had paid a price. "Lu Yi wanted to teach me something I could perform for a long time, an act that would sustain me for 20 or 30 years."

They went looking for a bike small enough that Diane's feet could reach the pedals when she sat on the handlebars facing backwards. BMX bikes were popular at the time, so they were able to buy one that didn't need a lot of customizing—just getting rid of the brakes and making it a "fixie," able to be pedaled backward or forward.

Pickle Family Circus rehearsals were no longer held in the church on Potrero Hill, so Diane decided to learn her bike act there. On the first day, Lu Yi told her to sit on the handlebars and pedal in a circle backwards. He trotted along beside, taking her weight. When she started to get the feel of it, he said, "Now practice."

"I practiced eight hours a day, seven days a week trying to figure out how to ride that damn thing. Pedal once, fall over, curse. One pedal, fall over, curse. Again. Again."

Two weeks later, when Lu Yi came to see how she was doing, Diane managed to ride three times in a circle before falling off. "I was so excited. I said, 'You see that—three circles in a row! How many times do I need to do this?' He stood there with his arms crossed, 'One thousand times. Every day. If you fall, start again.' So, I got back on that bike and started counting circles—one, two, three..."

Diane did her 1,000 circles a day, which took about 4 hours. And when she had the bike riding down, she started to learn how to kick metal bowls onto her head, first from standing and then while riding the bike backward. "I looked like a boxer—my eyes and my forehead had lots of swelling, and some blood."

The art of circus is built on the orthodoxy, and pain, of technique.

It took Diane over two years of regularly performing this bike act with the New Pickle Circus' *Jump Cuts!* to be able to catch the bowls on her head consistently. Luckily, because she was part of an ensemble, other performers could pick up the bowls she dropped, allowing her to stay on the bike and keep the act moving.

In 1996, Diane created a solo show with director Paoli Lacy.[102] They changed the bike act to make it work in the context of this new piece, first by adding the Baby character that Diane had been performing successfully for years. Because they also wanted it to be interactive, an American clown interpretation of a Chinese act, they invented Uncle Fred (or Aunt Frieda). This character was an audience volunteer who came on stage to play with the Baby, hand her props and, if the Baby had an accident, picked up the dropped bowls. The act was a success so, after her solo show closed, Diane took this routine on the road.

"Thanks to Lu Yi, I've performed my baby bike act for over 25 years in the U.S., China, Mexico, Greece, Indonesia, Malaysia, Australia, the Canary Islands, Panama, Venezuela and on cruise ships in the middle of two oceans."

---

102   Director Paoli Lacy was also a Ringling Clown College grad, a performer in Make*A*Circus, creator of Clown Therapy and the Director of The Clown Conservatory from 2010 - 2012.

ACT FOUR:

FROM SUNSHINE TO STAGE LIGHTS

14. HARD TIMES

1990 - 1992

Sanzang said, "I am scared. As the saying goes, if the mountain is high it's bound to have monsters; if the ridge is steep, spirits will live there." Monkey encouraged his fear. "I see no end of row upon row of craggy peaks, twisting beds of torrents. Tigers and wolves are running in packs, there are ten-thousand fathom snakes breathing monstrous winds. The towering cliffs are as ancient as the primal Essence; the majestic crags are cold even in the sunlight."[103]

Just as Lu Yi was settling into his new life in the Bay Area, with *La La Luna Sea* out on tour and the San Francisco Youth Circus training at home, all things Pickle became decidedly unsettled. For the next two years, the organization faced a host of craggy peaks and monstrous winds.

In December 1990, the Pickle Family Circus headed into its ritual of reworking their outdoor show for the Palace of Fine Arts stage. Because Judy Finelli was busy managing the effects of multiple sclerosis, she had to bring in an outside director, Don Jordan. Don had studied at the famous École International de Théâtre Jacques Lecoq which gave him the cachet needed to get the job. But before rehearsals began, Diane "Pino" Wasnak's partner Joan "Queenie Moon" Mankin left *La La Luna Sea* to focus on her acting career. This broke up the clown duet that was central to the plot,

---

103   Wu, C. Jenner, W.J.F. (2005). *Journey to the West*. (C. Fair, Ed.). Disruptive Pub.

one of the only all-female clown teams working at the time. And the Pickle community lost a beloved friend and colleague. Don Jordan replaced Joan Mankin with a clown he'd worked with before, but it was not smooth sailing.

Lu Na: "They hired an outside director, and it was problematic. He would get frustrated and blame the Chinese performers. It was hard for them to express themselves because of the language barrier, so my father had to speak up to protect them. And dance choreography was hard for the acrobats because, in China, they just did their act and left the stage. The director called them stupid because they couldn't follow directions in English. My dad was really angry."

Shana Carroll: "Don Jordan revamped *Luna Sea* and made it more of a clown show. Everyone had a character. It wasn't a bad idea, but Lu Yi was enraged."

Judy Finelli couldn't mitigate these issues nor could she continue running the circus because multiple sclerosis forced her to, as Karen Quest put it, "... go from not good, to one cane, to two canes, to a wheelchair very quickly."

Shana Carroll: "Judy liked working with Don Jordan so she named him as her successor. That's when things hit the fan. Many folks didn't like him as a director. It was Lu Yi's dream to become an artistic director, not just a coach.[104] This was a big blow to him and it created a civil war in the company. There was enough dissent that Judy had to unseat Don from the position. Some artists left because they disagreed. Others were 'Team Lu Yi' because he was the one unifying thing, with him the company was at its best. For a moment Lu Yi was given the reins as Artistic Director, but it became clear he wasn't quite ready to manage an American non-profit."

---

104   In Nanjing, Lu Yi was both the Artistic Director and the head trainer.

. . .

To keep growing, the circus leadership decided to change their model from performing in parks to performing in theaters. Because the skill level of the Pickle Family Circus was rising, in juggling as well as acrobatics, they needed to get out of the wind, away from the heat and off the uneven ground that were part and parcel of outdoor performing. So, after the holiday run at the Palace of Fine Arts, the indoor version of *La La Luna Sea*—without Joan Mankin—went out on tour, a theater tour.

The move from parks to theaters cost the Pickles their close relationship with audiences and community organizations up and down the west coast. They also had to change the way they did business, pivoting from working with non-profit sponsors to getting booked into theaters. Their circle of tents, stake pounding circles, and meals shared outside would be replaced by hotel beds and catered lunches at the theater. The trade-off, though, meant higher quality lighting and sound, local crews to help set up and tear down the more elaborate scenery, and a flat stage for tumbling, with no sun in acrobats' eyes and no wind blowing down jugglers' patterns.

Drummer Bill Belasco: "Playing in theaters was so much fun for the band. Musicians are used to playing in clubs and bars where people are talking and dancing; it was a break from all that. I was in heaven—the Cowell Theater, the Palace of Fine Arts, theaters out on the road. And we played all original music, plus three jazz tunes before every show!"

But there were business challenges with the new model. Since this was the Pickle's first foray into theater touring, they had trouble finding enough bookings and then, when they did get into theaters, they struggled to fit the *La La Luna Sea* set on the stages. Some theater managers complained that the show was not the one they had booked—theater bookings are done months and sometimes years in advance, so these presenters had seen video of the outdoor version.

Judy Finelli: "I was appalled when I saw a video of the indoor version of the show. It was no longer *La La Luna Sea*. It was 100% Don Jordan. Un-Pickle in the extreme."

. . .

The Pickles brought in William Ball to direct the 1991-92 show. Ball had recently retired as the founding director of San Francisco's flagship American Conservatory Theater (A.C.T.)[105] and was known for his work in classical theater and opera. He was an interesting choice for a circus, but clearly one that would raise the Pickle's stature in the arts world, offer new opportunities for the performers and help build the circus' nascent indoor theater-based aesthetic.

Peggy Snider: "I had hired the guy from A.C.T. to direct the holiday show. Two days before we started rehearsal, I woke up from this insane nightmare that I was going to die. I thought, 'I can't die, I have two kids.' I was a single mom since Larry [Pisoni] had left me and the kids and the circus. I called the head of the board,[106] and we met for breakfast. I said, 'I need to leave,' he said, 'I know. We are getting things into place,' but I was like, 'No, I need

---

105   The American Conservatory Theater (A.C.T.) moved to San Francisco from Pittsburgh in 1967. Founder William Ball's first season featured sixteen productions, with performances in San Francisco and tours to thirteen other California cities. In 1986, Ball, suffering from exhaustion and under accusations of financial mismanagement, was forced to leave the company.
106   Dr. Mark Snider, then head of the ER at San Francisco's St. Luke's Hospital, was the Board Chair of the Pickle Family Circus for many years. He is not related to Peggy Snider.

to leave today.' I left. At 7 am the next morning someone called, I don't remember who, telling me that Bill Ball had committed suicide."

Shana Carroll: "William Ball was going to direct the show, which I hoped would give the Pickle Family Circus new relevance. But then he killed himself right before he was supposed to come."

When William Ball passed in July 1991, the board rehired co-founder Larry Pisoni, who had left the company a few years before. When Larry took over, Diane "Pino" Wasnak lobbied him to hire me to be her clown and acrobatic partner. Larry Pisoni had been my first acrobatics teacher in the mid-70s, but we had never worked together on a show. Larry's image for the 1991-92 show included a clown trio, perhaps because of the success of the original Pickle clown trio, Larry, Bill Irwin, and Geoff Hoyle. He brought in two new clowns to work with Diane in *Pickles on Parade*, former Ringling Brothers clown Laura Pape and me, using the stage name "Razz."

I met Lu Yi at the first rehearsal, officially joining the story of the Nanjing/San Francisco circus affair. Before we look at *Pickles on Parade* and then the subsequent Pickle shows, I will give you a fast-forward glimpse of my early acrobatic career and how I found myself standing in a big, drafty San Francisco gym getting the once-over from a small Chinese acrobatics master.

15. PICKLES ON PARADE

Like Jennings McCown, the acrobat you met in the first "Spotlight," I had a typically haphazard American circus training. When I was a teenaged Berkeley street juggler in the early 70s, the Pickle Family Jugglers were my heroes. Larry Pisoni started teaching a circus skills class and I signed up right away. Each session started with 90 minutes of acrobatics, which I abhorred and swore I'd never do again. As a fat kid who couldn't master a simple forward roll in gym class, I was an unlikely candidate for an acrobatic career. Even the somewhat slimmer 6'2" frame I brought to Larry's class struggled with the basics and my overgrown head of hippie hair didn't make it any easier, getting yanked painfully when I tried a backward roll.

Luckily, the second half of Larry's class was juggling and balancing tricks like rola-bola and rolling globe. I loved those last 90 minutes so much that I would forget about the acrobatics. A couple of months later, I had short hair, new sweatpants, and a rudimentary knowledge of rolls, cartwheels, handstands and basing two-highs, flying angels, and Risleys. With my juggling skills, this was enough acrobatics to get me work in Everybody's Family Circus, a small show run by some of my classmates.

In 1978, I got a second round of acrobatic training, this time with Stu Goldberg, a child acrobat in vaudeville turned discotheque owner. Sunday mornings would find our trio, Wendy Parkman, Billy Kessler, and me at "Dance Your Ass Off" in San Francisco's North Beach, practicing on the deserted dance floor. The act we built with Stu had a good six month run until Wendy and Billy joined the Pickle Family Circus and I went to theater school. Thirteen years later, when I joined the Pickles, I got my third and final round of acrobatic training from Lu Yi.

That first week of rehearsal, Lu Yi was appalled at my mish-mash of techniques, my advanced age, and my lack of strength. But he saw I was excited to learn, and he needed me to base the Pickle teeterboard act, pedal the group bike, and to do partner acrobatics with his favorite flyer Diane "Pino" Wasnak. My American, Russian, and Chinese castmates enjoyed some laughs at my expense, and they helped me get ready for our opening, which was only a few months away.

Pickles on Parade was the first Pickle circus to be designed, from the beginning, for theaters rather than for parks.[107] Larry Pisoni imagined a show with a theme, rather than a scripted play like *La La Luna Sea*. *Pickles on Parade* featured better skills in pole climbing, teeterboard, and hoop diving—plus the addition of Chinese "meteor bowls"[108]—and Zhou Yue and Huang Zhen's handstand chair act. The cast also had some new performers, including an "audience volunteer," tiny Youth Circus student Sarah Fels scampering up and down the pole.[109]

The show began, not surprisingly, with a parade. A circus classic, but one with a very different sound and look. Led by drummer Bill Belasco, the cast entered playing an hypnotic rhythm on percussion instruments, dressed as

---

107   Mykaltlewis1. (2015, May 17) Pickle Family Circus *"Pickles on Parade" Highlights*. [Video]. YouTube. https://www.youtube.com/watch?v=TuJboxja3O8

108   Meteor Bowls are a Chinese act performed with two bowls attached to either end of a rope. The bowls are filled with water and the performer spins the rope; centrifugal force, and skill, keeps the water from spilling as the performer moves their body around the spinning rope.

109   Performers who worked in *Pickles on Parade*: Laura Pape, Mykal Lewis, Cindy Marvel, Huang Zhen, Zhou Yue, Diane Wasnak, Jeff Raz, Montana Miller, Charlotte Bachman, Jens Larsen.

everything from a frog to a giraffe. This opening was purposely contemplative, setting the stage for the theme of mysticism and animal spirits.

Zhou Yue and Huang Zhen were now more comfortable living in America and working in the Pickle Family Circus. The theater tours were closer to the way they had worked in China, too. They lit up stages with genuine smiles, smooth dance moves, and even improvisations with the clowns. Zhou Yue's *Pagoda of Bowls* act, which in China was a serious presentation of exquisite hand balancing skills, became, in *Pickles on Parade,* a snake that I was "charming." U.S. audiences loved this act—now sexy and funny yet still exquisite. When I half-jokingly said we should take our new act to China, Zhou Yue was shocked. She told me that this American approach would get her booed off the stage. "Audiences in China are like audiences for ballet dancers here—they want to see perfect form, not snakes and clowns."

. . .

Larry Pisoni's return to the Pickles was short lived due to conflicts with the board of directors, who were also dealing with serious financial issues. When the Pickles were ready to create the 1992-93 show, Judy Finelli was still not available. She was supervising the school long-distance from New York City where she was getting treatment, but she was no longer working with the performing company.

At this low point, the board turned to someone they—and the performers—knew and trusted: Tandy Beal had worked on *La La Luna Sea* two years earlier as the choreographer and she had a long international career as a dancer, choreographer, and Artistic Director of her own Tandy Beal & Company.

Tandy Beal: "I was walking on the beach with Peggy Snider, my husband Jon Scoville and Pickle board member Earl Crab, whom I've known since I was fourteen. Peggy said, 'We need a new artistic director,' and Jon quickly answered, 'I know exactly who you should get.' We all asked, 'Who?' Jon pointed to me and said, 'Her.' We laughed and went on to the next subject."

The Pickle board did offer Tandy the job, but she was concerned about the budget issues. She told herself: "I'm going to work for six months to make this new show, and probably not get paid. I'll do it because nobody is ever going to ask me to direct another circus, this is the last circus of my life."[110]

Tandy Beal and Lu Yi got to work planning the 1992 show, a show that would set the tone for the last eight years of the millennium. These years would be a second "Golden Age" as Lu Yi and Tandy Beal established and then deepened a dynamic partnership that combined rigor and discipline with creativity, humor, and even whimsy.

---

110   Since 1992, Tandy has created many circuses with the Pickles, Tandy Beal & Company as well as working for two years with the Moscow Circus in Japan.

16. TOSSING & TURNING

1992

"In the film The Nightmare Before Christmas[111]*... the director always loved the craziest version that I did... The circus is that way, too. Working in circus allows me to be so much broader than what the dance world prefers. In the dance world, where there are issues of high art versus low art, you couldn't possibly put in some of these scenes."*[112]

- Tandy Beal

Tandy Beal's "craziest version" of circus fit beautifully with Lu Yi's "bitter training" and innovative tricks. Together, they made *Tossing and Turning,* an exuberant show that combined high and low art.

Robert Taylor of the Santa Rosa Press Democrat wrote this about their work: *"Tossing and Turning* ...takes its name from the troupe's juggling and tumbling as well as the show's ingenious plot about a man's sleep interrupted by fantasies ...[It] includes acts and techniques usually seen only in touring Chinese circuses. Performers spin rice bowls and tumble through hoops, 10 of them ride in circles on a single bicycle, and acrobat Zhao Mei [recently arrived from Nanjing] balances on one side of a bike, then slips through the frame to the other ...[Razz], a big, rumpled clown ...can't sleep [while Pino as the 'sandperson'] attempts to cure his insomnia but is his prime nemesis ...

---

111   Tim Burton directed the movie *Nightmare Before Christmas* and Tandy Beal was the choreographer.
112   Tandy Beal interview in Schechter J. (2001) *The Pickle Clowns: New American Circus Comedy*. Southern Illinois University Press.

Some of the dreamlike fantasies suggest the illustrations of Maurice Sendak's book *In the Night Kitchen*, with pillow fights and tumbling bodies. There's also an ear-splitting parade of early morning trash collectors with twirling brooms, and trash can lids for cymbals ...Pino drives Razz to exasperation as a mosquito ...that sounds as loud as a World War II bomber."

Tandy Beal: "*Tossing and Turning* worked for children and adults—kids would laugh at some points, adults at another, everyone at others. We reached all the levels, and the ensemble level."

Princess Stepahanie of Monaco, who grew up in the International Circus Festival of Monte Carlo, says that circus is "...the only show where a family, everyone from children to their grandmothers, can sit together and all be entertained ...It's what real life should be like. It's sincerity, feelings, emotions. All real. There are no lies in circus."

Before joining the Pickles, Tandy Beal had created a solo dance and theater piece on the theme of 'insomnia.' She did so much research on *Night Life* that she had ideas left over for *Tossing and Turning*—sheep tumbling over the bed, climbing poles to the stars. "The central image was a man trying to sleep. The dreams were the acts, and the clowning was usually the insomnia. I saw Jeff [Raz] practicing with [musical] spoons and that developed into the 'food parade.' It turned into the short eccentric dance of the tomato sandwich, the pickle, and the piece of cheese ...my intention is to make our shows feel warm and intimate, with a sense of wonder and delight."

Diane "Pino" Wasnak and I were the clowns who would have to carry the theme of insomnia. We were not excited. At an early clown rehearsal, held at the church on Potrero Hill, Tandy told us about her successful solo show *Night Life*, and asked us to keep an open mind; Diane and I grudgingly agreed to explore possibilities. Tandy had seen a solo play of mine so she asked me to improvise a bedtime story. I did. It was awful. Before Tandy could move on to another insomnia themed idea, Diane offered to take a try at a story.

The brilliant *Goldilocks and the Three Bears* that Diane Wasnak improvised that day, using mime and gibberish, went directly into the show. It became a pivotal act in *Tossing and Turning,* and later in dozens of variety shows and in the Pino & Razz duet we later toured as *Eyes Wide Open.*[113]

. . .

Aloysia Gavre: "Tandy asked if I would audition to be an apprentice for *Tossing and Turning* and I boldly said, 'If I'm going to leave my dance scholarship to UCLA, I need to work in the air.' Even though aerial wasn't Lu Yi's specialty, he understood that is who I was. As an apprentice, I also did hoop diving, pole climbing, and general acrobatics. It made me feel a lot more comfortable, walking into a professional setting with only a little experience but knowing that Lu Yi and Tandy knew my skills and Jeff, who had been my circus teacher in high school, was also there. It helped me blossom. In the middle of the *Tossing and Turning* tour, we performed at Pepperdine University. I invited the dance teachers from UCLA, and they said, 'You are doing more than we could ever teach you.' I ended up being with the Pickles for six years."

Aloysia Gavre's Pickle castmate, Djeli (formerly Bill Forchion): "I first met Lu Yi at the church on Potrero Hill. He didn't look happy, like he was thinking, 'This is not the big black guy I ordered.' He started grabbing my arms, tapping my legs and asking me to touch my toes. He said, 'Not very nimble' OK, what do I do with that? I watched him working with the kids

113   Many acts from *Eyes Wide Open* are available on YouTube. Wasnak D. (2022, May 30) Pino & Razz "Tossing & Turning" 1992 Pickle Family Circus. [Video]. YouTube. https://www.youtube.com/watch?v=a5UbgwxV_ZA

and he had them doing stuff I thought was amazing. 'Oh, goodness gracious, I must be in the wrong place, because all I am is strong.' I wound up doing the kids' classes—25 years old, 6'4" and 210 pounds standing at the back of a line of eight-year-olds learning how to kick and stretch. Raphael Cruz looked back at me in one of those lines and said, 'You're old …and you're not very good.'"

Robert Taylor, Santa Rosa Press Democrat: "Since the Pickle Family Circus began 19 years ago, one of the hallmarks has been 'ordinary people doing extraordinary things,' and there's always a sense that the performers are doing their acts, discovering their talents, for the first time. When Razz begins juggling, he seems truly amazed …Pino appears to reinvent mime … the trapeze artists are graceful and precise, but their smiles and bodies are human."[114]

Working with a diverse company of 'ordinary people' is a guiding principle for Tandy Beal & Company. Tandy brought the idea that a multicultural and multinational cast is crucial to the Pickles. This made for some misunderstandings with Lu Yi around casting and struggles with the Chinese performers in rehearsals—we now had two new acrobats from Nanjing: solo bicycle artist Zhao Mei and hoop diver/pole climber Xu Xing Fa. Zhou Yue was still in the company but Huang Zhen had moved to Montreal.

Tandy Beal: "As a director, you try to feel from different peoples' point of view. When I would ask the Chinese performers to repeat a piece of choreography or a transition, it was tedious for them in the mind as well as the body. They were used to doing their acts, not walking around with a stupid prop or repeating dance moves or hanging out at rehearsal all day. And

---

114   Taylor R. (1993, December 26). Exuberant Pickle Acrobats Full of Juice. *Santa Rosa Press Democrat.*

there was a dissonance between them as high-level circus pros and basically Circus-101 acrobats. The trio from Nanjing did a yeoman's job of finding their way in, of sucking it up when I'd say, 'Let's rehearse that one more time.' Bringing the two cultures together, Chinese and American, as well as different kinds of theatricality and levels of skill; lots of worlds crashing together."

And it turned out that miscommunications between the East and the West weren't always international.

Djeli: "I didn't understand the language—I don't mean Chinese, I mean California language. The Pickles and Youth Circus folks spoke in a language that was different from anything I'd heard on the East coast. I was in New York working with Hovey Burgess and a bunch of folks who were deep in the circus scene there, but west-coast circus language was very different. Add in Lu Yi on top of that, I was completely lost, and he was not throwing me a lifeline whatsoever. Luckily, Tandy showed me how to get more flexible. It took a year until Lu Yi said he would work with me individually, and he said, 'You'll learn faster if you're my assistant.' I was in the gym from morning to night, rehearsing with the Pickles, doing my own training and assisting Lu Yi in all his group classes, adults and kids."

In its two years, *Tossing and Turning* also featured folks from three other countries. Russians Sergey Zenov and Youri Klaypotsky performed, and Youri's wife Elena was in charge of wardrobe (they traveled with her mother and their daughter). Austrian acrobats Doris Schwarzlmüller and Ulf Kaplaner, and Canadian handbalancer Denis Davio were also in the cast.[115]

---

115   The performers who worked in *Tossing and Turning* in its two seasons: Aloysia Gavre, Aidan O'Shea, Xu Xing Fa, Zhao Mei, Zhou Yue, Diane Wasnak, Jeff Raz, Serenity Smith-Forchion, Bill Forchion, Denis Davio, Jamie Adkins, Sergey Zenov, Youri Klaypotsky, Doris Schwarzlmüller and Ulf Kaplaner.

Lu Yi's other American students, the San Francisco Youth Circus, would join *Tossing and Turning* during the local holiday run. Youth Circus performers were featured in the teeterboard and hoop diving acts, doing some of the most spectacular tricks. They also took the group bike from an eight-person to an 11-person act.

As successful as *Tossing and Turning* was artistically, the Pickle's coffers—which had not been flush for a number of years—started causing real concern. This put plans for a 1993-94 season in peril.

17. "BANKRUPT!"

1993

"Can you imagine it? You're out on a bus-and-truck tour and you get a phone call, 'We're declaring bankruptcy. Pull up your stakes and come home.' That was the scenario that confronted the 21 members of San Francisco's 18-year-old Pickle Family Circus...which redefined the concept of circus for a generation of Americans and spawned such talents as Larry Pisoni, Geoff Hoyle and Bill Irwin."[116]

In January 1993, my *Tossing and Turning* castmates and I had recently finished a successful holiday show in San Francisco and were heading out to play Cleveland, with plans to tour for three months, finishing at the Kennedy Center in Washington D.C.

Djeli: "Sitting at SFO, we were all excited—we're off to tour the country with a beautiful show! Then one of the Pickle board members shows up, hands each of us a letter, says, 'Don't open them until you're on the plane,' and leaves. I'm thinking, 'Bonuses?!' She wasn't gone five minutes before we opened the envelopes."

The letters said the good news was that the board had deposited money with a travel agency to get us all home from wherever we were stranded. The bad

---

116   Schiffman J. (1994, January). The Pickles Take Over the Circus. *American Theatre Magazine.*

news was that we could get a call at any moment telling us to pick up those plane tickets.

...

The Pickle Family Circus' original economic structure—a non-profit circus sponsored by local non-profits—left them doubly vulnerable to fluctuations in funding for not-for-profit organizations. In addition, a vital source of support disappeared when the federal CETA program, which paid the salaries of a number of Pickle artists, ended in 1982. Finally, going from outdoor to indoor performances in 1991 exacerbated these economic challenges.

Co-founder Peggy Snider says "…it became more difficult to perform in outdoor conditions, (uneven ground, wind, sun in your eyes, etc.) as the performers' abilities increased under Lu Yi's tutelage. But moving inside required heftier budgets, not only for lights, but crews and housing—no longer tents pitched in the parks."

Former Pickle General Manager Ann Vermel adds that new audiences had to be developed since some long-term sponsors of outdoor Pickle performances were no longer able to host the circus. "Deficits became annual and stacked up. Not only were the CETA funds lost, but every local foundation I called refused to make a grant…They had, they told me, given enough to what they now considered an impossible situation…The Pickles were a major arts group but also an art form that did not fit the philanthropy of the times. $104,000 would have been an easy gift to make to, say, the opera, but not the circus. Not in those days."

Ann Vermel's last actions as General Manager, in early 1993, were to "… inform the parents committee that the [Pickle] school, separate from the production side of the Pickles, could be successful, and to stiff the Palace of

Fine Arts [where *Tossing and Turning* had premiered] for the rent so that we could meet payroll. We had no other resources."

. . .

The folks at Cleveland Playhouse Square welcomed us so warmly that thoughts of bankruptcy were forgotten—the city had renamed a street "Pickle Family Circus Alley" and we were going to perform *Tossing and Turning* for a whole month in a huge, beautifully renovated art deco vaudeville theater. Each of our dressing rooms had a bathtub and the walls were covered with signatures by the Marx Brothers, the Nicholas Brothers, Mae West, and many other old-school greats!

A week later the Pickle truck got repossessed in the middle of the night. The impending bankruptcy became all too real. Financial troubles had caught up to the company at the same moment we were out introducing a new show, with a new director, to the rest of the country. Back in San Francisco, the Pickle board of directors decided that the non-profit company couldn't keep the show on the road and told us, the cast and crew, to fly home. Right now.

We had other plans.

San Francisco-based theater critic and playwright Jean Schiffman: "The Pickles [had] a group of artists who liked—*loved*—working together, including two energetic regular performers, Jeff Raz and Diane Wasnak; a top-notch artistic director, dancer/choreographer Tandy Beal, who had run her own non-profit dance company for 20 years; a master trainer, Lu Yi; a devoted company manager, Brian Grove; a prominent San Francisco arts consultant, Barbara Kibbe, who actually called *them* to ask if she could take them on as a pro bono client; and a business, foundation and theatre community eager to help. [The touring company] cut costs in every possible way: They sold concessions to pay their own salaries, slept three to a hotel room...Their booking agent...personally helping them every step of the way."[117]

A group of us, performers and technicians from four different countries—China, Russia, Canada and the U.S.—met in hotel rooms after every show to strategize how to keep going. We ran the company like the original Pickle Family, as a collective. Many of us took on administrative work and we all sold concessions—Zhou Yue was our sales leader, standing in the lobby after every show in full costume signing autographs, but only on items purchased at our merch stand. Karl Marx's idea, "From each according to their ability, to each according to their needs," animated many of our decisions—if you had friends who could house the circus, you called them; if you couldn't miss a paycheck, like our technician whose child had special needs, you got paid first.

We received help from unexpected places: the Pickle's booking agent agreed to pay us for each show after we had set up in the next theater. The Pickle board chair, Dr. Mark Snider, sent us posters and other memorabilia to sell. The bus driver, Bob White, sold clown noses in the audience to help raise the $500 in cash that the bus company required we hand him every morning so he could keep driving us to a dozen theaters across the country, from Highland Park to Waco—during the Branch Davidian siege—and, finally, hopefully, on to the Kennedy Center.

In Lincoln, Nebraska, my aunt Hilda Raz, a poet, professor, and publisher, found housing for the entire circus and cooked huge pots of chili to keep us fed. In Maryville, Missouri, a small Chinese restaurant slapped a "closed" sign in the window when Zhou Yue greeted the owners in Chinese—the young couple hadn't heard anyone else speak their mother tongue in three

---

117   *ibid.*

years. While the two other Chinese acrobats went into the kitchen, Zhou Yue grabbed an order pad, told everyone what they were going to order and, after a feast, the young Chinese couple brewed tea that was so good the Russians almost cried. As we were saying our good-byes, Zhou Yue gave Youri Klaypotsky and his wife Elena a half pound of dry Chinese tea. Those tea leaves did more to ease the Sino-Soviet tensions than any diplomatic summit.

As we crisscrossed the country with *Tossing and Turning*, we didn't tell anyone outside of the company about the bankruptcy. No one knew that the 21 people they saw selling concessions, setting the rigging, playing the music, and performing on stage were the entire organization. In Washington, D.C. for our final date, company manager Brian Groves finished negotiating some details with the Kennedy Center's house manager and they both went to get the OK from their bosses. Brian stepped into an empty office, counted to 50, stepped back out and told the house manager that the San Francisco office said they were good to go. He later found out that, due to staffing cuts at the Kennedy Center, the house manager had done exactly the same thing. It worked. The show was a big success.

Tandy Beal: "I flew to Washington D.C. on my own dime because I'd wanted to see something I had a hand in creating at the Kennedy Center. Backstage, Youri Klaypotsky asked me, 'Don't you have your own 501(c)3?' I wondered how he knew about American non-profits, but I called the National Endowment for the Arts and made a flash appointment to say, 'Here's the situation, I think this is a worthwhile adventure; if the Pickle's dissolve, can we keep the art going? Can we continue getting funding for the dance company and the circus?'"[118]

---

118   Tandy Beal & Company was formed in 1974 to create "original concerts in dance, theatre, circus, and music. Since then, Tandy's company has toured 120 works from Anchorage to Zurich, Zagreb to Atlanta, Aptos to Zayante." https://www.tandybeal.com/history

Jean Schiffman: "When the artists came back to San Francisco ...Barbra Kibbe [had] paved the way for a New Pickle Circus by asking foundations for money to buy the name, marketing materials and assets of the defunct company. The artists are happy for the chance to learn new administrative and technique skills ...like the well-trained acrobats they are, each Pickle has a clearly defined role, trusts the others, and keeps the lines of communication open."[119]

Barbara Kibbe: "We went to the bankruptcy auction at the office of a bankruptcy trustee. I had two checks in my pocket, one for what I hoped we would have to pay and one for every penny we had. I tried to talk with the trustee but he was monosyllabic. We sat there, worried that Larry Pisoni or someone else might arrive and try to outbid us. After about twenty minutes, there were footsteps in the hallway. We all stared at the door as the footsteps came closer, and then faded away. We bid the lower amount and walked out owning a circus."

One of the first decisions made by the New Pickle Circus—now part of Tandy's non-profit, Friends of Olympia Station—was to remount our successful *Tossing and Turning* for a second year, adopting the Ringling Brothers' pattern of running a show for two years. Even though we were still a small company, we now had a show with the skills and creativity to compete with the "mind blowing" Cirque du Soleil.

---

119   Schiffman J. (1994, January). The Pickles Take Over the Circus. *American Theatre Magazine.*

18. NEW PICKLE CIRCUS

1993 - 1996

"The Pickle Circus works on a much smaller scale [than Cirque du Soleil] - one that may strike some as more human and accessible. Because the on-stage company numbers only 11, plus a five-person band, everyone wears many more hats...Lu Yi is credited as 'master trainer' and his training appears to have been masterful indeed."[20]

In the New Pickle Circus, we wore many hats, many costumes, and used many different skills. All circuses need a wide variety of skills to make their magic and, in the past, this meant a lot of different people and animals. For example, in 1939 the Federal Theater Project's Circus Unit[121] featured 125 human ring performers, from dog trainers to aerialists, hand balancers, contortionists, rope spinners, and clowns—plus 50 musicians, 42 technicians, 15 dogs, three monkeys, three ponies, two bears, and a "bucking mule."

The more refined art of Chinese acrobatics, with its centuries of tradition and its set repertoire of acts, still needs variety. The large person who pedals a bike with 11 people almost never flies off a teeterboard onto the top of a

---

120   Shirley D. (1992, October 21). Stage Reviews: Insomnia is fun and games for Pickle Circus. *Los Angeles Times.*

121   The Federal Theatre Project (FTP) was established in 1935 by President Franklin Delano Roosevelt's administration to provide work for unemployed theater professionals during the Great Depression. The FTP was a branch of the Works Progress Administration (WPA) and the Circus Unit was part of the larger FTP Variety Unit. The Circus Unit employed 250 performers in 60 acts from 1935 to 1939, including clowns, jugglers, tightrope walkers, cyclists, and aerialists. Among them was the future movie star Burt Lancaster.

three-high. In China, government-supported troupes have the resources to support large casts. So does Cirque du Soleil. Not so with the Pickles.

Lu Yi had to do a lot with only a few acrobats. In China, he had learned how to look for the different bodies he would need to fill the different roles. If he was looking for a base, someone to hold other people's weight, he would feel their arms and shoulders, testing for strength and balance. If he was choosing a flyer, he would lift them up to see if they were light enough and sturdy, not floppy. Once he had the right people in the right roles, he could teach them the proper techniques.

While a Chinese performer might fill one role, doing one act for their entire career, in San Francisco, being able to fill several roles was an advantage, and often a career necessity. Lu Yi had 60 acrobats in Nanjing so each person could specialize after their all-around training. In San Francisco, he was limited to a dozen or so performers for any given show. In their review comparing the Lu Yi-trained cast of the Pickle Circus favorably to Cirque du Soleil, the *Los Angeles Times* considered this limitation an advantage; seeing each performer in multiple roles made the show "more human and accessible."

To give a sense of how many different roles each Pickle filled, here are the acts that Diane "Pino" Wasnak performed in *Tossing and Turning*: hoop diving, teeterboard, group bike, pole climbing, and three different partner acrobatic clown acts. She also played music, told the story of Goldilocks in gibberish, and did most of the transitions between the other acts. For the acrobatic clown acts, Lu Yi used our different bodies—Diane's small one and my big one—to create innovative acrobatics, while Tandy Beal used them to create joy and wonder.

Tandy Beal: "I think Cirque [du Soleil] has done an astonishing job 'theatricalizing' circus [but] the Pickles are human size, both in the show and in the making of it ...[And the Pickles] can be an artistic home. Rather than come in, do your act, and leave, it is a place where, through yeasty collaborations, people can develop their acts and themselves even more. It is sometimes hard to tell where one person's idea ends and the next one's begins. There can be a great joy in the synergy of working like this."[122]

In Tandy and Lu Yi's "yeasty" creation, *Tossing & Turning*, people across the country saw the results of that synergy. If you had been in Cleveland or Waco or Washington D.C. in 1993, sitting in the audience of a Pickle show, this is what that synergy would have looked like during the acrobatic clown acts:

> The five-piece Pickle band starts playing an opening tune as lights come up on a large clown in a top hat and tuxedo/pajamas standing center stage. As the big clown gives a convoluted introduction, the petite Pino slowly makes her way up through the audience, onto the stage and then right onto the big clown's back. Razz keeps talking as the two clowns do a series of moves designed so that Pino's feet never touch the ground: a high arm-to-arm that Pino dismounts by sliding down Razz's back, taking his top hat along the way and returning it as she slides up between his legs. They do another series that takes Pino around Razz's body again, with another hat exchange, then Razz does a backward roll with Pino walking on him like a lumberjack on a rolling log. Finally, Razz stands up with Pino standing in his hands and the two of them walk off stage in lock step, Pino five feet in the air and Razz on the ground.

> A few acts later, the lights come up on the large clown asleep with his head on an oversized pillow (Pino in a giant pillow costume). The

---

122   Schechter J. (2001) *The Pickle Clowns: New American Circus Comedy*. Southern Illinois University Press.

Pino-pillow yawns and rolls over Razz, which leads to a series of lifts, including a jump into a Risley (Pino sitting on Razz's feet) as the big clown tries to get his delinquent pillow back under his head.

The final acrobatic clown number has Pino and Razz respectively playing accordion and baritone horn. They give some folks in the front row noisemakers and teach them how to join in on the chorus. Then the band plays and the clowns start dancing and doing complex acrobatic sequences, periodically playing their instruments and cuing the audience. This culminates with Razz on all fours with Pino standing on his back. Pino jumps four times as Razz gets a little closer to standing on each jump; she ends up standing on his head playing accordion while he plays the horn. Pino dismounts from Razz, they finish the dance, play their instruments, and cue the audience for the final chorus.

As the New Pickle Circus matured, Tandy Beal, Lu Yi, and those of us in the performing troupe, found more and more ways to use our limited number of different bodies. We also used different costumes, music, dance moves and story themes to create our own kind of circus magic.

Lu Yi had innovated a lot in the past, but the kind of innovation that the Pickles were doing was different. In China, Lu Yi innovated on Chinese acrobatics by taking tricks that were already part of the historic repertoire, *The Hundred Entertainments,* and recombined them. His goal was to make them "...better, smoother, and more impressive. More difficult." Lu Yi's famous *Picking Flowers on Top of a Head,* for example, combined three traditional skills—contortion, partner acrobatics and spinning plates.

Lu Yi: "I had seen acts where people used a backbend ...to pick a flower from a vase with their teeth ...I added a person, myself in this case, to the bottom of the trick. On the bottom person's head would be a vase filled with flowers …and balance points for a Chinese handstand bench …[one] acrobat …would stand on top of the bench, on top of the vase, on top of my head, and bend backwards to the flowers …Spinning plates gave our arms something to do."[123]

In San Francisco, Lu Yi worked with people who were already innovating before he arrived, creating New Circus by combining their repertoire—which included juggling, rope walking, trapeze, rudimentary acrobatics, trampoline, and clowning—with a wide variety of concepts and techniques from the world of dance, theater, and music. The results could get pretty wild.

"I had to chase people around and beat my chest," dancer and choreographer Kimi Okada remembers from the first two seasons of the Pickle Family Circus when she played "Ramona La Mona, the tap-dancing gorilla." "It wasn't what I was trained to do, but it was a lesson for me that it is okay to be silly …Eight or nine years later, Larry Pisoni asked me to choreograph a … clown dance for twelve gorillas …Busby Berkeley and Fred Astaire inspired me; but …many of the circus performers weren't trained in dance, and … when you have a gorilla suit on, it limits what you can do."[124]

Tandy's theatrical, whimsical approach to dance and circus, combined with Lu Yi's innovative use of the Chinese acrobatic repertoire, our composer Jeffrey Gaeto's music,[125] and our costume, set and lighting designers skills, defined the final phase of Pickle history. This marriage of discipline and wildness was on full display in *Jump Cuts! The Circus Goes to the Movies,* the New Pickle Circus's second creation.[126]

---

123   Lu, Yi., Holt, D. (2023). *Training is Bitter*. Periodgraph Press.
124   Schechter J. (2001) *The Pickle Clowns: New American Circus Comedy*. Southern Illinois University Press.
125   Jeffrey Gaeto arranged his own music as well as music composed by Paul McCandless, Lou Harrison, Art Lande, Richard Marriot and Jon Scoville.
126   Performers who worked on *Jump Cuts!* over its two seasons: Aloysia Gavre,

Corinne Flocken of the Los Angeles Times reviewed *Jump Cuts!*: "Tandy Beal, working in tandem with acrobatic trainer Lu Yi, makes the scenes in *Jump Cuts!* flow instead of startle. The elaborate moves in the detective story, with the players darting in and out between a cluster of sneakily scuttling building fronts in quest of a purloined secret letter, turn choreography into cinematography."[127]

"*Jump Cuts! The Circus Goes to the Movies* ...featuring eight multifaceted performers...is the story of two lost tourists who, locked inside the Mon-U-Mental (MUM) studios after-hours, are swept through scenes ranging from black-and-white western shoot-em-ups to spoofs of film noir to splashy musicals. These adventures are all conjured up by the studio's resident ghost and brought to life by circus acts, comedy, outlandish costumes and live jazz."[128]

Even the costumes, which had to be designed to allow for a lot of moment and copious amounts of sweat, were wild, as Steven Winn of San Francisco Chronicle pointed out: "Beaver Bauer's costumes, including all black-and-white cowboy duds, shoulder-baring mummy wraps, an organ grinder's monkey suit (for the capering Wasnak) and a brassy yellow trench coat (for Razz's befuddled private eye), belong in some circus hall of fame."[129]

And, in keeping with New Circus' established mixture of theater and circus,

Aidan O'Shea, Xu Xing Fa, Zhao Mei, Zhou Yue, Diane Wasnak, Jeff Raz, Serenity Smith-Forchion, Bill Forchion, Jamie Adkins, Teresa Dinaburg, Doris Schwarzlmüller, and Ulf Kaplaner.

127   Flocken, C. (1996, January 18) You ought to be in Pickles: The circus goes to the movies, older audiences get reeled in. *Los Angeles Times*.

128   *ibid*. (Editor's note: *Jump Cuts!* was created a decade before *Night at the Museum*, which had a similar plot device.)

129   Winn, S. (1995, December 12) Pickle Circus Goes Off to the Movies. *San Francisco Chronicle*.

Jump Cuts! eschewed some circus traditions in order to tell a story. Corinne Flocken of the Los Angeles Times noticed that the pacing of *Jump Cuts!* was different. "The members of the New Pickle Circus don't put a lot of stock in ta-dahs. Instead of the trick, ta-dah, trick, ta-dah pacing of most American circuses, the Pickles prefer a smoother approach that owes more to the theater than the center ring."[130]

Tandy Beal: "By the time we were making *Jump Cuts!*, Lu Yi and I were two horses trying to get to the same place, but with different maps. We saw each other's gifts and honored them. He was delighted that I could make narrative out of a series of tricks. If you just do a series of tricks, you must be really good; if you go through a trick sequence and something charming comes out of that, you can make it work even if you aren't experts. In *Jump Cuts!* I used different movie worlds to give the circus a framework. Diane and Jeff carried the narrative through their characters, 'What movie world will we put in front of the clowns for them to enter?' These worlds were the springboards for the circus acts. For example, in the western section, how do you keep it all in the cowboy vernacular, different from the ballroom scene, the detective scene or the adventure scene? The whole black and white saloon sets it up, then hearing footsteps, everyone getting terrified and Diane walking through the saloon double doors. Then the table sliding act as a bar fight with the embellishment of each trick, a little coda, that is charming and advances the narrative: finish the trick, land on the ground, do something that defines the character and the world, and take the story forward."

. . .

---

130   Flocken, C. (1996, January 18) You Ought to be in Pickles: The circus goes to the movies, older audiences get reeled in. *Los Angeles Times*.

After the New Pickle Circus had launched *Jump Cuts!*, Lu Yi hosted a formal meeting at his home with Tandy Beal and her administrative partner, Sheila Baumgarten. Over a huge Chinese meal, Lu Yi pitched the idea that Tandy Beal & Company abandon the difficult and financially risky business of touring shows with adult performers, and instead focus on touring with the Youth Circus.

Tandy Beal: "I knew that it is difficult for Lu Yi, and me, to work with so many green performers, with a limited time to move the art forward. But touring with children, who everyone loves, also meant we couldn't make a substantial narrative circus show."

Even though she understood Lu Yi's pragmatism—in Nanjing, having a group of well-trained kids was a good economic model—she knew that in the U.S. there are many hurdles to going out on the road with children that have nothing to do with the art. In the end, the San Francisco Youth Circus did a lot of local gigs and joined the adult shows for their S.F. holiday runs.

Around this same time, the Pickles' booking agent—who had taken a lot of risks to help the company on the "bankruptcy tour"—was pushing Tandy to stop doing original shows in favor of well-known stories. He suggested a circus based on *Rumpelstiltskin* would be easier to market.

Tandy decided to keep creating original circus with us, her New Pickle troupe. "I felt great that our shows were working for everyone in the audience, kids and adults. Peter Brook[131] cites an ancient Hindu quote that says something like, 'Great theater illuminates life, and entertains the drunks in the audience.'

---

131   Peter Brook was an English theater director and writer. One of his most famous productions, *The Mahabharata*, based on the Sanskrit epic, was 11 hours long and toured the world for four years.

We were on it. We could reach to all levels—people who were sophisticated theater goers and people who had never been in a theater."

After two years of *Jump Cuts!*, the Pickles produced several more original shows, including *Step Right Up!*, which featured six new acrobats from China—three of whom had medaled at the Wuqiao Festival and another three who had toured internationally—as well as a new Russian duet, four American clowns, and three American dancer/acrobats.[132]

Lu Yi embraced the Pickle's more extreme forms of innovation. He had become famous as an innovator in China when he began inventing new tricks influenced by Eastern European acrobats. Later, he and his Nanjing colleagues created "revolutionary circus performances" by adding narrative, theater, and music. When they went to Australia, they experimented with "setting the mood or intention but not telling the whole story, keeping it vague," an approach that Cirque du Soleil later adopted. Now, working with Tandy Beal and the New Pickle Circus, he could innovate with dance, music, costumes, clowning, sets, and stories—lots of stories.

---

132   *The Step Right Up!* cast: Chinese acrobats Cai Guang Yi, Cao Liang, Zheng Bo, Chen Feng Shun, Hou Chun Yana and Gan Pau Chan; acrobatic duo Svetlana Gololobova and Yuri Gololobov; clowns Diane Wasnak, Jeff Raz, Ben Allen and Amos Glick, acrobat/dancers Saki, Jonathan Nosan and Josh Larson.

19. MONKEY KING AND LADY LIBERTY

I shared a hotel room with Lu Yi when the New Pickle Circus was in residence at the Cincinnati Playhouse. We talked a lot. As usual, Lu Yi steered the conversation towards the future of circus. One day, before I left for the theater, he asked, "What is the most important story in America?"

I paused for a few moments, stumped, and he shifted into full *lǎoshī* (teacher) mode. "The most important stories make the most important shows. In China, *Journey to the West* is the most important story."

Lu Yi created *The Big Apple Circus Meets the Monkey King* because of the importance of *Journey to the West*. Its 100 chapters have inspired the most famous Peking Operas, which in turn have inspired circus artists around the world with their mix of acrobatics, theater, singing, instrumental music, dance, clowning and mime, all with amazing costumes and make-up.[133] Lu Na says her dad's dream was to do a *Journey to the West* show, but it never happened.

Lu Yi: "So, Jeff, what is the American *Journey to the West*? What story should American circuses tell? You need to know this."

I tried a few possibilities—*Paul Bunyan, The Wizard of Oz, Alice in Wonderland* (British, I know)—until I realized that there is no easy American equivalent

---

133   Pickle Circus shows *Tossing and Turning* and *Jump Cuts!* also had all these elements, albeit in a very different style.

for the epic journey of Sanzang, Monkey King, Pigsy and Friar Sand. Desperate, I blurted out, "The Statue of Liberty?"

Lu Yi waited for me to explain.

"There is a poem, *The New Colossus*, on the statue. It was written by a Jewish woman." Lu Yi knew I was Jewish and often said that this meant I was smart—I never challenged his stereotype. Ancestors of the poet, Emma Lazarus, had come to America fleeing persecution by the Inquisition: "A little like how you and your family came here, Lu Yi."

He nodded and waited. I mumbled something about needing to get to the morning training, adding that *Journey to the West* and the Statue of Liberty are both about travelers, and raced out the door. Later, I realized that the 100-chapter novel and the 14-line poem are also about creating community with people who are strange to you. They shine light on a particular way of living, be it Buddhism or democracy … or circus.

Lady Liberty was designed and crafted in France, 3,600 miles from where it now stands in New York harbor. She is, according to the poem, "…a mighty woman with a torch, whose flame is the imprisoned lightning, and her name Mother of Exiles."

"Give me your tired, your poor,
Your huddled masses yearning to breathe free,
The wretched refuse of your teeming shore.
Send these, the homeless, tempest-tost to me,
I lift my lamp beside the golden door!"[134]

---

134   Lazarus E. (2002) "The New Colossus" In *Emma Lazarus: Selected Poems and other Writings*. Broadview Press.

When they came to the U.S., Lu Yi and his family were not "wretched refuse," but they were tossed by the tempest of Chinese politics. Nanjing acrobats were not "huddled masses," but they struggled to earn a living on "Gold Mountain" and thrived on the freedom of expression they found here.

The grandeur of the Statue of Liberty and its poem have thrilled millions of people—many of them immigrants, some of them my ancestors. A future team of acrobats and clowns, trainers and directors, composers, costumers, and choreographers might find a circus language that can match—and perhaps extend—the poem's celebration of America as a vibrant and diverse country, as vibrant and diverse as the circus.

But they might need to find a different story.

Even before she arrived, Lady Liberty was not popular with some Chinese-Americans. In 1885, the year before the statue arrived, Saum Song Bo wrote, "I consider it as an insult to us Chinese to call on us to contribute toward building in this land a pedestal for a Statue of Liberty. That statue represents Liberty holding a torch which lights the passage of those of all nations who come into this country. But are the Chinese allowed to come? As for the Chinese who are here, are they allowed to enjoy liberty as men of all other nationalities enjoy it? Are they allowed to go about everywhere free from the insults, abuse, assaults, wrongs and injuries from which men of other nationalities are free?"[135]

And then there's the troubling fact that focusing on the Statue of Liberty plays into the problematic idea of "America, land of immigrants." The truth is that many generations before the immigrants in Emma Lazarus' poem

---

135   Richardson, H.C. (May 6, 2024) *Letters from an American*. Substack.

were born, the land between New York Harbor and the San Francisco Bay teemed with towns and cities full of music, food, philosophy, cosmology, and clowning—created by people who had lived here for millennia. Perhaps that is the most important, and most untold, story of America.

. . .

Circus is an art-form that is more welcoming of metaphor than narrative. This hasn't stopped many of us, all over the world, from trying to tell stories with acrobatics, juggling, clowning, and aerial arts. We have already looked at how Lu Yi and his colleagues, influenced by the cultural revolution, started producing "revolutionary circus performances." Then there was the Moscow Circus teeterboard act that offered "playlets that give spectators not only the flavor of our life, but also reveal the soul of Soviet man" and Tandy Beal's *Jump Cuts!*, which told the story of two clowns lost in a movie studio. Even Lu Yi's B-movie-fueled idea for a San Francisco Youth Circus "Cowboys and Indians" show was his attempt to tell a core American story through acrobatics.

I have been part of circus plays based on epic adventures, including The Clown Conservatory's *Journey to the West* and *Alice in Wonderland,* and worked in theater/circus hybrids with a more abstract sense of narrative, like the unifying theme of insomnia for *Tossing and Turning* and a clown's funeral in Cirque du Soleil's *Corteo.* And once, I used Shakespeare's *Seven Ages of Man* speech to frame a circus performed by the entire school-aged population of St. Michael, Alaska.[136]

---

136   This show, and other adventures, are in my book, Raz, J. (2018) *The Snow Clown: Cartwheels on Borders from Alaska to Nebraska.* Adam's Court Press.

The circus arts can also enrich existing plays, like Wendy Parkman and her castmates did in *Comedy of Errors* and the Marin Theatre productions of *A Midsummer Night's Dream* with Diane Wasnak as Puck, myself as Bottom, and the rest of the "rude mechanicals" played by other Pickle performers (plus Len Pettigrew, an NFL linebacker-turned-sparring partner for boxer Muhammad Ali-turned-actor).

Addressing social issues, using both narrative and metaphor, also works in the circus world. From the San Francisco Mime Troupe's early play about the dehumanizing effects of assembly lines, using juggling club passing as the central image, to Make*A*Circus' *Lungman and Windpipe's Excellent Adventure*, which addressed secondhand smoke, to the 2022 S.F. Youth Circus production *Circus at the End of the World*, with circus acts based on the seven stages of grief. As of this writing, Veronica Blair, a San Francisco Youth Circus and Make*A*Circus alum turned aerial star with Universoul and other circuses around the world, is developing *The Rainbow is Enuf*, a circus inspired by Ntozake Shange's famous play.

On one level, circus is all about bodies moving—jumping and flipping, throwing and catching, flying through space. On another level, it is all about the metaphors and stories that all these moving bodies create. And then there are personal and national identities of the artists which, when things go well, create the exciting, global texture of a great circus. All of this—bodies, metaphors, stories, identity—add up to community, to family. From Monkey King to Lady Liberty, Nanjing to San Francisco, circus as an art-form thrives on metaphor and characters. It is a catalyst for identity and community.

Acrobatic clown Calvin Kai Ku:[137] "In San Francisco, there is a question of my identity as an American; in China, the land of my heritage, there is also

---

137   Calvin Kai Ku started as a magician, then became an actor, clown and acrobat

a question of my identity. This is a strange void. Being in China allowed me to ask myself, 'Where do I truly belong?' That question has shaped me as a person. Lu Yi gives me a sense of belonging. One day he asked me to help him fix a screen door, which made me very happy because, in our culture, you would only ask that of someone who is part of your family. My relationships are my belonging. Circus is my community."

---

performing around the world. Back in the Bay, he spent 15 years with the Medical Clown Project, five of them as the Artistic Director.

SPOTLIGHT ON...

ZHOU YUE

It is near the end of the last show of a *Tossing and Turning* tour. Zhou Yue is standing on my shoulders with three sticks in each hand and a plate spinning on each of the six sticks. I climb to the top of a small stair unit and she steps onto a bench that Zhao Mei is balancing on her head. Zhao Mei is also spinning three plates in each hand. They are now ready to perform Lu Yi's famous *Picking Flowers on Top of a Head*.

Zhou Yue bends backwards as Zhao Mei balances her. When Zhou Yue's face is a few inches below her feet, she picks up a silk rose with her teeth. She slowly stands back up and the crowd roars. A technician offstage tightens Zhou Yue's aerial spotting line and I grab the bench, protecting Zhao Mei's neck as Zhou Yue's weight shifts. She is now supposed to float down to the stage on the spotting line, gently lie her six plates on the deck, and take a bow with Zhao Mei.

Tonight, this won't happen.

Because the trick is a backbend, the spotting line attaches to a belt near Zhou Yue's belly-button. Because the line is in front, the carabiner that attaches that line to her belt can't be too large or clunky. The one she is using tonight doesn't have a safety lock. It somehow gets twisted.

When Zhou Yue gives weight to the line, the carabiner opens, and she falls 10 feet onto her back. The theater freezes, shocked. In the wings, Youri Klaypotsky hears the thud, sees Zhou Yue lying on the stage, and grabs a six-foot folding prop table. Juggling clubs, hats, and a giant mosquito swatter prop scatter as Youri closes the table legs and runs with it onto the stage.

I put down the bench and signal the band to play the music for the last act, Group Bike. The stage manager hears the music and sends the bike rolling on stage. I start riding the bike in a circle and the cast starts climbing on while Youri and a couple of technicians use the table as a backboard to get Zhou Yue safely into the wings. The EMTs will arrive backstage in a few minutes.

Six of the eight acrobats are on the bike when, pedaling hard under a pile of human flesh, I remember that Zhou Yue always jumps on the bike last, paired with Zhao Mei, one on each side to keep the balance. Out of the corner of my eye, I see Zhao Mei in position—if she jumps alone, we will all need EMTs.

I feel the bike wobble and hear "Oh, shit!" in a Russian accent. Then the crowd cheers as all of my castmates, including newly minted Group Bike acrobat Youri Klaypotsky, raise their arms in what the Chinese call "The Peacock Opening."

My castmates dismount, two by two, and exit. Zhou Yue goes to the hospital with Aidan O'Shea, a young American acrobat who speaks some Chinese. We don't know when we'll see her again.

The crowd goes home. We tear down the show in silence. No one wants to speculate on how badly Zhou Yue is hurt. No one wants to say the word "paralyzed."

As we are loading the last piece of the set into the truck, we hear, "Why so quiet?" Zhou Yue walks across the stage, a little stiffly, shouting, "Just bruise, no worry." There were a lot of tears at the hotel that night.

ACT FIVE:

EACH ONE, TEACH ONE

20. INCREDIBLE! ACROBATS OF CHINA

Because Zhou Yue retired after her back injury, Lu Yi started training a replacement contortionist named Leslie Tipton. He needed her for a new show, *Incredible! Acrobats of China*, which wasn't a Pickle production. Lu Yi was representing Spring Circus, a company he created soon after arriving in the U.S. in order to help acrobats from Nanjing—and elsewhere in China— who also wanted to journey west. He used his international connections to get auditions for performers so they could book their acts in shows on cruise ships, in theme parks and, when they managed to get green cards, in casinos.

An American magician-turned-producer, who had befriended Lu Yi when he toured in China in the early 1980s, asked Lu Yi to cast and direct *Incredible! Acrobats of China*. It was a rare opportunity for Spring Circus to create an entire show from scratch. Lu Yi cast Leslie Tipton and asked her to tell people her father was Chinese so the producer could call her an "Acrobat of China."

Leslie Tipton: "It was my first circus contract, and I knew nothing. Everyone else was Chinese; they didn't speak English and I didn't speak Mandarin. In addition to my act, there was a pole act, tight wire, hoop diving, diabolo, unicycle bowl kick, 'Mongolian' knife balancing, a magic act, meteor bowls, and a Monkey King who came on in the transitions. The show started with a dragon running through the audience."

In 1994, *Incredible! Acrobats of China* was slated for an open-ended run in Branson, Missouri, which is like the Vegas strip but without gambling and with a large dose of well-packaged, down-home Americana. Lu Yi gathered a cast of Spring Circus performers to Branson—mostly former Nanjing Acrobatic Troupers who already lived in the U.S., including some who had defected after the Big Apple Circus gig, and some from different troupes around China. Lu Yi's name still had a lot of power in Chinese acrobatic circles. With only two weeks of rehearsal, he decided to put together an act-to-act show, no story. The *One Hundred Entertainments* of Chinese acrobatics was enough of a theme to separate this show from the other Branson offerings.

Pickle veteran Aidan O'Shea, skilled in Chinese acrobatics and with a working knowledge of Mandarin, joined the cast soon after the show opened. He was just in time for "Free Branson Week," when locals got seven days of complimentary tickets to all the shows in town. Branson-ites loved *Incredible! Acrobats of China*, even though it was radically different from anything they had ever seen in the Lawrence Welk Champagne theater, in *Stars of the Ozarks*, or at the Mutton Hollow Crafts Village. In the "greet line" after full-house performances, many locals said, "You're going to be a big hit!" This was a good sign that the acrobats would do well long term.

Aidan O'Shea became the group's unofficial translator and Leslie Tipton started tutoring former Cirque du Soleil star Sung Hong Li in English. Aidan taught English to Monte Carlo Festival medal winning hand-balancer Kong Hong Weng who, in turn, taught Leslie some basic Mandarin and handstand techniques.

Leslie Tipton: "I would get into my handstand and Kong Hong would jump into her handstand. Then she'd contort her body to show me how bad my position was, all the while looking at me and talking. She was a great teacher.

She also taught me a very valuable phrase for a girl working with a lot of Chinese men, *Wǒ bù xiāngxìn nǐ; nǐ yǒu lǎopó* [I don't believe you; you have a wife.] Kong Hong liked to practice her English in the greet line after the show. One time she said, 'Thank you, blouse' to everyone."

Aidan O'Shea: "It was a pleasure being with the Chinese performers, helping them open bank accounts, go shopping, try to make our living conditions better. It was amazing to be accepted in a second language, a language and a culture that is so different. I couldn't get enough of the beautiful saturation and acceptance in that culture. And I really could help, I could make things better. Here were ten people who didn't speak English, exhausted from doing 14 shows a week and getting no help from the producers. They were wising up to what was going on, and, with my help, we could get things done."

Unfortunately, none of the performers were wise to all that was "going on." First, there was the issue of money.

Leslie Tipton: "I was the only one who got paid and I only got paid once. There was one round of checks but all the checks but mine had problems and couldn't be cashed. We were all there because of Lu Yi so we didn't leave. Lu Yi was friends with the show's producer from back in China, so he thought the guy was honest."

Aidan O'Shea: "We got per diem only, but there's a pride in Chinese culture, a toughness for getting through. 'We have twenty bucks for a week, there are ten of us. We've got this!' The hours of laughs and fun we had trying to get through. I laughed so hard at that kitchen table; huge fights and lots of fun."

Then the producer got cocky and stopped advertising. Audiences stopped coming. It got bleak. 12 performers living together in a three-bedroom house, doing two shows a day, seven days a week to a sea of empty seats. Aidan

O'Shea found a silver lining; "When shows would get canceled because we didn't have an audience, there was this cute boy who did the tech, so the two of us would hang out in the hot tub."

Doing so many shows, even without audiences, took a toll on Leslie's body.

Leslie Tipton: "It felt like getting stabbed by a knife in my back. I'd be warming up and crying. Aidan was like a man with a pregnant wife; there was nothing he could do. Luckily, Troy Aikman's[138] back doc was in Branson. I said, 'I can hardly walk without pain.' He said, 'So, you do this for a living?' I figured he was going to tell me to stop performing, like other doctors had, but he said, 'Let's get you back to work.' I had no insurance, but he treated me for free, for comp tickets. So did the x-ray guy."

But then came the flood.

Aidan O'Shea: "The river rose, and it flooded our floor, soaked the carpet. We had to wade through water to get to our beds. No part of that was enjoyable. The homeowners wouldn't allow the right people to come inspect the house, so here were world-class acrobats doing shows seven a week, only getting paid per diem and living in a lake. These are things they couldn't do to white people but most of us were Chinese."

Leslie Tipton: "Whenever Aidan or I had a panic attack, which was every day, the other one would say, 'It will be OK, we'll see the stars tonight.' At the end of every night, on the walk home, Aidan and I lagged behind and he taught me about the constellations. We would also joke about the water park

---

138   Troy Aikman was a three-time Super Bowl winning quarterback for the NFL's Dallas Cowboys.

right across from our theater. Its theme was rainbow flags, and they were everywhere. We'd ask each other, 'Do you think they know?'"[139]

Finally, the performers' luck changed.

Aidan O'Shea: "A week after the flood, someone found kilos of coke in the ceiling of the Elvis revue that was in the other half of our theater. Both shows, the Elvis impersonators, and the Chinese acrobats, got canceled. There was an ongoing investigation, so we didn't do anything for three weeks. The folks who owned the theater also owned our flooded house, and a hotel. They finally got us away from the molding carpet and into hotel rooms."

Slowly, the cast slipped out of Branson, most of them heading to Las Vegas. For the Chinese performers who hadn't trained in Nanjing, this was a last chance to work with the legendary director, Lu Yi—a way to go out on top. It didn't turn out that way.

A few months after *Incredible! Acrobats of China* closed, Lu Yi started working with a local "comedy, talk show guy" to restart the production. The local comic became the emcee for a smaller cast in a smaller theater. Former Pickle performer Huang Zhen left Cirque du Soleil to join his Nanjing colleague—and future Pickle acrobat—Xu Xing Fa in Branson. Xu Xing Fa had been company manager for the original Branson show, representing Lu Yi's Spring Circus, and he had plans to go into business with Huang Zhen.

The two acrobats-turned-businessmen were joined by Xu Xing Fa's wife, Xu Qiu Yue, the foot juggler Wong Hong, a future Pickle performer, and

---

139   Rainbow or "Pride" flags, are symbols of support those who identify as Lesbian, Gay, Bisexual, Transgender, Questioning, Intersex, Asexual and Two-Spirit (LGBTQIA-2S). Branson would be an unlikely place to find a Gay Pride themed water park.

Xiaohong Weng, who you have already met in a the first "Spotlight" with Jennings McCown. The final performer was a Malaysian juggler, clown and unicyclist who was nicknamed *Xiao Di* (Little Brother). Their new theater was a 500-seat house in a shopping center under a Walmart.

Xiaohong Weng: "The biggest audience was 100 or 200 people; the smallest was eight people, all developmentally delayed, sitting in one row with their caretaker. People who saw it liked the show, but we couldn't get audiences. Everybody loved country music. I remember this guy who was 75 years old and fake singing 'Moon River.' He still had 5000 seats full. Nobody in Branson knew about China. One day in the greet line, a teen-aged girl asked me, 'Why don't you guys have a little beanie, with a long braid and a long skirt? You're supposed to look like that, but you guys look different.' There was only one Chinese restaurant, and the food was junk. To us, it was not Chinese food. We made friends with the owner, he'd jumped off the ship illegally but eventually got a green card and opened his restaurant. He'd let us go to the kitchen and cook for ourselves."

Advertising on Branson billboards was prohibitively expensive, so Huang Zhen decided to print flyers for the cast to leave at convenience stores and gas stations, as well as handing them to people at red lights and in front of the neighboring Walmart. No one was getting paid. They were doing one or two shows a day, just to stay in practice. Luckily, the local comedy emcee was putting them up in his house—no molding carpet and everyone had their own bedroom.

Xiaohong Weng: "I loaned Huang Zhen and Xu Xing Fa the money I made on the cruise ship, $20,000. They didn't have money for us, even for our daily costs. I was the richest person there because I had saved money for two years. They used my loan for groceries and gas, everything. Eventually they returned it, over a couple of years."

Finally, Lu Yi called Huang Zhen and Xu Xing Fa to say he would never be able to pay them. Instead, he offered to give them the circus equipment and what was left of his company, Spring Circus, so everyone could keep their work visas. Lu Yi also told them that the Rio Casino in Las Vegas was looking for bungee jumpers. Xu Xing Fa and Huang Zhen had done a bungee act for Cirque du Soleil—and they had green cards—so they could work in the casino. The rest of the cast couldn't and now there was nothing for them in Branson.

Xiaohong Weng: "We said, 'Let's go do Vegas.' I got a restaurant job and sometimes worked for Huang Zhen and Xu Xing Fa's new company, Dynamic Acrobatic Troupe. But every time I got a performing job, I lost my restaurant job. I needed to keep my visa with Dynamic Acrobatic Troupe, but I couldn't apply for a green card because they didn't offer consistent income. They couldn't support me and my family. One of the reasons I moved to San Francisco to work at Circus Center was to get my green card."

Lu Yi wanted to take care of everybody, all his families—his wife and daughters, his Nanjing family and his growing San Francisco family—but he didn't have the clout or connections in the U.S. that he had in China. When some of the Chinese acrobats became card dealers in Las Vegas, he was disappointed that they had left performing. Xiaohong Weng had to work restaurant jobs. Xia Ke Min had to work as a delivery driver for a few months when the Pickle school was under-enrolled. Some of the Chinese performers in Vegas got help from the juggling clown Little Brother *(Xiao Di)* who had a friend from back in Malaysia who had friends in Vegas who paid cash for under the table jobs. World-class acrobats, whose artistry was an inspiration to hundreds of American circus performers, working on the cheap in restaurant kitchens. And they were resourceful—many of them have now made good lives for themselves in the U.S.

By the mid-90s, a strong community of former Chinese acrobats was growing in Las Vegas, a city that has become a haven for circus performers from all over the world. And five years after Lu Yi immigrated, San Francisco was growing a second generation of young Americans with world-class acrobatic skills.

21. YOUTH CIRCUS, GEN TWO

1995 - 2000

> Monkey King plucked a handful of hairs from his own body, chewed them to tiny pieces and spat them into the air. "Change!"he cried, and they changed into three hundred little monkeys. For you see, since the Monkey King had become accomplished in the Way, every one of the eighty-four thousand hairs on his body could change into whatever shape or substance he desired. The little monkeys he had just created were so keen of eye and so swift of movement that they could not be wounded by either sword or spear. Look at them! Skipping and jumping, they rush at the Monster King and surround him, some pulling, some crawling in between his legs, some tugging at his feet.[140]

"We would watch videos of Chinese acrobats and know that we were never going to be that good. But we were training for different lives than they were because Lu Yi let us be creative. That was what we brought to acrobatics."

- Maya Kesselman (Cruz), Dear San Francisco *cast member*

Francis Cruz, father of the acrobatic Cruz brothers: "When I see my son Dominic do acrobatics and dance, play the banjo, drum, and sing in *Dear San Francisco*, I think, 'My god, he started by doing a back handspring.' My other

---

140   Wu, C. Jenner, W.J.F. (2005). *Journey to the West*. (C. Fair, Ed.). Disruptive Pub.

son, Raphael,[141] was directing, going to France to write music for a dance group, playing banjo in the opera house in Sydney—all because he learned to do a back handspring. Francisco now works with The 7 Fingers, an artistic manager and doing some directing, because he learned a back handspring, and because he learned to love that back handspring."

Lu Yi had journeyed to the West and met his Monkey Kings (and Queens). He was now raising a second generation of highly skilled, highly creative, ensemble-minded American circus performers. He still hoped to use the trust he had earned from his earlier students—and the trust they had with each other—to revitalize acrobatics in China with American creativity. Lu Yi also dreamed of building an American acrobatic school/performing troupe that was similar to—and on par with—the Nanjing Acrobatic Troupe.

Djeli, one of Lu Yi's teaching assistants: "Lu Yi's whole idea was that we need a mix of people; he didn't want a homogeneous troupe. 'What we do here needs to look like this community. It is not Chinese, it is American with a Chinese infusion.' I really appreciated that. There was a kid, a brown kid, he was just great, he was energized. After this kid was training for a few weeks, Lu Yi turned to me and said, 'Now, get more brown people here.' He had a vision but, due to language and cultural barriers, he couldn't fully express what he wanted to see."

. . .

Pickle Family Circus School had split into two schools right before the bankruptcy. Acrosports, led by Sergey Zenov, Youri Klaypotsky and their business partner Dorrie Huntington, moved into the East Gym of the old

---

141   Raphael Cruz also played the lead role of "Buster," a Buster Keaton-inspired character, in the Cirque du Soleil production *Iris*.

Polytechnic High School. Just one long block down on Frederick Street was the West Gym, where the San Francisco School of Circus Arts began under Lu Yi's leadership.

The West Gym was humming. Serchmaa Byamba trained contortionists upstairs in a former classroom, just down the hall from the business offices. Two stories below, in the basement, a circus library was growing in one room. Another room became the student lounge. Costumes were getting hung in a third. The large, low-ceiling space between these rooms filled up with circus camps and dance classes. On the main floor, the old theater was attracting audiences again—now for circus recitals instead of high school musicals. The big gym, where seven decades earlier the Polytechnic high school football team had warmed up before crossing the street to Kezar Stadium and playing the 1928 championship game in front of 50,000 people, was now always packed. Elena Panova in one corner of the gym and Hélène Turcotte in another—both teaching trapeze—while the Pickles constantly wrangled with the Youth Circus, individual artists and the school's robust class schedule for the rest of the space. When Jennings McCown and the other flying trapeze teachers set up the huge net for their classes, everyone else was relegated to watching from the old cement bleachers built high on the east wall.

A second trainer from Nanjing was now working at the San Francisco School of Circus Arts. Lu Yi's long-time performing and teaching partner, Xia Ke Min, had moved to the Bay Area with his wife, Lin Qing, and their teenaged son Laurence. Lu Yi had been like an older brother to Xia Ke Min when they came up together in the Pan Family Acrobats' "three bitters" system in Shanghai.

Lu Guang Rong: "Lu Yi is influenced by the traditional Chinese family; if you are the oldest, you take care of the younger ones. Lu Yi was my boss in

Nanjing, and he treated me like a family member. He gives you everything he has. Anything you ask him, he helps. When he came to America, he brought that nature with him. He took care of technique, and he took care of life as well."

Lu Yi and Xia Ke Min shared a small office down the hall from the gym and became the teaching team at the center of the San Francisco School of Circus Arts, now San Francisco Circus Center, for the next 20 years. According to Lin Qing, Xia's wife, "...to the students, Xia was a happy face. Lu Yi was scary."

The second generation of Youth Circus acrobats remember Lu Yi as a strict, mysterious man, who also genuinely enjoyed being with his young American students. "He wanted us to be the best; he put everything into us."

Any time the flying trapeze net was down, you could find Lu Yi in the gym, dressed in a white shirt and a blue tracksuit that sported a red stripe. A jar of tea was always in his hands, except when he needed to grab the spotting lines; then he put down the jar and put on a pair of gardening gloves. He trained the new group of Youth Circus students the way he had trained the first generation and how he had trained his students back in Nanjing.

At the start of every class, the Youth Circus lined up in height order, shortest to tallest, and listened to Lu Yi talk for a few minutes. Then came flexibility—students standing on the floor stretching their legs up onto the side of a trampoline, first facing front, then to the side, and finally facing away from the trampoline with a leg stretched backward. This prepared them for the next exercise, which turned these three stretches into kicks, a series that is now called "Chinese kicks" by many students.

For "Chinese kicks," the group lined up on one side of the gym with Lu Yi clapping in rhythm. The first line started doing front kicks across the gym, followed by the second and third lines. When they got to the other side, the lines turned around and returned with side kicks. They turned again and went back across the gym with fan kicks and ended the series with back kicks.

Judy Finelli: "My first acrobatic teacher, Joe Price, an ex-vaudevillian contortionist and acrobatic dancer in the 20s, 30s and 40s, used a warm-up progression that was basically an abbreviated version of the progression that is done in every acrobatic school in China."

The next section looked a lot like a gymnastics class as the group, still moving in lines across the gym, did forward rolls, backward rolls, handstand walks, handstand hops, handstand rolls, back roll extensions to handstands, in progression of difficulty. They then did barrel turns with kicks, cartwheels, round offs, and back handsprings.

At this point, the students went to different areas of the gym where Lu Yi and Xia Ke Min gave them detailed instruction on physical and mental aspects of their specialty acts. During an interview in his kitchen, we asked Lu Yi to give us an example of the instructions they would give the students. He told Ori Quesada and me:

"There are two groups of acts: relatively calmer acts and the more active ones. Ori is more suitable for a calm act, Jeff for a more dynamic act. Ori, you always need to bring a dynamic approach to a calm act. Now, if you two are working together on a hand-to-hand act, and Ori is the top, he has to be connected to Jeff and Jeff has to give Ori a sense of protection. The top needs his back and core to be strong, with energy from his core going up and down. The base has to give the top stability and that sense of protection.

Jeff, lie on the floor. Ori, do a handstand in his hands and Jeff will do ten push-ups with you."

I stayed in my chair and steered Lu Yi back to the Youth Circus class.

After the students finished their specialties—hand-to-hand, contortion, handstands, pole climbing, hoop diving—they reconvened for a final 15 minutes of conditioning: V-ups, pushups, burpees, donkey kicks and, for those who were ready, standing back tucks and then back tucks right into front tucks.

Devin Henderson and Dominic Cruz, the younger brothers of two acrobatic families: "Lu Yi always knew when you were ready. He had his steps and you had to finish them before you could go on. It was hard to trust it when he said, 'Okay you got it,' but you sometimes trusted him more than you trusted yourself."

Ron and Or Oppenheimer, siblings who were in the third generation of Youth Circus students, what they call "the end of the Golden Age of Lu Yi training":[142] "My favorite Lu Yi quote is, 'In India you don't eat cow, cow is God. Here you don't eat Lu Yi, Lu Yi is God.' That was the atmosphere of the youth circus program—we all worked hard and took it seriously, but it was lighthearted. No one cried. In gymnastics people cried. In Youth Circus, when I did a really good back tuck, I got a lot of corrections. When I did a bad one, Lu Yi just told me to do another."

---

142   Or Oppenheimer has a masters degree in engineering from MIT and is now a senior staff engineer at Carbon; Ron Oppenheimer has played principal roles with Cirque du Soleil and Cirque Éloize and now specializes in flying pole and Chinese pole, as well as acrobatics, aerial rope and straps.

The content of Lu Yi's training sessions hadn't changed much since his first day in the Pickle Church, but he did adjust his style when working with American children. For example, early in his first summer in San Francisco, Lu Yi looked at a nearly empty gym and asked Francis Cruz: "Where is everybody?" Francis said, "They're on vacation." "What is vacation?" When Francis explained, Lu Yi was puzzled and upset, "They have to be here every day so they can train to be the best acrobats." 20 years later, when Or Oppenheimer asked Lu Yi about going on a school trip, he said, "Go have fun! You are kids and you have other things to do."

These adjustments helped Lu Yi and Xia Ke Min train three generations of American performers who, even without the other-worldly skills of troupe-trained Chinese acrobats, became circus stars—exquisite, multi-faceted artists who love their work. Even Youth Circus performers who left acrobatics behind, like Or Oppenheimer, use their training in different ways. "Lu Yi's 'back to basics' mentality applies to college. My engineering classes were hard and a bit boring, and you don't get to do the interesting stuff until junior or senior year. I understood that and I have patience and perseverance. Other students didn't."

Acrobatic clown Jonah Katz:[143] "When they traveled west, the Nanjing acrobats took a real step down. Lu Yi went from teaching the best in the world, and inventing acrobatic acts that have never been replicated or have become standards, to giving us Americans a jumpstart. Lu Yi is responsible for spreading Chinese acrobatics to the rest of the world, with the help of Xia Ke Min and Xiaohong Weng. He remains a legend worldwide."

---

143   Jonah Katz graduated from both The Clown Conservatory and Lu Yi's Professional Acrobatic Program. As a professional, he is based in Europe and has performed around the world, including a number of trips to China.

22. FAMILY MATTERS

"In 1977 I was eleven and Zhou Yue was seven. We were picked, with four other boys and six other girls, to join the Nanjing Acrobatic troupe after we auditioned at our school, the Nanjing Sports Institute. One of the acts I did as a student and a professional in the Nanjing Acrobatic Troupe was basing Zhou Yue in hand-to-hand."

- Xiaohong Weng

Xioahong Weng, Zhou Yue and the ten other young acrobats who joined the Nanjing Acrobatic Troupe in 1977 spent most of their waking hours together. In China, almost all acrobats work with the same ensemble for their entire career. This used to be true for most circus performers around the world, but the "ensemble" they worked with was their family. Although there are still many circus families, the advent of New Circus brought an era of freelancing to North America and Europe—a circus "gig economy" that challenges some of the core concepts of the art-form.

At 11 years old, Xiaohong became an employee of a government-supported troupe. He trained six days a week, the standard work week in China at the time, from eight in the morning until six at night with a two-hour lunch break. His cohort sometimes trained extra hours in the evening because, as Xiaohong says, "We were students, and we were young so extra practice was necessary. The leaders and teachers thought it was good for us, that they were doing the right thing."

The 12 students in Xiaohong's "class" trained together for four years at the Nanjing Acrobatic Troupe before taking exams on acrobatics foundations, basic circus skills, and specialties acts so they could become performers in the shows. Before he left China at age 28, Xiaohong was teaching the new students, stage managing, running the lights and sound for the Troupe's shows, and still performing from time-to-time.

Like the San Francisco Youth Circus, Chinese acrobatic students worked on basics in the early morning—warm-ups, stretching, tumbling, hand balancing—before they divided up, going to the teachers who worked with them on their individual specialties. In the afternoon, they focused on teamwork and group acts—hoop diving, choreography for contortion partners, ten people on a bicycle, and other classics from the Chinese acrobatic repertoire.

The Nanjing acrobats who went through this training with Lu Yi and his faculty got to know one another's habits, skills, timing, fears, and joys. They were in sync on stage, they had an element that is an essential part of Chinese acrobatics, *mòqì*, pronounced moo-chi, which literally translates to 'tacit agreement,' although 'being in sync' or 'being on the same wavelength' might be more accurate.

The idea of *mòqì* is based on a simple physiological principle. The Scientific American article *Brain Waves Synchronize when People Interact* explains: "When people …share an experience, their brain waves synchronize…like dancers moving together …The experience of 'being on the same wavelength' as another person is real, and it is visible in the activity of the brain."[144] Acrobats need to synchronize their brainwaves as well as their bodies.

---

144   Denworth, L. (2023, July 1) Brain Waves Synchronize When People Interact. The Minds of Social Species are Strikingly Resonant. *Scientific American*.

Lu Yi: "Timing is crucial in acrobatics and there is different timing for different tricks. Connection is essential—look in their eyes, focus, establish *móqì.*"

Actor Colman Domingo performed with Make*A*Circus in the early '90s: "I went to the audition, and…Master Lu Yi said, 'Colman, you have *móqì.*' I said, "What is *móqì?*' He said, 'You have a big heart'…If you look at my career now, [my circus background] explains a lot." Colman's career recently led to an Oscar nomination for Best Actor.[145]

Maya Kesselman Cruz and Marta Henderson: "Lu Yi-trained acrobats are good at working in a group. We've done it since childhood, and it reminds us of being a kid. You were never a soloist in Youth Circus, so we don't have a soloist mentality. All our tricks were together, so there was trust."

Outside of the Youth Circus, most American acrobats find it hard to manifest *móqì,* even if they know the word. In the U.S., circus partners usually don't grow up together. This makes such a high level of connection harder to create. In addition, the culture in the States is more transient and the government doesn't sponsor circus like it does in China and Canada, so performers move around to different jobs, different regions, and different companies. In the years I was working with the Pickles, I almost always needed—and wanted—to work at least three other part-time jobs.

---

145   Colman Domingo was nominated for his title role in *Rustin*, making him the first Afro-Latin man to be nominated for a Best Actor Oscar, and only the second openly gay man to earn an Oscar nomination for playing a gay character. Former Pickle clown Bill Irwin plays A.J. Muske, whose heated conversation with Colman's character Bayard Rustin is one of the crucial scenes in the movie. Q with Tom Power. (2024, January 8) *Colman Domingo on his journey from circus performer to civil rights leader Bayard Rustin.* [Video]. YouTube. https://www.youtube.com/watch?v=qUgx0eGxwXk

...

Developing circus skills to the highest level takes generations. For many years, in many countries, these generations were self-contained, within families. In the United States, until recently, most circus performers were born into circus families. The New Circus movement, started by the Pickle Family Circus and Make*A*Circus in the early 1970's, spawned a generation of American circus performers who didn't have family connections to the art-form. Many of them, however, came into circus with a formal education in theater, clowning, mime, dance and/or music so they could train the next generation in these disciplines.[146] Judy Finelli wanted to bring in master acrobatic trainers from abroad to add formal acrobatic training to the mix, supercharging the process of creating a new kind of New Circus at a higher level of acrobatic skill.

There are still great circus families who have reached amazing levels of skill and artistry—the Wallendas on the tight wire, the Gaonas on flying trapeze.[147] Most Russian and Chinese circus performers have acquired world-class skills through a different kind of generational learning since their countries' revolutions in the 20th century.

---

146   Most colleges didn't offer courses in animal training, so there were very few animal acts in the early New Circuses. Later, Cirque du Soleil and others used "animal free" as a marketing tool despite the fact that Cirque du Soleil had produced animal shows with Circus Knie, and owner Guy LaLiberte and former CEO Daniel Lamarre are both on record saying that they wanted animals early on, but that it was too expensive. "Animal free" isn't usually the result of progressive politics; it is mostly PR.

147   Circus families: In 1922 Karl Wallenda, the son of a German circus family, started a high wire act with his brother Herman and two others. In the '40s the family act became known as The Flying Wallendas and there are still Wallendas performing today. The Gaonas are a Mexican circus family. Their trapeze act, The Flying Gaonas, made its debut with the Clyde Beatty-Cole Bros. Circus in 1962, appeared with the Big Apple Circus in the '80s and they are featured in the 2015 movie *The Flight Fantastic*.

Before the Russian revolution, many of the circuses in Russia were owned by families who were not considered Russian—mainly Italians and Jews.[148] When the Soviet government took power in 1917, they exiled many of these "outsiders" and created a national infrastructure for training Soviet performers.

After the Chinese revolution in 1949, the government there also created a national infrastructure, training people outside of circus families in the traditional skills of Chinese acrobatics. Some family circuses evolved into government-sponsored troupes; Lu Yi's first troupe, the Pan Family Acrobats, evolved into the Red Acrobatic Troupe and eventually into the Nanjing Municipal Acrobatic Troupe. Other family troupes stayed independent. Lu Yi's dislike of the Qian Brothers' provenance in a family circus speaks to the tensions between these two systems.

In both the Soviet and Chinese circus ecosystems, generational learning happens between teachers and students rather than from parent to child.

Neither the Soviet or Chinese structures eliminated circus families any more than the NBA has eliminated basketball families like the Currys and the Thompsons.[149] But these institutions opened an avenue for people with no circus in their families to join the profession and to get trained by top artists. These students perform at a high level of skill—sometimes even higher than

148   Dominique Jando: "The great Russian circus families that date from before the revolution were practically all of foreign origin, mostly Italian, and a few German Jewish families such as Salamonsky (who created what is today Circus Nikulin). Gaetano Ciniselli (Italian) created a circus in St. Pétersbourg, the oldest circus building in Russia, which is still extant. Other families of note are Truzzi, Ferroni, Bedini... The only pre-revolution purely Russian circus family was the Nikitin family."
149   Basketball families: Klay Thompson and Steph Curry were teammates on the NBA's Golden State Warriors, a professional basketball team in San Francisco. Both of their fathers were also professional basketball players, Steph's brother Seth Curry plays in the NBA and both of their mothers were college volleyball stars.

their teachers. As it happens, seven of the Youth Circus performers who became professionals are from two singular families—Francisco, Rafael and Dominic Cruz; Brad, Sadie, Devin and Marta Henderson. Dominic Cruz even recently married his fellow Youth Circus student, and *Dear San Francisco* castmate, Maya Kesselman Cruz. New Circus families.

. . .

The Soviet and Chinese models, although different from each other, are in stark contrast to the individual free-lance careers of most American performers. The first two models were—and to some extent still are—immersive and largely supported by the government. This is unlike most circuses and circus schools in the U.S.[150]

Francisco Cruz and Will Underwood: "Lu Yi would show us videos of insane tricks from China. We were teenagers so we'd say, 'We want to do that!' And he would tell us, 'Your training is too soft. North Americans will never do this. You could have all the passion in the world but in China they do 10 to 12 hours of training a day.' We realized we were doing a fraction of what it took to do those tricks. He wasn't bummed though. He was excited that we were the first Americans to do a 'leg catch,' a 'dolphin,' or a 'tornado' on the pole."[151]

---

150   Canada and France are among the "western" nations that famously support the arts—and circus arts in particular—which is why many performers from the U.S. finish their training in those countries, if they're lucky enough to be accepted into programs abroad.

151   A "Leg Catch" is jumping backwards from one pole, leading with your feet, and catching another pole with your legs; a "Dolphin" is jumping backwards from one pole, leading with your chest, doing a half backflip and catching another pole with your legs; a "Tornado" is climbing up and down a pole in a spiral movement using only your hands, without your feet touching the pole.

In China, Lu Yi and his leadership team had always planned far into the future for the organization—new acts, new shows, the troupe's touring schedule—as well as for each individual in the company. They were creating a multi-generational circus family, and, because of the funding from their government, they knew there would be a future for their troupe. They knew that they would all be together for the long run.

Compare this to an American arts organization—even a "family" circus like the Pickles. Almost all the performers join the company after training elsewhere, they usually work on short contracts, and they are free agents at the end of every contract. This means that Lu Yi's American colleagues have an entirely different set of challenges, usually with a much shorter horizon—next week or next season rather than ten to twenty years in the future. American circus Executive Directors and General Managers are not expected to plan their auditions five years in advance, nor are they necessarily inclined to map out careers for their performers or to hire them as coaches when they retire. They are usually not tasked with creating a circus family. What they do have to do is spend a lot of time getting the money needed to keep the company afloat.

Lu Yi was completely committed to working within the American system since, with the help of his immigration lawyer, he had filed naturalization papers and, eventually, received his U.S. citizenship. He had navigated many hurdles, including the question, "Have you ever been a member of the Communist Party?" which is asked of every applicant for naturalization. Lu Yi had to answer, "Yes, I have" since being a member of the Party was essential for his career in China.

When Lu Yi became a U.S. citizen, he lost the option to move back to China, but with the San Francisco Youth Circus, he created a program that had Chinese-style advantages for his students. His American students would grow up together, starting as young as five years old. They would train together, create ensemble acts together, and perform as an ensemble around the Bay Area. Their work together was based on Lu Yi's philosophy: "Training someone is passing love to that person. You are hard on them, and you love them." Youth Circus performers were, and in some ways still are, a family.

Francisco Cruz and Will Underwood: "We were a team. I was one-thousand percent with the others all the time, the same way Lu Yi caught you when you fell. He taught us to throw focus on each other when the other was doing a trick. He gave us those instincts to be aware of each other."

The Pickle performers were also a family.

Djeli (formerly Bill Forchion): "We all ended up on Cirque du Soleil's *Saltimbanco*, lumped together as the "San Francisco Crew": Shana Carroll and Gypsy Snider, Sam Paine and Sandra Feusi, twin sisters Elsie Smith and my wife at the time—Serenity Smith Forchion—and me. We were a scrappy bunch of acrobats, but in Montreal we met a lot of medalists in international gymnastics and partner acrobatic competitions, the elite of the elite, and here we were the kids in the canvas Converse rolling up saying, 'OK, let's do this thing!' But we had heart and it turns out that's what Cirque du Soleil wanted, they wanted to infuse heart into the show."

Lu Yi was able to work with a core group of Pickle performers for most of the '90s and had two decades with the San Francisco Youth Circus. For the Americans, this was a surprisingly long and fulfilling part of our careers. But for Lu Yi, it was too short of a time with too little financial support to bring his long-range plans to fruition. When many of the New Pickle Circus performers left to join Cirque du Soleil in 1997, it was doubly painful for Lu

Yi—Huang Zhen, one of the first of his Nanjing troupe to join the Pickles, had left to join Cirque du Soleil a few years earlier.

Huang Zhen: "Lu Yi didn't speak to me for two years. I felt guilty because he was like my father. When my Cirque du Soleil show performed in San Francisco, he came to see it. After that he was really proud of me, and I felt so good. After he saw that show, he wanted to create a show like that."

Leaving the Pickles for Cirque du Soleil made perfect sense to any American-of course highly skilled, ambitious performers would audition for the biggest circus organization in the world. In a traditional Chinese context, however, performers leaving their home company—their family—was a betrayal. For Lu Yi, this was a blow to the hard-won longevity in his adopted country.

23. GENERATION TO GENERATION

2001 - 2005

After Cirque du Soleil hired most of the New Pickle Circus ensemble in 1997, Lu Yi started talking about the need to build a performing troupe in San Francisco that would be on par with Cirque du Soleil—both in size and financing. This would give performers—acrobats, clowns, and aerialists—a chance to thrive as professionals at home and have continuity between their student and professional lives, like acrobats in China. They would have the added advantage of *móqì*, of being on the same wavelength with the people with whom they perform.

Lu Yi wasn't sure the Pickles could be that troupe. The bankruptcy, something he had never faced in his career in China, gave him an unsettling sense of the fragility of American circus organizations—especially small non-profits with big ambitions. But the Pickles kept trying to find ways to grow as both a performing company and a school.

By 2000, the New Pickle Circus was sharing the gym on Frederick Street with the San Francisco School of Circus Arts (formerly the Pickle Family Circus School) and Make*A*Circus. Peggy Ford[152] and I started The Clown Conservatory that year as part of the school. A few years later,

---

152   Peggy Ford was one of the first women to graduate from Ringling Bros. and Barnum & Bailey Clown College in 1974. She toured in Ringling's famous clown alley, then settled in the Bay Area and became the Artistic Director of Make*A*Circus, Program Director of the San Francisco Circus Center and co-founder of The Clown Conservatory.

Make*A*Circus faced its own financial crisis and closed. The San Francisco School of Circus Arts then merged with the New Pickle Circus, forming the San Francisco Circus Center.

San Francisco Circus Center produced shows for a few years under the Pickle name, working with several different directors, including former Pickles Gypsy Snider and Aloysia Gavre. Aloysia's show featured Youth Circus veterans the Hendersons, the Cruzes, Maya Kesselman (Cruz), and some Nanjing acrobats brought in by Lu Yi to perform a ballet acrobatic act and a teapot balancing act.

Aloysia Gavre: "For the balancing act, I came up with the idea that she's having a tea party and pouring for the guests.[153] I also asked Lu Yi if we could dress the Chinese acrobats as cowboys. He said "yes" to both ideas. The Nanjing acrobats had so much fun because it was so far from their usual. We were making extraordinary things seem ordinary, relatable to the public. This was my strength, not the technical part."

In the mid-2000s, Moscow Circus veteran Elena Panova launched the Professional Aerial Program for adults at San Francisco Circus Center; soon after, Lu Yi started the Professional Acrobatic Program, also for adults. With The Clown Conservatory, which Peggy Ford and I were still running, Judy Finelli's dream of an American school based on Russian and Chinese circus techniques, and American clowning, was almost a reality—the "almost" being that these were three separate programs rather than a unified school.

The faculty at Circus Center decided to bring the acrobatic, aerial, and clown programs together. The three directors, Elena, Lu Yi and I, started to talk

---

153   A few weeks after Stephanie Greenspan interviewed Aloysia Gavre, we saw her Troupe Vertigo in an engagement with the San Francisco Symphony; one of her acrobats did this tea party contortion act.

about combining our programs into a complete circus school. The three of us met regularly with Judy Finelli, Dominique Jando, Xiaohong Weng, Clown Conservatory co-founder Peggy Ford, and former Cirque du Soleil aerialist Hélène Turcotte, hoping to return to Judy's initial dream. We even had the possibility of expanding the dream to include trainers from France, Canada, Mongolia, and other circus cultures, incorporating their traditions into the successful methodologies that we were pioneering at Circus Center.

Lu Yi's dream of a company on par with Cirque du Soleil still hasn't happened. Neither has the Circus Center senior faculty's idea of building a unified international circus training program in San Francisco. As Lu Yi feared, the economic base and administrative structure of Circus Center couldn't bring either of these dreams to life. If new government programs that support American circus are enacted, like the Federal Theater Project in the '30s and the CETA in the '70s, these dreams might still come true.

Unfortunately, many people in the U.S., including many performers, believe that being a "starving artist" fosters creativity and that surviving in the "gig economy" that has been our reality for decades is necessary to be a "real artist." This belief is belied by the dynamic, creative and economically viable circus cultures in China, the Soviet Union, Canada, Australia, and many places in Europe. Clearly, circus as an art-form can grow and flourish with government support.

Even with these challenges, San Francisco Circus Center continues to be a destination for in-depth training and an artistic home for innovative performers, acts and shows. Some of the artists that Lu Yi, Xia Ke Min and Xiaohong Weng trained are now coaching the next generation. Some have even started their own circus schools.

Pickle aerialist Aloysia Gavre started the Cirque School in Los Angeles with her husband and ex-Pickle stage manager Rex Camphuis. Their mission is "For Anybody with Any Body." The New England Center for Circus Arts (NECCA) in Brattleboro, Vermont, was founded by Aloysia's former trapeze partner, Serenity Smith Forchion, and her twin sister Elsie Smith. Over the years, NECCA has featured many ex-Pickles on their faculty, including Djeli, Aidan O'Shea, Aimée Hancock, Jan Damm, Joel Baker, Sandra Feusi and Sam Payne (Sam and Sandra's duet Chinese pole act, "Vertical Tango," won gold medals at four European circus festivals in 2005, making them the MVPs of that year.)

In 2009, Lu Yi visited a class at NECCA led by his old teaching assistant Djeli. There was a framed picture of Lu Yi on the wall of their gym, a converted cotton mill in Brattleboro, Vermont. The class was structured exactly like a Lu Yi training, what Djeli now calls "my dogmatic practice."

Djeli: "After the class, Lu Yi said, 'This is very good, very traditional. What you need now is to do it your way. This is America, not China, and *you* have to be the master trainer.' At first, I was insulted, 'Are you telling me I'm not doing it right, so don't put 'Lu Yi' on it?' He said, 'No, you know what you're doing, now do what you know.'"

It took a while for Djeli to figure out what this meant and how to take Lu Yi's advice.

Djeli: "I needed to put my spirit into the techniques, this is the real Lu Yi way. What I do now is acrobatics of the mind. It's letting our minds do those acrobatic twists and flips to help us flow in our everyday state. It's part of the healing process; when the mind isn't acrobatic enough to shift through difficult times, or even smooth peaceful times, and it worries about what's coming next, it's not, as Lu Yi would say, nimble. I now work with school

214

children, mainly boys, and adults. The work looks a little like philosophy and a lot like play. Sometimes we're solving Rubik's cubes—I could feel my brain shifting when I first moved a cube in three dimensional space. Watching the kids learn to see the back side, the side they can't see, based on what they can see, that's acrobatics. It's flipping and tumbling through the air and knowing how you're going to put your hands down and what your legs are going to do—tuck? stretch? straddle?—that same thing is happening in your mind. 'How am I going to adjust for the next moment? How can I be nimble?'"

At Circus Center, the legacy is still alive. Jennings McCown still teaches flying trapeze, Elena Panova still runs the aerial department and Jeremy Vik,[154] a graduate of both The Clown Conservatory and Lu Yi's Professional Acrobatics Program, trains Youth Circus students alongside Youth Circus veteran Ori Quesada. The American students-turned-performers-turned-teachers are following the same path as generations of Chinese acrobats, albeit in the more haphazard free-lance style of the American circus world.

Jeremy Vik: "Chair stacking is something that needs a coach that you trust to spot you, encourage you, and hold your safety line. My student, Masai, and I both had a joy of handstands, but it took a coach with the right knowledge, at the right moment of our lives, to give us the gift of an act. Xia Ke Min was my coach and I'm proud I was that coach for Masai. When I see her finish a handstand on five or six chairs, her face says, 'I did it. I did that scary, satisfying thing, and I want to do it again!' I am honored to be able to pass on what I learned from Teacher Xia, Master Lu Yi, and Xiaohong Weng to the next generation. I think about the teachers who passed the knowledge of Chinese acrobatics to my teacher, Xia Ke Min. How far back does the chain go? How far forward will it go? In a decade or two, will my student Masai,

---

154   Jeremy Vik was an actor, singer, dancer, and clown before adding handstands on chairs to his resume. He returned to Circus Center as a Youth Circus coach for juggling and hand balancing.

who is only 14 years old, teach some kid who will be stacking chairs late into the second half of this century?"

From one generation to the next, the family of circus.

24. SEND IN THE CLOWNS

2000 - 2010

"At 9:00 on our first day at The Clown Conservatory we started our first class — acrobatics. By 9:05, my classmates and I were lying face down on worn-out blue tumbling mats on the floor of a repurposed, but not renovated, high school theater, stretching our ligaments beyond where ligaments should stretch. At 9:30 I was balancing on my head with our teacher, a former Chinese circus star, holding my feet and encouraging me to 'Be strong!' I just wanted to live long enough to eat lunch."

- Jake[155]

The fictional character Jake is a student at The Clown Conservatory in my book *The Secret Life of Clowns*. Xiaohong Weng is the "former Chinese circus star."

Xiaohong Weng: "Sometimes I had to babysit the clown students—I'm talking about adults. In the U.S., students don't follow directions as well as they do in China. Discipline isn't as good. It's just the culture."

Xiaohong's clown students grew to love him, though they also remember him saying on the first day of school; "All of you are probably going to get

---

155   Raz, J (2017). *The Secret Life of Clowns: A Backstage Tour of Cirque du Soleil and the Clown Conservatory*. Adams Court Press.

hurt, because you're so old. I'm not supposed to say that, and I know I'm not supposed to call you fat, but I probably will. I can't help it, I'm Chinese."[156]

The Clown Conservatory started in January, 2000, at the dawn of the new millennium. My co-founder Peggy Ford and I modeled the school on my alma mater Dell'Arte International, a venerable physical theater school in California's Redwood Empire, 300 miles to the north. We created an in-depth professional circus clown training program for adults, the only one in the U.S. The Clown Conservatory offered a two-year program that included Chinese acrobatics and juggling (these classes were taught by Xiaohong Weng and Judy Finelli respectively), mime, dance, music, body awareness and classic clown entrées taught by Dominique Jando.

Most of our clown students came into the program with creativity, spontaneity, and wildness; what they needed was discipline, physical skills, and structure. Chinese acrobatics was the first class of the year and the first class every week. Xiaohong set the tone for the rest of the classes. Over the years that he taught acrobatics to clowns, Xiaohong grew as a teacher and adapted the millennia-old techniques of Chinese acrobatics to fit these "nontraditional" students.

Xiaohong: "At the Clown Conservatory, I got good at adjusting my teaching. I had to be friends with the students, sometimes I had to think about their emotions. Sometimes they disagreed with me or said they couldn't do the classwork physically, so I had to find ways to encourage them, calm them down or find a different way to teach. If a clown student cannot do a handstand, what else can they do? Maybe a headstand? A triangle headstand

---

156   Xiaohong Weng, like Lu Yi and Xia Ke Min, is beloved in San Francisco despite often being so blunt he sometimes offended his American students. I've come to think that their Chinese bluntness was a relief from, even an antidote to, our Bay Area culture of trying hard not to offend. Speaking bluntly may have been their secret sauce.

or a yoga headstand? If they can't put their legs straight up in the air, how about scissor legs or straddles? How about waving their legs?"

Some of the clown students struggled with acrobatics and others excelled. Some of the more acrobatic students were invited to train with Lu Yi.

Calvin Kai Ku: "Andrew P. Quick and I were in clown acro class when Xiaohong told us to go upstairs. We went from being clowns in the basement to training in the big, sunny gym with all these beautiful aerialists and acrobats. Lu Yi shaped our bodies—stretching us, pulling us, pushing us, sitting on us, so our bodies would conform to the flexibility and needs of the tricks he knew we were capable of doing. Lu Yi can examine you and say, 'your body can do this, do that.' He will look at your shape and know how to strengthen it to do the tricks he wants it to do. He also sees your habits and tendencies, what your mind does when you're contorting or when you're flipping. He'd say, 'Calvin, your mind wants to do everything; you are a wild horse that is too crazy. You need to be in handstand jail.'"

Working with acrobatic clowns, Lu Yi showed Americans his wilder side, the side he was famous for back home. In Nanjing, Lu Yi was more Monkey King than the monk Sanzang. He was an old-school master who had trained in a harsh, pre-revolutionary family circus and then was sent out to represent his newly Communist country around the world. When he got home, he used what he'd learned from performers in Europe and Africa to bring never-before-seen innovations to the cloistered world of Chinese acrobatics.

Lu Yi helped Calvin Kai Ku create new pole tricks and a whole new style of pole act. After Calvin seriously injured his left arm "...Lu Yi opened my eyes to the possibility of going on, of continuing to strive after my injury. My view of Lu Yi is that he's always about possibilities. Wild ideas. 'What if we do this?' When I had the injury, he helped me figure out a one arm monkey climb for a segment in a student act he set on a pirate ship—all of us climbing up and down the pole (the mast) with *Pirates of the Caribbean* playing in the background."

Calvin eventually created a solo act combining pole climbing, clowning, and magic.

Calvin Kai Ku: "When I healed, I kept training and the one hand climb became my closing trick, holding a coat on a hanger in my other hand. The act was me trying to hang a coat at the top of an 18-foot pole, but to hang the coat I need the hangers, and they are at the top of the pole. I had learned a magic trick of linking coat hangers from Mike Caveney[157] so I put it all together and Lu Yi taught me a bunch of pole skills to use. I figured out how to do the tricks in a way that looked clumsy and then wove in impressive pole tricks. A mix between skill and clumsiness and magic, on a Chinese pole."

As Lu Yi watched the clown students grow, he hatched a plan with his partner Xia Ke Min, himself a famous clown back in China, and with the clowns' acrobatics teacher Xiaohong Weng. They would use American clowns to fulfill Lu Yi's dream of giving Chinese circus an infusion of humor, emotion, and warmth. Their earlier plan of sending the first generation of Youth Circus acrobats on a Chinese tour, performing to a hip-hop soundtrack, was on hold since most of them were out touring the world with other circuses.

Lu Yi always planned long-term: Working with his connections back in Nanjing and around China, waiting for newbie clowns to get good, slowly, carefully building to the moment when the teachers, the students, the money, and the schedule were all aligned. For years, Lu Yi kept working and watching,

---

157   Mike Caveney is an American magician, author, publisher, magic historian, and collector.

ready to send his American students—all acrobatic clowns—to reinvigorate Chinese circus back home.

25. "ANOTHER LAYER HARDER"

"Acrobatic clowning is very difficult. Acrobats have to perform an act with grace and skill, but when clowns do tricks, they need to interpret them differently, make them fit with the clowning, which is harder. Training acrobatic tricks, that's hard; add clowning and it is another layer harder."

- Lu Yi

John Gilkey: "In the world of clown, and perhaps everywhere, there is a paradox of discipline and wildness—you need the discipline if you want to be professional, but you've got to have wildness if you want to find something new, original, and engaging. So, there is always a push and pull with discipline."

Discipline and wildness underpin the entire art-form of circus, not just clowning. The importance of discipline and wildness combining is a key reason why the Nanjing/San Francisco relationship has been so successful. Lu Yi's deep understanding of the art of circus, both the bitterness of training and the joy of wild innovations, meant he was uniquely positioned to see new ways these two qualities could merge, bringing new acts, new styles, new flavors into the circus world.

Lu Yi believes that every circus must have three elements—"Wow!" moments, humor, and teamwork. The "wow" moments are amazing physical feats which make the audience gasp (inhale). The humor is clowning, which makes the audience laugh (exhale). This is why acrobats and clowns go so well together—they get the audience breathing, inhale for the acrobats, exhale for the clowns. Inhale, exhale; together, acrobats and clowns are life.

Dominique Jando, clown and historian: "[In the circus] you see one extraordinary feat after another and every now and then [they] send in the clowns and everything comes down to earth and you just feel relieved."[158]

And then there is the third element, teamwork. The Pickles started as a collective, a team that worked together to run, set up and perform a circus. They were inspired, in part, by Maoist thought. Lu Yi came of age in the Maoist era of collectivizing and spent his life performing, training and directing group acrobatics acts. For Lu Yi, teamwork, *mòqí*, is essential to all acrobatics. Teamwork is also essential for clowns—even for solo clowns since the team a clown works with extends to include the audience, the band, and everyone in the tent or theater.

Other physical art-forms—vaudeville, variety, drag and burlesque—use the elements of "wow," humor, and teamwork to amaze and delight audiences. There can be more elements in any given circus—cute moments, scary moments, sweet moments, plot points, and politics—but without "wow," humor, and teamwork, circus simply doesn't work.

Acrobatic clowning brings all three of these elements—"wow," humor, and teamwork—together into a single act, sometimes all three are contained within a single performer. The acrobatic clown numbers in *Tossing & Turning*—the opening where Pino climbed all over me as I tried to introduce the show, the act where she played my pillow, and the musical number with dancing and

---

158   Dominique Jando in Samels, M. (Executive Producer). (2018) *American Experience: The Circus*. [TV mini-series] A Winter Pink Films Production; PBS. https:// www.pbs.org/wgbh/americanexperience/films/circus/

doubles acrobatics while playing instruments—all had the "wow" acrobatic factor and comedy, as well as teamwork that extended beyond the two of us to include the band and the audience. Tandy Beal gave the framework for these acts. Lu Yi designed the acrobatics. They both helped us make the acrobatics fit with the clowning.

The *móqì* Diane and I needed to perform the acrobatics helped us get laughs with our clowning. This was important because acrobatics can put humor at risk. For an acrobatic clown, the "layer deeper" is staying connected to the audience, making sure that every human in the theater or tent is included in your teamwork, at the same time that you are doing difficult and dangerous acrobatics. Since being in-sync with the audience is necessary for laughs, the "wow" factor can overshadow both humor and the kind of expansive teamwork clowns need to employ.

For *Jump Cuts!*, Lu Yi trained Diane and me on shoulder pole. I balanced a 15-foot pole on my right shoulder, Diane scampered up the pole and then did some "wow" moves, including holding the pole to her shoulder while upside-down in a ball, kicking her legs up and "hopping" towards the ceiling. She finished the routine by sitting cross-legged on the pole, flourishing to the audience, and then sliding down head first into a handstand on my hands.

The framework Tandy gave was a classic adventure movie with Diane as a monkey and me as a would-be Tarzan. For the first few weeks we performed this act, the acrobatics were new enough and hard enough that I couldn't be a clown. I wasn't able to play a comic Tarzan or connect with the audience or even connect with Pino the clown; only with Diane the acrobat. Luckily, in a few weeks my shoulder pole technique got good enough that I could go that layer deeper, teaming up with Pino and with the audience to get some laughs.

Acrobatic clown Faeble Kievman found that the opposite is also true, that humor can put the "wow" at risk. A Russian acrobat once told him that his act was good but the audience didn't pay much attention to the tricks because his character was too strong. For acrobatic clowns, keeping these three elements in balance is crucial.

. . .

To Lu Yi, all performers, even the clowns, have to remember that training is bitter. This was not easy for many of us in San Francisco. Starting in the 70s, ideas about spiritual growth through physical movement, like yoga, often blended into the circus ethos, but these concepts were anathema to Lu Yi: "Acrobatics is not good for you. It is good for the audience." In order for the audience to enjoy our acrobatics, and acrobatic clowning, he put bitterness into our rehearsals.

Lu Yi would test us to make sure we were physically and mentally ready to perform dangerous tricks. Especially the clowns, since we needed to go that layer deeper in performance. Diane and I had considerably less acrobatic training than the Youth Circus "kids," even though, as the Pickle clowns, we were among LuYi's most visible American students.

One day, a month before we were scheduled to premiere the group bike act, Lu Yi told me to start riding the heavy-duty bicycle in the counterclockwise circle that defines the act. He then told everyone in the company to get on, even people who didn't perform Group Bike. I kept trying to go faster, the technique needed to compensate for the hundreds of pounds of Pickles as they climbed aboard.

When they were all on, Lu Yi said, "10 circles," which is at least triple what we would do in a show. He stood in the middle of the circle slowly counting in English. "One... two... three..." When he got to six, I was ready to give up; when he got to eight, I would have happily crashed the bike, injuring everyone, to stop the burning in my legs. By 10, I was ready to run over this small, calm Chinese man. But I kept pedaling for another two circles as everyone dismounted safely.

Lu Yi came over, punched my shoulder and said, "Remember that." A few minutes later, he said, "Again!"

In the years we performed that act, I never dumped the bike, even when we performed outside at the opening of Yerba Buena Gardens on a too small, eight-foot high stage that released just enough moisture from the overnight rains that the bicycle wheels started to hydroplane.

In 1997, I had the joy of helping Xia Ke Min teach Group Bike to the last class of students at the Ringling Bros. and Barnum & Bailey Clown College. The newbie clowns loved Xia Ke Min because he embodied circus—"wow," humor, and teamwork. He was an acrobatic star, a clown, and a great partner to Lu Yi—his "older brother"—as well as to his clown teammate Yang Xiao Di. In the next chapter, I'll shine a spotlight on Teacher Xia before we follow a quartet of clowns on their journey to the East.

SPOTLIGHT ON...

XIA KE MIN

Many of us in the '70s San Francisco circus scene knew Xia Ke Min and Lu Yi from two books about Chinese acrobats,[159] the only ones available back in the day. None of the Chinese performers were credited, though, so we didn't know their names. The photographs inspired us for years and, since we didn't have teeterboards, climbing poles, or giant urns, we focused on trying to learn from the pictures of group acrobatics as well as the ones showing rola-bola, diabolo and other juggling acts.

The picture of Lu Yi basing *Picking Flowers on Top of a Head* made our jaws drop, but we didn't even understand what was happening in the picture of a teeterboard trick Xia Ke Min did with Lu Yi. Later we learned that Lu Yi would jump onto one end of a teeterboard to shoot Xia, standing on the other end, into the air. Xia would fly and land headfirst on Lu Yi's head …without either man using their hands. In the picture, taken the moment before their heads touch,[160] both men's arms are out to their sides and Xia is already in position to balance in a free headstand. A free headstand is a difficult trick; flying headfirst toward someone else's head, landing skull to

---

159   Yongxue, S. (1981) *Chinese Acrobatics*. China Books & Periodicals.

160   This picture can be seen on page 81 in Lu, Yi., Holt, D. (2023). *Training is Bitter.* Periodgraph Press.

skull and then balancing in a free headstand is exponentially more difficult and dangerous.[161]

We were shocked when we met Xia Ke Min in person—he seemed much bigger than Lu Yi, making this teeterboard trick, possibly the greatest of all time, even more impossible. It wasn't until Xia's mother visited from China that we understood why the Pan Circus had made him Lu Yi's flyer. She was tiny—well under five feet tall. Xia wasn't actually much taller than Lu Yi, but his body was rounder and his laugh was bigger. It is fitting that, after they stopped performing together, Lu Yi became a director and Xia Ke Min became a clown.

Xiahong Weng: "Xia Ke Min and his clown partner Yang Xiao Di were famous in China. Yang was the talk, talk, talker, the top banana, and Xia was the second banana. They were in a popular movie with circus acts from all around China, done like an old stage show with a curtain and an emcee. In one act, Yang Xiao Di walked through the curtain with a beer bottle half full of water and an umbrella that opened by pushing a bottom—these weren't common in China in those days. Yang tossed the bottle, caught it on the umbrella tip and opened the umbrella. Water poured out of the bottle just as Xia Ke Min came through the curtain. Yang stayed dry under the umbrella and Xia got soaked."[162]

This was Xia Ke Min's life in China—a famous clown who used to be a famous acrobat with full-time work at the Nanjing Acrobatic Troupe, one of

---

161   Lu Yi and Xia Ke Min have both wondered aloud if training and performing this trick wasn't a contributing factor to the Parkinson's disease that afflicted both of them later in life.

162   This is a Victorian-era juggling trick, credited to Paul Cinquevalli, the Prussian juggling superstar who divorced 'juggling' from 'magic' in the English language. For more information, see: Wall, T. (2019). *Juggling—From Antiquity to the Middle Ages: the Forgotten History of Throwing and Catching*. Modern Vaudeville Press.

the best circuses in the world. He was surrounded by the people he grew up with and by the younger performers he'd taught. A good life.

Then he went to New York City in 1988 with Lu Yi and other acrobats from Nanjing to perform in *The Big Apple Circus Meets the Monkey King*. Xia Ke Min's clown partner Yang Xiao Di played Monkey King; Xia fell in love with America.

Lin Qing, Xia Ke Min's wife says that when he got back to Nanjing, "...he told me that he wanted to move to America. In the bookstore, he showed me a picture of the beautiful city San Francisco. He always followed Mr. Lu Yi. He is the younger brother.[163] They slept in one bed. They had a very close relationship. He came to America first in 1992 and then after seven months I was able to join him."

In San Francisco, Xia Ke Min was originally slated to perform with the Pickle Family Circus or on cruise ships with Lu Yi's Spring Circus. He ended up only performing occasionally, doing acts from the traditional Chinese clown repertoire called the "Happy Chef" at events around the Bay Area. His main job became Lu Yi's teaching partner, training the Youth Circus and working with individual adult students—and occasionally with the Pickle cast.

Xia Ke Min: "If they needed the basics—strength and stamina—I would teach them. If they were ready for skills, they would go to Lu Yi. Teaching American kids, you can't be that strict. Chinese kids can hold handstands a long time, American kids say, 'I'm tired.' In America, students are coming for recreation first, but in China, most kids are studying to have a career; once they are accepted into a school, they already have a job. In America it's the

---

163   Lu Yi writes, "I was older [than Xia Ke Min] and had been in the troupe longer. That made me an elder circus brother." Lu, Yi., Holt, D. (2023). *Training is Bitter.* Periodgraph Press.

opposite, parents are paying to have their children participate. In China, the kids have something to lose. In America, the school has something to lose; if the parents pull the kids out, they lose revenue."

Xia Ke Min found a niche training young adults who had their eyes on a circus career—people who had something to lose. Faeble Kievman was one of them. After he graduated from The Clown Conservatory, Faeble asked Xia Ke Min to teach him the spinning plates section of the "Happy Chef." Xia said that lots of people had asked "...but I would say 'no' because they are not funny enough. Now I am thinking about who I wanted to pass 'Happy Chef' down to. Faeble, I've been waiting for you to ask."

Xia Ke Min taught Faeble Kievman the spinning plates routine (a clown running up and down a long table that eventually holds ten sticks with plates precariously spinning on their ends), balancing three eggs on a chopstick on one's nose, and juggling a pot, ladle, knife. Xia taught the acts with Chinese opera movements, his version of "Happy Chef." Although this isn't Faeble's style, he still finds Xia's movements have become ingrained in him.

Xia Ke Min also trained a trio of adults—Fleeky Flanco, Dominik Wyss and Christopher "Chrissy" Roguskie. Christopher Roguskie, who went on to train in China, was the only student Lu Yi taught spinning plates as a specialty and the only person outside of China he taught *Picking the Flower with Spinning Plates*. Dominik Wyss is now San Francisco Circus Center's Acrobatics Department Co-chair and Fleeky Flanco, who also trained with Mongolian contortionist Serchma Byambaa, is performing in Europe and North America using elite handstand and front-bending contortion skills while playing an over-the-top character.

Fleeky Flanco: "I saw a picture of a contortionist in Cirque du Soleil, and I said, 'I'm going to do this or die.' I didn't know how to get to train with Lu

232

Yi, so I talked to Xia Ke Min. He looked me up and down, 'You want to do contortion? No, no, no, no. I don't think this is going to work. Not for you.' I was destroyed. I had moved to San Francisco with nothing because I wanted to train. Then Devin Holt told me, 'Xia says that to everybody.'"

Fleeky Flanco signed up for a contortion class with Xia Ke Min and one other student. "My first class, after we do some handstands, he says, 'You really want to do contortion?' I'm like, 'Yes.' and he's like, 'Really? You really want to do contortion? You sure?' I said, 'Yes!'"

Xia Ke Min set a piece of PVC pipe covered with foam between two tall benches and told Fleeky to lay across it to warm up his back. Five minutes later, Xia stood by Fleeky's head and the other student grabbed Fleeky's hips. "…I'm looking upside down at Xia, 'You really want to do contortion?' 'Yeah!' 'OK' and he grabs my shoulders, and they squish me together. One minute into this, I say, 'Stop. Stop!' but Xia says, 'No, no, you want to do contortion.' He pushes more. A hot ball of lava flows into my stomach and shoots out through my whole body. I was on fire and my eyes were rolling back in my head. I said, 'I'm going to pee myself' and he stopped. That was the first six months of training with Xia. It was so crazy, so much work. Every day I felt like I was 70 years old, I was in so much pain. But he didn't do it in a mean way. He's like, 'Do you want to do this? Because I don't really care.' He doesn't help you unless you put out the effort."

As Xia Ke Min taught Fleeky contortion, fellow student Dominik Wyss helped him create a wild character based on a painting of a red-headed ghoul by Gerald Brom.

Fleeky and Xia Ke Min's other adult students also got career advice from their teacher. Fleeky says that, "…Xia was very much about the money. He'd say, 'You're training with me now, so you better make ten times what you pay me, minimum.' People in San Francisco were getting screwed left and right and he was always trying to get us to think realistically about money. 'Never have a doubles act; you have to split the money.' 'When they pay you money, that when you know if they really like you or not.'"

Faeble Kievman and Fleeky Flanco continue to use traditional acts from the Chinese *One Hundred Entertainments*—contortion, handbalancing, Happy Chef, jar juggling and various balancing acts—in the context of wild American clowning.

. . .

If Lu Yi is the monk Sanzang of our story, Xia Ke Min is Pigsy—the third companion on the *Journey to the West*. Pigsy, whose Buddhist name means "pig who rises to power," was once an immortal banished to earth. He is "... generally goodhearted, although he often lets his vices, food and laziness, get the better of him."[164]

Fleeky: "Xia Ke Min would say that he was the laziest coach, but he also had a brilliance that most people didn't notice. His laziness and brilliance were hand-in-hand. For instance, he didn't know much English, but he could talk with you for hours and still make a joke about you that cut so deep. He's always clever, and clever about getting out of work. He'd say it himself, 'I was born a rat[165] and rats sneak around. I get my cheese and then I hide.' For me, hearing stuff like that became aspirational—'Don't overdo it.'"

The idea that a great trainer can, and even should, be "lazy" is a core concept for Dr. Sivasailam "Thiagi" Thiagarajan, a major figure in the consulting

---

164   Wu, C. Jenner, W.J.F. (2005). *Journey to the West*. (C. Fair, Ed.). Disruptive Pub.
165   Xia Ke Min was born in 1948, Year of the Rat in the Chinese zodiac.

world. The president of The Thiagi Group, Matthew Richter, explains: "The best trainer is a lazy trainer. The more a trainer does, the less the participants learn... We talk a good game when we say 'engagement,' but what works best is when we sit down [and] stop talking."

Fleeky: "After I'd been training with Xia for a while, he took me aside and said, 'Fleeky, you stay with me one year; different Fleeky.' And I was like 'Wow! He really thinks I'm special.' Then there was a new student a few months later and Xia was like, 'You stay with me one year, different you.' He said that to everybody. But when he said it to me, he changed my life. You have to buy into it. He had so much inside of him about performing and no one here in San Francisco to talk to. I think by hanging around him for fifteen years, it came out. I learned so much and he slowly became one of the most important people who was ever in my life."

Xia Ke Min now considers Fleeky Flanco one of his biggest successes as a teacher.

ACT SIX:

JOURNEY TO THE EAST

26. CLOWNS IN NANJING

2008

> After traveling for fourteen years and overcoming eighty-one ordeals, Sanzang, Monkey King, Pigsy, and Friar Sand reach the Western Heaven. They climb the mountain of Vulture Peak; they take a bottomless ferry steered by the Conductor of Souls. Finally, they reach Thunder Monastery, where Buddha hands Sanzang 5,048 holy scrolls. Buddha then orders deities to take the pilgrims home, and they all fly east on a magic cloud.[166]

In September 2008, the Clown Conservatory acting teacher Joan Mankin, who first met Lu Yi in rehearsals for *La La Luna Sea*, flew east with two other Americans. They were heading for Nanjing where they would lead the first Western-style Clowning Workshop in China.[167] Joan Mankin's team from San Francisco Circus Center was Caroline (Linie) Orrick, a Lu Yi-trained acrobat, Clown Conservatory grad and former Circus Center board member, and Jonah Katz, still in his teens and already a Clown Conservatory grad, a Lu Yi-trained acrobat, and a tap dancer. I planned to join the team two weeks into the month-long workshop.

---

166   Wu, C. Jenner, W.J.F. (2005). *Journey to the West*. (C. Fair, Ed.). Disruptive Pub.
167   The workshop was hosted by the Nanjing Acrobatic Troupe, Lu Yi's old company, and the Jiengsu Provincial Arts organization with additional sponsorship of the Chinese Arts and Cultural organization.

Joan, Linie, and Jonah were beginning the final phase of the two-decade long circus affair between Nanjing and San Francisco. During his time in San Francisco, Lu Yi often talked about bringing American circus to the East, back to China. He wanted to unite his "Chinese and American families," and had identified the techniques of San Francisco clowning as the key skills that Chinese acrobats needed to excite and surprise their audiences and gain new fans.

The day after arriving in Nanjing, Joan Mankin taught a clown class. She began with a warm-up designed to connect the students' emotions and thoughts with the various parts of their bodies. Joan's translator, Ma Li, a staff member of the Nanjing Acrobatic Troupe, interpreted instructions like "paint the ceiling purple with your breath" as "okay, she's at it again; just do something weird." Ma Li's skill as a creative translator between two languages, and between two cultures, proved to be both invaluable and occasionally baffling.

Jonah Katz: "American circus folks going to China better have something the Chinese performers don't have! If you're an acrobat, aerialist, juggler, or contortionist, you'll never live up to the Chinese standards. Where Americans get ahead in China is clowning, mime, audience participation, and the art of performance."

To be clear, China already had a rich tradition of circus clowning, but it was different from the San Francisco style. Circus clowning in China has a set repertoire, including "The Happy Chef," acts that Xia Ke Min performed on-and-off in the San Francisco Bay Area.

20 Chinese acrobats—18 men, one woman and an eight-year-old boy-formed the student body of the Nanjing Western-style Clowning Workshop. They were all top students and performers from acrobatic troupes across China:

Beijing, Wuhan, Yin Chuan, An Hui, and Tai Yuan. For the San Francisco teachers, working with a group of world-class acrobats was exciting—and a little intimidating. In a month, these 20 acrobats needed to be knowledgeable, vulnerable, and funny enough to perform San Francisco-style clowning in front of live audiences. In circus time, a month is an incredibly small window to learn any discipline—clowning included—but it was our turn to try to do what Lu Yi had done. We were on a similar mission—go to a far away land to quickly give the artists there the gift of our discipline. Lu Yi brought Chinese acrobatics to San Francisco; we were trying to bring American clowning to Nanjing.

Before the trip, we were told that China was going through a transformation, letting go of some of its attachment to tradition and seeking out new artistic channels. That's why we were invited. Our task: raise the level of comic acting and encourage the performers to connect on a more personal level with their audiences.

In her opening speech, Joan Mankin asked the students to bring their whole personalities to every class—their funny side and their serious side, their good and their bad, their ugliness and their beauty. All of these are necessary for clowning. Ma Li translated this diligently. Then Joan, Linie and Jonah started teaching six hours a day, five days a week, in a rehearsal room on the ground floor of the arts center that also housed the Nanjing Acrobats, four floors above.

Along with the daily acting work, Jonah taught tap dancing, Linie trained the group in specific Western clowning techniques (falls, slaps, trips, and smashing into walls), and the students watched videos of Western clowns: Bill Irwin, Carol Burnett, Buster Keaton, and others. The acrobats especially loved tripping, sometimes covering 20 feet a trip, arms windmilling—"a thing of terrifying beauty."

Joan Mankin: "The students throw themselves with tremendous dexterity and gusto into every trick we ask them to do… but ask them to reveal something true and vital about themselves in front of other people and they run into a wall of a different kind."

Joan, Jonah and Linie quickly felt comfortable in Nanjing, a city of five-and-a-half million people, in part because they had heard a lot about it from Lu Yi and the other Chinese acrobats they knew. The streets were crowded with thousands of pedestrians and vehicles—two- and three-wheeled bikes, scooters, motorcycles, cars—all moving quickly through small spaces. Stepping off the curb required trust, full focus, and a keen sense of the rhythm of the street. Stop to think, and you're dead; stay in the flow and you get to the other sidewalk. We decided that a Nanjing intersection was Lu Yi's inspiration for the fast-paced ensemble table sliding act that he created for the cowboy section of *Jump Cuts!*. It took a lot of *mòqí* to survive both that act and these intersections.

The second week started off well, as the students turned a quick field trip around Nanjing into a series of short, comic scenes. They went to a nearby mall to try San Francisco-style street performing, doing their scenes and playing human sculptures for big audiences. Some clown students giggled and watched at a safe distance puffing on their cigarettes, but the group clearly enjoyed their first taste of clowning in public.

. . .

On the flight to Nanjing, I had started reading Iris Chang's *The Rape of Nanking: The Forgotten Holocaust of World War II*. I learned that the war had scarred more of the world than I was aware of, despite growing up Jewish in America and the son of a veteran. After I landed, images of Japanese

242

atrocities from the book gave the vibrant city of Nanjing a gut-wrenching pall, which helped me understand why Lu Yi had once refused to join the Pickles on a tour to Nagoya, Japan. Later, when Lu Yi was training the American women's synchronized swimming team for the Olympics, he surprised and impressed me by agreeing to coach the Japanese team, too.

Soon after I landed in Nanjing, Joan and I started designing the final student show. Inspired by the earlier field trip, we framed the various clown acts with a simple, flexible story: Jonah, lost in Nanjing, is befriended by the eight-year-old Chinese acrobat who had nicknamed himself "Banana." The pair discover different clown acts on the street, the bus, the park, the zoo, and at a soccer game. We decided a big tap dance number would kick off the show. We would also include an ensemble piece using "animal forms" from martial arts, which Joan had studied for years. Both of these full-cast scenes were inspired by the opening ceremony at the recent Beijing Olympics.

On a day off, I stumbled on the Jiangsu Province Kun Opera. Kun Opera (*Kunqu*) is a 16th century ancestor of the more famous Beijing opera, making it one of the oldest extant forms of Chinese opera. The theater was an easy walking distance from the Nanjing Acrobatic Troupe's headquarters, so I went to see a free performance with English subtitles. I was amazed. Kun Opera looked less like Beijing Opera and more like Italian Commedia Dell'Arte. The characters were similar—the wily maid, her mistress and her mistress's lover, the overbearing father, the pedant and his mischievous servant. A comic slice of feudal life. The acting style was also similar to Commedia, with broad physical action—sometimes even slapstick—and direct address to the audience.[168]

---

168   Commedia dell'Arte is an Italian theatrical form with roots in 16th century Venice. It flourished throughout Europe for two centuries-a popular theater, often performed outside, that emphasized ensemble acting, improvisation within a scenario, masked characters and lazzi (set routines, usually for one or two characters that often involved

Joan and I were both trained in Commedia Dell'Arte and we were thrilled to find a Chinese art-form that featured many of the ideas and techniques we were now teaching in our Western-style Clowning Workshop. I tried to set up a field trip to the Kung Opera so our Nanjing students could ground the "strange" American clown concepts they were learning in a long-established Chinese context. This idea got nixed by the leaders of the Nanjing Acrobatic Troupe. They told us that everyone knows about *Kunqu* and that no one will go to see it—certainly none of these acrobats. *Tell us, who was in the audience today, besides you? It was all old people and some students who were forced to be there, right?* They were right but we argued that most of the material we were teaching was already in Nanjing, a few blocks away, and free. "Why spend all this money and time to fly in American clown teachers when you've got excellent Chinese actors performing and teaching the same techniques right in the neighborhood?"

Sadly, the Nanjing leaders were right—the idea of going to the Kun Opera was scorned by everyone. I realized that Lu Yi's plan to reinvigorate Chinese acrobatics was based on the cachet and novelty of American teachers; our "otherness" was part of the excitement.

. . .

The Chinese clown students needed to perform—to season their acts in front of friendly audiences before the big final show, which would be attended by several high level Chinese acrobatic officials, including the army general who oversaw the three military acrobatic troupes. Unfortunately, the Nanjing Acrobatic Troupe's leaders hadn't booked any shows, as they had

physical virtuosity). Many European clown entrées came from commedia lazzi. It may not be a coincidence that Kun Opera and commedia dell'arte are similar—16th century Venice had close economic and cultural ties to China.

promised, so we decided to take the students back to the mall—this time in makeup and costume. When I announced this to the group, Ma Li refused to translate. For the next half hour, the Nanjing leaders made one odd excuse after another—"the weather isn't right," "the mall will close early today"—in quiet, friendly tones as I got more and more shrill. Finally, Ma Li had given me enough hints that I got it—there was no way the students were going to the mall that day and everyone was trying hard to give me a way to save face.

I said, "You know, I think it is a good day to run the acts here in the rehearsal hall." Ma Li translated, the tension dissipated, and the students got ready to rehearse. The problem turned out to be the makeup. Apparently going outside in clown makeup was never going to happen. Joan Mankin started her career performing in parks with the San Francisco Mime Troupe and the Pickle Family Circus; I started as a street juggler. Walking the streets in makeup and costume was normal for us—even an essential part of our histories and identities. The Chinese acrobats had grown up in schools and on stages. When they were in makeup, the public came to them, not the other way around.

One evening a few days after the aborted mall performance, I got called into a meeting with the leaders of the Nanjing Acrobatic Troupe. Ma Li sat with Mr. Chao, who had Lu Yi's old job as the Troupe's leader, and a couple of other administrators. They poured tea and we sipped for a few moments before getting to the point. Ma Li translated, "Mr. Chao says that they are concerned about the way the training is going, if the students will learn anything that Chinese audiences will want to see." I told them that clowning, like acrobatics, takes time to develop—but unlike acrobatics, you only know if the clowning is good when it is presented in front of an audience. "We need to schedule shows for these clowns so they can learn to listen to, and respond to audiences." Many cups of tea were consumed. Even though the conversation was full of cross-cultural crossed wires, Mr. Chao finally agreed to complete the program.

Once I knew we weren't getting sent home, I pushed hard to get them to book a theater for the final show, which was coming up in 10 days. They agreed, but I didn't hold out much hope. Even if Mr. Chao miraculously found a venue, there was no way we'd get an audience on such short notice.

27. SHOWTIME

2008

> After many years of traveling to the West, and then eight days flying back to the East on a magic cloud, Tang Sanzang and his companions arrived in China. They presented the Emperor with the 5,048 holy scrolls they had received at the Thunder Monastery. Buddha rewarded each traveler with a new title—Monkey King became Buddha Victorious in Strife and Sanzang was the Buddha of Precocious Merit.[169]

Lu Yi landed at the Nanjing airport after a long flight east from San Francisco, just in time for the fourth and final week of the Western-style Clowning Workshop. He settled at the hotel and then invited Joan and me to join him and the Nanjing Acrobatic Troupe's leadership on a trip. We were going to a technical university where there might be a theater for the final clown show. Leaving Linie and Jonah to teach the rest of the day, we got on a bus and headed to the university, 90 minutes outside of Nanjing.

As we drove past a small, weedy field, Lu Yi said, "This is where I dreamed up the act *Picking Flowers on Top of a Head*." We asked why he was designing new circus tricks in a field. "After every international tour, we artists had to work on farms. It was part of our reintegration, to remind us of our roots, and the roots of the Chinese revolution in farming. While my body worked in that field, my mind invented new acrobatic tricks."

---

169   Wu, C. Jenner, W.J.F. (2005). *Journey to the West*. (C. Fair, Ed.). Disruptive Pub.

As the sad little field flew by and we drove on through semi-rural suburbs, I kept thinking about my teacher as a young man, a star performer, forced to work on a farm. He didn't sound bitter—it was just the way things were—and it clearly didn't hurt his body, his spirit, or his career. I wondered if I would have accepted taking a few months out of my life to shovel dirt in the same way he did, but the worlds we grew up in were too different to speculate. Finally, I was left with an image of a young Lu Yi, shovel in hand, dreaming up new tricks for an acrobatic tradition that was started by other farmers a few thousand years before.

At the university, the Nanjing group sat down with the Dean and his team, drinking tea, smoking, and talking. After 15 minutes, Ma Li told Joan and me that they were just doing introductions—and that she would translate again when the subject of a theater came up. An hour later, Ma Li was still silent, and the Chinese men were all standing up to leave. Joan stood up, too, "We need to see the theater. Now." Ma Li balked at telling the school officials that this American woman with wild red hair was trying to order them around, but she somehow managed to get the group to walk to the theater. It turned out to be perfect for the final clown show: 200 comfortable seats, a large stage and good lighting and sound equipment.

We gave the thumbs-up and the whole group walked to the Dean's spacious office. More tea and more smoking. Joan and I asked Ma Li to translate as they made the final arrangements, but she said they were still in the getting-to-know-you phase, which was necessary to build trust with the head guy. We drank more tea. Lu Yi must have had many meetings in San Francisco that were as frustrating to him as these were to Joan and me. But Joan and I were going home in a week; Lu Yi had to keep living in San Francisco.

When the bus took off for Nanjing, we were still not sure if we had a theater for the clown students' final show. Joan and I were confused and disappointed but when we arrived for class on the Monday of our final week, Ma Li told us that everything was set for the big show at the university's theater. We were sure that no one would come on less than one week's notice and that our poor students would play to an empty theater on Saturday night, but we had to focus on our final week in Nanjing: a mall gig that afternoon (without make-up), two shows at an elementary school that we had booked ourselves, and a high school show the following day that Joan set up with an English teacher she had met on the train to Shanghai.

The mall show was shaky, but the students learned a lot about where the laughs were—or could be. Our Chinese clowns got better each of the next two shows and then, when they looked out at 1,000 high school kids laughing, screaming, and cheering, they knew they were getting the hang of San Francisco-style clowning.

After these performances, we had a technical rehearsal at the university in preparation for their final presentation, which had turned into an extravaganza featuring the clown students' show plus four acts from the Nanjing Acrobatics troupe. This meant we needed to weave a contortionist, a trio juggling large jars, a version of a famous ballet doubles acrobatic act,[170] and a magician[171] into the story of Jonah and Banana wandering Nanjing.

---

170   In 2002, Circus Center Executive Director Pat Osbon, Lu Yi, and I attended the International Circus Festival of Monte-Carlo where an acrobatics act from Guangdong won top honors performing a circus version of a ballet *pas de deux*. The flyer, a woman, was in a tutu, en pointe, doing pirouettes and attitudes on the base's head and arms. After the festival, other Chinese troupes created their own versions of this act, as is customary.

171   Unlike western circus, magic acts are part of the core repertoire of Chinese acrobatics.

An hour before the big show, there were two chairs in the third row draped in red cloth, each with an orange and a bottle of water on a small table next to them. One was for Lu Yi, the other for the General. All of the other seats were filled with young people. We were amazed, grateful, and worried that the audience was there too early. It turned out that students at technical university were accidentally told an earlier start time. They were happy to sit patiently through the last hour of technical rehearsals, and the young soldiers guarding the front doors didn't seem to bother anyone but me.

At showtime, the sound technician hadn't arrived, so I went into the booth to run the music cues. I lowered the master volume so the clowns could establish their own rhythms and create relationships with each other. They would also be able to hear the audience better. When the technician finally arrived, he tried to turn the volume back up—loud music playing continuously was the accepted style, a way to make the show feel well-packaged and to drown out any mistakes. For exactly these reasons, loud music would ruin the clowning, so I kept my body between the sound board and the sound technician.

The Nanjing clowns got real laughs. They created real relationships with one another and with the audience. The transitions ran smoothly, even the ones that were added at the last-minute to integrate the new acrobatic and magic acts into the clown show the students had been performing. This was important because doing acts—also called entrées—is only half a circus clown's job. Transitions are the other half, and just as important. For shows that are put together quickly, the transitions are created at the last minute, during the final rehearsals, when the clowns and directors finally see the acts in order. Then they can get ideas about stitching the show together. This part of the "American clown canon" would also be featured a year later when San Francisco clowns, including Linie and Jonah, would appear on the biggest circus stage in China.

Although clowning was new to these Chinese acrobats-turned-clowns, they had been on stage since childhood—and it showed. Angel, the only woman clown, improvised a bit in the audience where she flirted with—and then rejected—Lu Yi. She was breaking Chinese gender, age, and status norms, playing with—and then insulting—a famous older man. Even her flirting, mild by American standards, was surprising in the context of Chinese circus. These shocking moments brought gales of laughter. Improvising-being in the moment, and reacting to what is going on around you—is a core clown skill. It was new to these acrobats who were used to rehearsing for perfection. Clowns rehearse in order to know the material well enough to be able to improvise. Angel clearly honed this difficult skill in record time.

Before we left Nanjing, Joan Mankin and I visited the park at Xuanwu Lake, right in the middle of the city. In a bandstand near the water, we stopped to listen to a large group of people singing to recorded music. When they finished a song, Joan asked for the mic, stood on my shoulders, and belted out a show tune. The crowd loved it.

In the previous four weeks, our team from San Francisco Circus Center had taught 20 Chinese acrobats the basics of our style of clowning and helped them create and perform a show with a storyline that got laughs and cheers from Chinese audiences. In their final performance, these newbie clowns also created transitions that integrated—and strengthened—four classic Chinese acrobatic acts.

Together with our Nanjing students, we proved Lu Yi's theory that there is a Chinese path to Western-style clown techniques and that Chinese audiences would love the combination of classic acrobatics and San Francisco clowning.

After the final show, several of the Chinese students planned to apply to The Clown Conservatory at San Francisco Circus Center, which had recently received a Homeland Security accreditation that allowed us to accept international students.[172] The Chinese government also invited San Francisco Circus Center to send professional clowns to perform in their 2009 Wuqiao International Circus festival.

Lu Yi's two families had finally met, and they were getting along beautifully… for the moment.

---

172   Unfortunately, this journey to the West didn't work out.

28. WUQIAO INTERNATIONAL CIRCUS FESTIVAL

2009

Dozens of faces, half old and half young, stare though plate glass windows into a theater lobby, laughing and pointing. They are grandfathers out for a stroll in the city of Shijiazhuang, each with one grandchild.[173] They laugh at the American clowns, one dressed as a baby and another a grandma. One juggling, one jumping on stilts and—their favorite—Kung Fu Panda, all rehearsing under the watchful eye of an older Chinese man.

Lu Yi had used his clout in Chinese acrobatic circles to get six American clowns booked to perform at the Wuqiao Festival, although they would not be eligible for awards in the festival's competitions. The upside of this arrangement was that the San Francisco Circus Center team would be in all nine shows, working closely with the festival director, lighting designer and conductor to create transitions between the other acts. This would help the two different circus programs flow smoothly, and give the clowns a chance to show off their entrées as well as their improvisation skills.

We were at the festival to solidify San Francisco's circus reputation internationally, to get more tours to China, and to inspire Chinese acrobatic

---

173   In 2009, China was still under a policy that restricted most families to only one child. The "One-child policy" started in 1979 and was amended in 2016, when all Chinese couples were then allowed to have two children.

troupes to use more San Francisco-style clowning skills. Lu Yi also wanted to lay the groundwork for a Chinese branch of The Clown Conservatory.[174]

This is what I wrote in my journal on the third day of rehearsal in Shijiazhuang: "After a few hours of refining our ideas and eating a huge and wonderful lunch, we are back in the lobby to show the assistant director the whole megillah. In addition to dozens of kids and their grandpas behind the glass doors, we now have camera crews in the lobby, swarming over Lu Yi and the performers as they try to show their stuff. Lu Yi is as happy as I've seen him in years, with microphones in his face and cameras all over his students. We'll be on TV tonight and, if things go well, we'll be doing San Francisco proud in front of thousands of Chinese circus fans and international agents in the next week and a half."

Every odd year, the Wuqiao International Circus Festival is held in the capital city of Hebei Province, Shijiazhuang. On even years, the festival is in neighboring Wuhan, the city where the COVID pandemic began in 2020. Hebei Province is considered the birthplace of Chinese acrobatics, making these festivals major international events.

Shijiazhuang was a small town until the railroad arrived in the early 20th century and transformed it into a city. Since the 1947 "Chinese Civil War," Shijiazhuang has grown to 11 million people. The weather in November 2009 was mild, except for one snowstorm, but the smog was so thick that it wasn't until the last day that we realized there was a huge office building across the street from our hotel. Despite the air quality, I walked the mile from the hotel to the Hebei Arts Center to join the performers from France, Russia, Uzbekistan, Ukraine, Kazakhstan, Latvia, Armenia, Australia, Poland,

---

174   This project, a Chinese campus of The Clown Conservatory, didn't get past the early planning, partly because I didn't want to spend months every year away from my family.

the Czech Republic, Columbia, Cuba, Mexico, both North and South Korea, Taiwan, Mongolia, and many cities across China. The Joka Boys, a comedy acrobatic duet from the Zip Zap Circus in Cape Town, South Africa, became friends and mentors to the less-traveled American performers.

The six clowns from the San Francisco Circus Center, plus the four Chinese acrobats who were booked to work the pre-show in Transformer stilt costumes, arrived in Shijiazhuang a week early to acclimatize and rehearse. Circus Center designer Chris Weiland came, too, helping with makeup and costuming, as well as painting audience faces before each show. Lu Yi and I were there to direct the clown acts and manage our ever-changing relationship with the festival leadership.

The clowns were all Clown Conservatory grads except my long-time clown partner Diane (Pino) Wasnak. Linie Orrick and Jonah Katz (who had been on the Nanjing trip) were joined by Christopher Keller as a satyr on bounding stilts; Xia Ke Min's student Faeble Kievman as Kung Fu Panda; and his performing partner Calvin Kai Ku. Calvin's parents also came to see the shows, and the "United Nations of circus" backstage, before flying on to Hong Kong for a long-awaited family reunion.

Calvin Kai Ku: "Here I was, Calvin, a Chinese-American guy, going to China. You're going to this country, this land where everyone looks like you, and like your relatives, and yet you don't identify with them. Someone backstage said to me, 'You look Chinese, but you aren't Chinese.' I was blown away. I am one of Lu Yi's only Chinese-American students, which is very special to me. And Lu Yi is also Chinese-American, he immigrated to the Bay Area just like my parents. I needed a connection with him because our blood is from the same hemisphere. But my family is from Hong Kong, and I couldn't find that 'uncle' kind of feeling with Lu Yi because it's different with people from the mainland."

In the months leading up to the trip, Lu Yi had worked with the clowns to customize their material for a Chinese audience. Calvin and Faeble did a balancing number about selling Chinese "lollipops" in a traditional tánghúlu display.[175] Christopher added a monkey puppet because of the long tradition in Hubei province of strolling performers with trained monkeys. Diane and Linie capitalized on the strong Chinese affection for babies and grandmothers, and they added Chinese dialogue to their routines, as did Jonah Katz.

In the days before the festival started, the clowns and a team of American balloon twisters shared the big lobby. The smiling people crowded outside the lobby's wall of glass windows buoyed the clowns' spirits and gave them a chance to test material on a Chinese audience.[176]

Another entry in my Wuqiao journal: "I watch the director, Mrs. Liu, as she watches our 'audition.' Jonah starts his act, and her face relaxes when she sees that he moves with an acrobat's grace, and then there's a hint of a smile as he tap dances and juggles. She wants to see more, so Christopher comes out with the monkey puppet, which gets a real smile of recognition and, when Diane goes into her baby bit in Chinese, Mrs. Liu is laughing out loud and repeating each phrase after Diane. The day is won; Lu Yi's crazy idea of having a group of American clowns do the transitions at a major international circus festival in China is now making Mrs. Liu a very happy festival director."

---

175   *Tánghúlu* is a traditional Chinese street food made of five or six small hawthorn berries covered in colorful, shiny hard sugar and served on a stick. In Hebei, vendors carry long poles with dozens of *tánghúlu* sticks bristling out of them.
176   Clowning is both universal and very local, so clowns working in a new country—or even a new region—need to test their material on locals to find what works for this new audience.

For me, the week before the shows started was a whirlwind of amazing sights, international politics, schedule changes, and power plays:

On the street in front of the theater, I see a woman pedaling an adult-sized tricycle, a very popular mode of transportation here. She has a full-sized black Naugahyde couch strapped to the back and when she gets closer, I see the matching armchair strapped to the couch. A group bike act with furniture instead of acrobats.

Walking home late at night on a busy street, now deserted, when suddenly the sidewalk becomes an outdoor cafe—seven tables with two chairs each, patrons sipping hot soup that was cooked on a stove built on a large tricycle. Another trike has the sink. The next morning, there is no sign of soup or chairs or the wheeled kitchen on that stretch of sidewalk. The proprietors must have loaded the entire café on the two trikes and pedaled home.

The horribly fixed stares on the North Korean performers' faces when I say "hello" as we pass each other in the halls backstage; their handlers always just a few steps behind them. It reminds me of the days I taught juggling in San Quentin. Before coming to the festival, I had thought, naively, that international tensions would melt away when everyone was in costume and makeup, sharing the same dressing rooms and the same stage.

During the technical rehearsal, a French juggler is standing on stage arguing about his lighting, trying to get it just right. On one hand, I sympathize with his passionate attempt to make his act great, and on the other hand, I see that he is teetering towards arrogance—and making me late for lunch. Finally, the director, Mrs. Liu, steps forward, says something into her mic and 20 Chinese women in gold costumes and elaborate headdresses walk onto the stage to rehearse their act. Our French friend is toast. He says something that, from the look on his translator's face, clearly crosses the line. Mrs. Liu walks away and sits down. My heart is with her—this is what I would have done were I directing. But then, when it's our turn to rehearse, I am arguing with Mrs. Liu, trying to get a spotlight on Diane. The irony registers in time for me to tone down my rudeness. We get the spotlight because of Lu Yi, who still has respect here. I presume that the French performer will be cut from the festival, but he is still in the show that night. His lighting is terrible and his act suffers.

. . .

A 15-foot sculpture of the festival logo, an acrobatic lion, is the first thing the audience sees when they enter the lobby. It is made entirely of balloons. A balloon fashion show, also created by the American balloon twisters, gives the festival a touch of glamor even before the first circus act is performed.

Pino's "Baby" is a big hit with the Chinese audience, as is Linie's grandmother character, Nai Nai. Before leaving San Francisco, Lu Yi had insisted that Faeble perform as Kung Fu Panda, an idea that would have been trite coming from anyone else. Of course, Lu Yi knows Chinese audiences—they love Faeble's Panda, especially in a knockabout act with Calvin, who is half his size. Jonah does his bounce juggling while tap dancing act, something no one in the audience, or backstage, has ever seen before. Christopher, in a satyr costume built over jumping stilts, impresses even the Chinese acrobats with his flips.

Christopher Kellor: "Seeing other acts helped me to gauge where I was and what things I needed to work on; being thrust into an environment with a huge language barrier showed me many of my strengths, as well as my weaknesses."

Calvin Kai Ku: "I saw the other performers backstage in their natural way, the way they are when they're not performing. Growing up you only see the stage personality. There were wonderful clowns from Italy, on trapeze, and a bizarre trampoline act with a bouncing bicycle and unicycle. I met the Chinese acts in passing but they were always sleeping backstage, like they're trained to do. I wanted to meet this pole climber from France and see his rigging. He didn't speak English, but his translator spoke French and Mandarin and my translator spoke Mandarin and English. We had a playful four-person game of telephone—very silly! Once, I was in the hallway when a Russian clown, who had just finished his act, ran off stage. I got a glimpse of how hard clowns work—from the audience, his act didn't look very hard but backstage he was panting like he'd run a marathon."

There were two different programs—each running over three hours in length—that rotated during the week-long festival. When we arrived at the theater for the first public performance, the show order had been changed— the Russian tiger act would now start the show. This left Jonah Katz doing his solo tap dance/juggling entrée three feet downstage of 30 roustabouts madly dismantling an enormous metal cage. Because they had trouble with the cage in rehearsals, they left the stage lights on. The tigers were also on stage, staring at the audience from cages with their yellow eyes. Jonah held his own in this chaos, winning applause from the audience and respect from our Chinese hosts.

My journal: "The 'A' show lasted four hours tonight and most of the audience left before the final bow and it is now after midnight and I'm just getting home and I have a meeting with Lu Yi at 7:30am to figure out how we're going to do it all again tomorrow for the 'B' show."

Diane and Linie, the Baby and the Grandmother, both spoke Chinese as they greeted people walking into the theater. Linie would see a child and say, "I am your grandmother, I love you, grandson/granddaughter," in Mandarin well enough to be understood—and get laughs. Often the parent would say that their child speaks the English that they learned at school, so Linie would ask, "How old are you?" in English. Depending on the child's ability, she would keep going with questions in Chinese or English: "What is your name?" "What is your father's name?" "What is your mother's name?" She'd finish with, "I am excited to see you, thank you for coming, have a good day" in Mandarin. Then she would start again with the next family, and the next and the next, until the 3,000 seats of the Front Hall of Hebei Arts Center were filled.

Linie: "I was relieved. I had a character that worked in China, and I had stuff to say, in Chinese and English, for an hour and a half. The meet and greet before the show was just the start because each program had one particularly long transition in the middle and another long one near the end. We had to fill them by each going into a section of the audience to entertain. Luckily, Diane and I had lavalier mics so we could talk to our sections."

The second long transition, which often stretched past ten minutes, was right before the final act, flying trapeze. There were two flying acts, one from Kazakhstan for the "A" show and one from North Korea for the "B." They both had long set-ups. The audience had already sat through nearly three hours of circus when the house lights came up, a bunch of wires dropped from the flies, dozens of technicians flooded the stage, and six San Francisco clowns raced into the audience to try to keep the crowd from going home before the big finale.

Linie Orrick: "I was assigned a corner of the balcony. By the time I got there, most people had already gone to sleep. As 'Grandma' I didn't wake them up; they looked too peaceful. And I had already done my job because they weren't going to leave before the trapeze flyers because they were asleep."

These sleepy circus fans missed a circus singularity. The North Korean flyer's final trick was a quint—five somersaults in the air from the moment he let go of the trapeze bar to the moment he grabbed his catcher's hands. It usually took them four or five tries to land this amazing feat, with long pauses between attempts as the flyer climbed slowly back up the rope ladder. You could almost hear the judges' teeth gnashing as their "three tries only" rule was flaunted. But the quint, when they made it, was breathtaking.

An incident at the end of the festival gave Lu Yi's American "family" a glimpse of the power and prestige their teacher used to have in China, and how much moving to San Francisco had cost him. The foreign participants were paid in cash, sitting in a large room backstage until their name was called. Lu Yi was made to wait until the end to get his envelope. We were furious that our trainer was treated with this level of disrespect, a man who had been the festival director's boss's boss. Lu Yi laughed. "I learned something new about China today."

Lu Yi could laugh at being slighted; his plan had succeeded and his dream was fulfilled. Lu Yi took a huge risk bringing us to the Wuqiao Festival, trusting that we could "make it" on the biggest and most international stage in China. His risk had paid off: San Francisco clowns won over thousands of Chinese circus aficionados. They impressed the other performers with their energy and emotion, and the festival directors with their entrées and improvisations. Lu Yi knew that news of our success would spread quickly to every acrobatic troupe in China, and they would start to incorporate San Francisco-style clowning into their work, reinvigorating both their performers and their audiences.

. . .

As I write this chapter, tension between China and the U.S. is high. Person-to-person relationships, although small in comparison to international agreements, remain crucial to shrinking the gap between the countries. For example, in November 2023, The New York Times, reporting from the Asia-Pacific Economic Cooperation (APEC) summit in San Francisco, noted that Chinese leader Xi Jinping's "...face lit up as he greeted the man who had driven him around rural Iowa, when Mr. Xi was a young party official from Hebei province hoping to glean insights into America's agricultural technology. Earlier, [Mr. Xi] thanked Mr. Biden for reminding him that his wife, Peng Liyuan, a famous Chinese soprano and folk singer, has a birthday on Monday, as does Mr. Biden."[177]

The Nanjing/San Francisco circus affair is part of a larger sweep of Sino-American cultural exchanges, including the Shanghai/American Conservatory Theater exchange we explored earlier and Xi Jinping's agricultural trip to Iowa, as well as the Philadelphia Orchestra's many Chinese tours. Matías Tarnopolsky, president of the Philadelphia Orchestra, remembers a Chinese Foreign Affairs minister telling him that the orchestra's 1973 visit had been the subject of joyful dinner table conversation throughout his childhood. "'Keep doing what you are doing,' [the Chinese official told Mr. Tarnopolsky]. 'It's beautiful, and I feel like it's the only thing that's working.'"[178]

After teaching in the first Nanjing workshop and performing at the Wuqiao Festival, Jonah Katz and Linie Orrick went back to Nanjing for a second clown workshop, this time with Diane (Pino) Wasnak as the lead trainer. Of their 24 students, four had been in the previous workshop and 12 were from the Beijing International Arts School (the Beijing group was joined by

177   Pierson, D. Swanson, A. Sanger, D. E. (2023, November 17). A Rare Opportunity to see China's Leader Up Close and (sort of) Personal. *The New York Times*.
178   Tarnopolsky, M. (2023, November 16). American musicians are doing something profound in Beijing right now. *The New York Times*.

a teacher who specialized in American musicals). Since then, San Francisco performers have traveled to China many times, including a Lu Yi-led tour of nine circus schools in three different Chinese cities.

Jonah Katz: "I truly feel we are starting an artistic revolution in China. It will be written in the history books that people from San Francisco Circus Center brought emotional and creative innovation to all forms of performance in China."

Lu Yi: "Now there are a lot of clowns performing on TV in China; this is different than before. San Francisco has good clowns and their trips to China had an impact. Shanghai acrobats, some of the best in China, are doing more clowning, they are more focused on clowning. The clowning in China has been influenced by the U.S. and this could elevate the field of Chinese acrobatics and circus in general."

29. THE NEW FACE OF CHINESE ACROBATICS

"A great acrobat needs to love acrobatics. Training is hard work, it hurts in 1,000 different ways, and takes many years. Teacher Xia used to tell me that it is better to cry in training and laugh on stage than to laugh too much in training and cry on stage."

- Ori Quesada

Ori Quesada and Dominik Wyss are now the face of Chinese acrobatics in San Francisco. As the co-chairs of San Francisco Circus Center's Acrobatics Department, they share the position that Lu Yi held for 26 years, making them responsible for training the next generation of the Nanjing/San Francisco circus affair.

Dominik and Ori came to this job, this responsibility, on two very different paths.

Dominik Wyss: "In 2001 I was in Switzerland studying economics and planning to be a physiotherapist or chiropractor. My parents went to see a small caravan show and invited some of the circus artists over for lunch. These performers told me circus school was a real thing and I thought that sounded a lot more fun than economics. Then I met the wire walker David Dimitri, who said, 'A man I met on the Big Apple Circus taught me flips and one-arm handstands on tight wire. Go find Lu Yi in San Francisco.'"

Ori Quesada: "Mr. Lu Yi asked me to train in acrobatics when I was seven years old, and it changed my life. I was different from the other kids he chose to train; I was thick and short and didn't fit into the gendered roles Mr. Lu Yi was used to teaching. But we had a special relationship, and we challenged each other a lot. When I stopped growing at four-foot-eight, Mr. Lu Yi said I didn't have a future as a hoop diver. But he could see that I loved acrobatics more than anything. He said I had the heart."

Dominik Wyss: "In a weird way, I fit in very well at San Francisco Circus Center. I trained with a Chinese opera acrobat the last year I was in Switzerland, so the way I did the kicks and the warm-up was what Lu Yi and Xia Ke Min had seen when they were kids. In Switzerland, we trained on a concrete floor with a carpet; for very advanced tricks our teacher would pull out a kid's mattress. I was a skateboarder, so I was used to falling on concrete. In San Francisco, I trained on the wooden gym floor with Lu Yi, and also with Vladimir Nazarov."[179]

Ori Quesada: "Mr. Lu Yi didn't pay the same attention to me as he did some of the others. He told me I wasn't suited to learn things the others were learning. A lot of the time, especially in the early days, it was because he would only teach certain tricks to the boys. As a trans kid, I was still trying to figure out who I was and how I fit into the world, and into acrobatics. It was painful. So, I sat and watched. A lot. I would focus on how he taught the tricks, which is how I learned to hoop dive. The first time I was able to do a hard hoop diving trick, I surprised us both. Something shifted for Lu Yi then, and he changed his mind about what he would choose to teach

---

179   Vladimir Nazarov and his partner Vladimir Alimanov consistently won international competitions in Pairs Acrobatic Gymnastics for much of the '70s. In 1975 they performed with Olga Korbet and other Soviet Olympians at Madison Square Garden. Vladimir Nazarov taught at Circus Center for a few years in the aughts.

me. Spending those years watching Mr. Lu Yi teach the others made me the acrobat—and the teacher—I am today."

Dominik Wyss: "I've always had a complete lack of self-preservation to reach a goal. In San Francisco, I would train seven days a week. I had to prove the point because growing up in Switzerland I was the only black child in the village and there was a very strong degree of racism in Switzerland. They were not bad people they just didn't know, but I had a constant battle to fit in."

Ori Quesada: "Mr. Lu Yi wanted to teach me an act that would help me succeed as an acrobat. We tried a lot of things before he chose *Rola-Bola Kick Bowls* when I was 16. Training this act was hard and lonely. I would warm up and tumble with everyone, and then spend an hour in the corner by myself trying to balance on a rola-bola against the wall. Sometimes I would get so angry and frustrated because everyone else was having fun together training hoop diving or teeterboard, and I was alone in the corner. I would secretly glare at Mr. Lu Yi whenever I took a break from getting hit in the face with metal bowls while trying to kick them onto my head. Then I would hear him call to me from across the gym, 'Again!' But I knew that he loved me, and he wanted me to be able to make a living as an acrobat for the rest of my life."

. . .

Lily Janiak of the San Francisco Chronicle described Ori's *Rola-Bola Kick Bowls* act in her December 2023 review of Circus Bella: "I can't quite explain how, but for a brief few moments, whether a spoon flips into a metal cup becomes the most important thing in the world. There Ori Quesada is… perched atop a rola-bola—a balance board rolling back and forth on a cylinder—like a surfer riding a wave. Charmingly, he's already dressed himself while balancing on the mechanism: shirt overhead, pants and shoes on while seated, which must activate gluteal muscles most of us don't know exist. As a finale, he flips bowls and cups from the tip of the board to a growing stack on the crown of his head. On opening night, he'd already missed a few, so the sweat was beading. But then, when the spoon hits its target with a satisfying clink, you and the preschool stranger next to you might have found yourselves roaring with the same rabid triumph, like military victors fresh from the battlefield."[180]

...

Dominik Wyss: "My teachers, Vladimir Nazarov and Lu Yi, had such a passion about acrobats, living and breathing acrobatics and circus. They couldn't turn it off. At that point I couldn't either. Once, when Lu Yi saw me being obsessive, he put his arm around me and said: 'I feel sorry for anyone in a relationship with you.' I would stay up all night trying to figure out, intellectually, why I couldn't get a trick, then go to the gym in the morning. But it wouldn't work. I learned later that it would have been better if I just slept—the body implements, we just need to give the body the bigger picture. I am an observer. The better I observe, the faster my body will learn."

Ori Quesada: "If Mr. Lu Yi had not gotten Parkinson's, I think I would still be working with him now. He mentored me as a teacher in my early 20s, and was always looking for teaching opportunities for me, even when he got sick. Today, training the new generation of the San Francisco Youth Circus is surreal. I can hear Mr. Lu Yi's voice in my head. None of my current students ever met him, so their mentality around training is different than what I grew up with. It is hard for them to accept that learning acrobatics

---

180   Janiak, L.(2023, December 16). Review: 'Kaleidoscope' is an Analog Circus Feast Amid Digital HQ of SoMa. *San Francisco Chronicle.*

takes a long time, is incredibly difficult, and sometimes lonely. A lot of my job has been teaching my students how to train."

Dominik Wyss: "Lu Yi told me to forget about all the books. 'In the moment, what will overrule all your technical knowledge is what is right in front of you.' He is incredible at observing and perceiving things. He could tell you stuff about people's bodies; everyone had their little quirks, and he would imitate and show the little things in each person. He also had a lot of knowledge of Chinese medicine, maintaining the body, energy wise. He worked really long hours, but he knew exactly how to keep his body balanced. He was very aware if the energy in the room was balanced. Even the colors he had in the gym reflected that."

Ori Quesada: "What I love about the Youth Circus is that I get to build relationships with each of my students, like Mr. Lu Yi did with me. Every student needs the fundamentals to be a great acrobat—strength, flexibility, endurance, balance, and explosive power. For these things they need basics: stretching, conditioning, tumbling and handstands. No matter what, every acrobat needs these fundamentals, but each person's body is different and needs specific care and attention. Mr. Lu Yi would try to figure out what specialties were best for each student's body type and personality, and he would guide us towards where he thought we would be most successful in the long-term."

Dominik Wyss: "Vladimir Nazarov and Lu Yi both had an ego and didn't want to share the glory. Vladimir was okay with students also working with Lu Yi, but Lu Yi was not okay with people training with Vladimir. These days, I have to assume my students are trying to train with everyone, through workshops, Zoom, etc. especially since the pandemic. But Lu Yi and Vladimir both agreed; 'Learn the basics first, then do what you want.' The tricky thing was, I was stubborn. I would argue with Lu Yi, same with Vladimir. Vladimir would say, 'You can, but you don't want!' Sometimes I would storm out of the room with my personality. I know now they were panic attacks, but I couldn't manage my anger."

. . .

Lu Yi: "Training with someone, or training someone, you are projecting love onto each other; you need this mentality, you need to work things out with love."

. . .

Ori Quesada: "The core of my job is balancing standard foundational training and individualized teaching—and I need to modify both of these for the new generation: I can't tell someone they will never be successful because of their anatomy, but I can take the essence of Lu Yi's pedagogy into my approach for the long-term curriculum. I didn't get much choice about what I trained when I was their age, so getting to have regular conversations with students about their training goals makes me happy."

Dominik Wyss: "Mr. Lu Yi and I argued over training approaches and techniques. Luckily, he entertained my annoying probing. Mr. Lu Yi's answers were often abstract, information got lost in translation and I wasn't ready to process the wisdom he generously shared with me. In 2010, I started my own gym where I could really experiment. Some of it was a disaster, but it allowed me to rediscover what Lu Yi and Vladimir Nazarov were trying to teach me. Chinese acrobatics has incredible wisdom; they figured out long ago what we're learning from science now. A lot of knowledge got lost in the Chinese revolution,[181] but if you go further back and look at the basic

---

181   "In an effort to reform the acrobatics sector, certain performances that were

concepts, they fit in the newer framework. I am rediscovering Mr. Lu Yi's wisdom, knowledge, and passion."

Ori Quesada: "No matter how talented a Youth Circus student is, if they don't trust the other students, if they don't trust in their own abilities, and especially if they don't trust their teacher, they won't be able to learn. This is why I love the model of Youth Circus as an ensemble-based program because it builds trust by just showing up and participating every day. We need that trust because teaching fundamentals is so difficult, but also so important. Many people come to circus looking for very specific coaching in a specific discipline, and they believe they only need to train in that one area. This often leads to plateauing in their skills and getting injured by overtraining and neglecting the body as a whole."

Dominik Wyss: "I'm eternally grateful that Vladimir Nazarov and Lu Yi put up with me. The way they cared about their craft and the people—that inspiration sticks with me. What they did was incredible, standing there from early in the morning to evening every day. The dedication! Lu Yi did what I do now in his 70s! It's incredible. Vladimir Nazarov and Lu Yi were both absolute masters and kind humans. I expect Master Lu Yi will guide me for a long time."

---

considered harmful to the mental and physical health of the performer and unworthy to represent China, were banned. Performances that displayed 'deformity or excessive stimulus' such as *Eating an Electric Light Bulb, Swallowing Five Poisonous Creatures* (scorpion, viper, centipede, house lizard and toad), *Dwarf's Comic Acts* ...and many more, were prohibited. Instead, acts that were considered fine traditional presentations were approved: *Jumping through Hoops on the Ground, Handstands on a Pyramid of Chairs, Juggling with the Hands,* and *Cycling,* among others. However, these were only the first steps that were taken. After the founding of New China [1949], policies... were introduced by the Party Central Committee to make significant changes in the acrobatics sector." Ala-Rashi, M. (2022). *China's Bending Bodies.* (T. Wall, Ed.) Modern Vaudeville Press.

Ori Quesada: "A good foundation builds a body's capacity to specialize later. This is hard for teenagers who are trying to find their own identity as artists and want to experiment with what is exciting to them rather than doing the same boring thing every day. I try to find out what each student is passionate about learning and use that to guide how I approach their training. This is an adaptation of Mr. Lu Yi's approach but, for my students, this cultivates the love and passion for acrobatics, which is what Mr. Lu Yi held above everything. I do try to guide my students towards the skills I think they can succeed in, but if a natural contortionist tells me that they are in love with hoop diving, I do everything I can to give them the tools to be a hoop diver. It may take them longer to be a hoop diver than it would to be a contortionist, but if they love acrobatics enough, they will endure the frustrations and failures. As a teacher, I want to continue to pass on the legacy of my teacher to the next generation and keep Mr. Lu Yi's style of acrobatics alive in San Francisco."

Felicity Hesed, former Artistic Director of San Francisco Circus Center, says that what Lu Yi did was "...absolutely groundbreaking, not just for San Francisco but for the world. But it's no longer groundbreaking—once the ground has been broken, it changes. Ori now brings all the training he learned from Lu Yi, but he does it from a contemporary standpoint of social and emotional development. Dominik brings a better understanding of exercise science, how to be more efficient, with less repetition and faster results, within Lu Yu's 'it's all about the fundamentals' ethos. Dominik is making sure to not to break students physically; Ori is making sure to not break them emotionally and mentally. It's brilliant."

CODA

Club Fugazi, Opening Night

October 21, 2021

A Chinese yo-yo flies off its string, high into the air above the Club Fugazi stage, landing effortlessly in Enmeng Song's right hand. With a calm, slightly accented voice, Song says: "This little toy has given me a job, a life, and a family. And it has now given me a home here in San Francisco."

Enmeng Song and his wife Shengnan Pan grew up together in the Shandong Acrobatic Troupe and journeyed throughout the West with Cirque du Soleil and The 7 Fingers. They have now immigrated to San Francisco with their two children, following the path of Lu Yi and his family. They embody the marriage of 2,000-year-old Chinese acrobatic skills with the American-style stage presence and audience engagement.

Song is facing away from the audience, looking at the three rows of people who chose the on-stage seating for the opening night of The 7 Fingers' show, *Dear San Francisco*. He tells them about learning the Chinese yo-yo, which in English is called a diabolo. He throws the diabolo again, spins halfway around and catches it on the string. He now faces the main room of Club Fuzagi, a fabled theater with a few hundred seats on the floor and a skinny upstairs balcony that runs in a horseshoe well above the other patrons. This room has seen beat-poet jams and Italian weddings, Grateful Dead album releases and Thelonious Monk recording sessions—all before becoming home to the "longest-running musical revue on the planet," *Beach*

Blanket Babylon. Finally, in 2021, the theater became The 7 Fingers' West Coast outpost.

Enmeng Song tells the opening night crowd that the diabolo is considered a child's toy or a woman's act back in China, and how he fell in love with it as an adult. He offers the balcony a shy smile before flipping the yo-yo up again, this time whipping the string through the air to catch it.

Applause.

"I knew about San Francisco even before I came here because a famous Chinese acrobat and teacher lives in this city. He was not my teacher, but every acrobat in China knows Lu Yi."

Applause.

"In fact, Lu Yi is here tonight."

The applause turns to a roar when a small man in the second row jumps up out of his wheelchair, turning around to wave to the audience. Lu Yi's wife, Wang Hong Zhu, and I reach forward to spot him—but the love of the crowd has taken Lu Yi back to his days as a star acrobat. He stands solid, arms raised, beaming.

On stage, Enmeng Song realizes that Lu Yi is now the star of the show, at least for the moment, and takes a few steps back. Offstage, American dancer, musician, and acrobat Isabella Diaz sees Song move, hears the applause, and assumes that the act is over. Isabella walks on stage with a microphone stand for the next act, looks at Lu Yi standing and gives the audience a puzzled smile. Understanding slowly washes over the artist's face and, with a knowing look, Isabella backs off stage holding the mic stand.

Laughter.

A week before opening, Xiaohong and I had taken Lu Yi to a rehearsal at Club Fugazi. Refusing to use either a walker or wheelchair, Lu Yi strode up the ramp and into the theater. He took everything in—the size of the stage, the complex rigging for pole climbing, hoop diving, and trapeze. Gypsy Snider was directing an act with some Youth Circus alum; when they saw Lu Yi, they all rushed over to greet their old friend and mentor. When the performers got back to work, Lu Yi told Gypsy how she should redesign her rigging. For the next hour, Lu Yi was 10 years younger, getting strong and steady off the skills and grace of his former students.

Back at opening night, the audience keeps applauding for Lu Yi after Isabella Diaz backs off stage. He eventually sits down. The crowd reluctantly ends their standing ovation. Enmeng Song finishes his diabolo act with a flourish. His ovation lasts until Isabella Diaz re-enters with the microphone stand and a proud little smile that says, "I got it right this time," and the audience laughs again. The show goes on.

This nightclub in North Beach—at least for one night—is the nexus of the Chinese/American circus connection. Lu Yi is celebrated as a circus maven who traveled half-way around the world to light up the Bay. Enmeng Song, a young man who started performing in China in the post-Lu Yi era, woos a San Francisco audience with his stage presence, open heart, and acting skills as much as his circus prowess. An American acrobat uses clown techniques to get laughs while messing up a cue.

The rest of the show featured Junru Wang—another Chinese artist who has a strong, emotional rapport with the audience—as well as a couple of Lu

Yi's Youth Circus alums, one third-generation Circus Center performer, and acrobats from Canada and Australia.[182]

This show, The 7 Fingers' *Dear San Francisco*, could never have happened without the Nanjing acrobats' journeys to the West. It takes the plans Judy Finelli and Lu Yi made in 1990 further than they could have imagined— American performers wowing the audience with their Chinese acrobatic skills, while Chinese performers hold the emotional core of the show.

The entire genre that The 7 Fingers pioneered—*Contemporary Circus*—is a mix of the Nanjing acrobatics credo "go high and know where you are in the air" with San Francisco-style audience interaction; the Chinese "land quietly" with American vulnerability.

---

182   2021 cast of *Dear San Francisco*: Enmeng Song and Junru Wang (China), Maya Kesselman, Dominic Cruz, Kalani June and Natasha Patterson (San Francisco Circus Center), Isabel Diaz (U.S.), Melvin Diggs (Circus Harmony, U.S.), Ruben Ingwersen (Australia) and Jérémi Levesque (Canada).

ENCORE

Remembering Lu Yi

Lu Yi died of Parkinson's disease on Wednesday October 25, 2023, just shy of his 84th birthday. His Berkeley home was filled with extended family, including some of his American students. I had COVID so Lu Na and Lu Yue called and I said, "I love you" and "good-bye" over FaceTime. Later that day, and in the weeks following, many other people gave thanks and said their good-byes on social media memorial pages and in interviews for this book and for Lu Yi's obituary in the San Francisco Chronicle.

Xiaohong Weng: "Lu Yi's life story starts before the revolution when there were old-school family circuses. Then in 1957, when circus became all government owned, Lu Yi transitioned from old-style to new-style. In the 80s he started doing business outside of China, foreign money coming into his troupe. A first for China. Lu Yi will be remembered by younger Chinese acrobats as a generational leader."

Lily Janiak, San Francisco Chronicle: "'I don't know where I would have found my voice had I not worked with Lu Yi and his students,' said Gypsy Snider... Lu Yi cultivated in his students not prettiness and grace, with toes turned out and ta-da razzmatazz, but rawness and creativity, added Snider, noting that her own gritty, stripped down aesthetic, on such vibrant display in *Dear San Francisco*, where she is co-artistic director, is a result of that teaching."

Abigail Baird: "When I was standing in a high hand-to-foot, or on my base's head, Lu Yi would say, 'Oh, you are just waiting to die.' If I accidentally kicked my base, Andy, in the balls, Lu Yi would say, 'Oh, international problem. Now you buy him pizza.' The week he died, I could hear him laughing and saying, 'Oh, now you miss me. Yes, international problem...'"

Judy Finelli: "Lu Yi didn't have the life here he thought he would have, but I hope he is glad he moved to America. I could not have predicted that his teachings would spread and branch out nationally, and internationally, in the way they did."

Serenity Smith: "When I would pride myself on straight legs and pointed toes, Lu Yi would remind me that agility is different from rigidity. 'Nimble Arts,' the name of my sister Elsie and my company, comes from that saying."

Francisco Cruz: "I can still hear his voice telling me how a round off should sound, to stop having a crooked body, to land like a cat. I can still hear you whispering new English words to yourself over and over again in the back seat of our car when we drove you home. I wince as your hand slaps the back of my neck. You taught me that 'training is bitter,' but more importantly how to love the bitterness. I want to say goodbye, but I also want to walk into that old church and see you there in your coaching clothes sipping green tea. You'll remind me once again to eat less cheese, always wear warm clothes outside, do more handstands. I owe it all to you. We owe it all to you."

Jaron Hollander: "*Me*: 'This is too hard. Maybe I will get it in my next life.' *Lu Yi*: 'No, next time around, you will be my teacher.'"

Shana Carroll: "It makes me sad that Lu Yi felt he never did the things he intended to do, because what he did was transform the circus landscape for forever. The cast of our show *Traces*, all students of Lu Yi, had an urban quality naturally to their movement because of breakdance and basketball; we even had a skateboarding act. Inconceivable that this could exist anywhere else in the world."

Abigail Munn: "When you worked handstands, he would put a chunky, not real gold watch between your hands so that you could see the seconds go round very slowly. Then he'd kind of hit you on the thigh and say, 'Persist.' Persist is my daily mantra as I work, train, and create circus. My consolation is that now Lu Yi will be able to see all the shows, and watch all his students. His teachings are still here."

Kirsten Gerding: "Lu Yi was so strict, strong, sweet & funny as hell! He was always dead honest & blunt with his instructions & feedback. Old school in every way. He got me to do things I never dreamed I was strong enough to do. When I told him I wanted to sing while doing pole he said, 'Oh, that will be so beautiful, as long as your technique is clean.'"

Lily Janiak, S.F. Chronicle: "Lu Yi had no interests outside of circus, his daughter Lu Yue said, aside from a foray into helping Olympic synchronized swim teams develop their acrobatic abilities. He never learned to drive, taking BART from Berkeley to work. He was bad with numbers, having had little formal schooling, but he frequently gave pocket money to his students or bought them snacks with it, according to Lu Yue."

Jeff Sensabaugh: "I met my best man through Lu Yi. And thanks to Lu Yi, I became a professional lion butt (I made enough money one year I had to declare 'Chinese lion butt' on my taxes). After evening classes I would drive him home—he taught me scraps of Chinese and I helped him study for his citizenship exam. He made an indelible mark on my life."

Huang Zhen: "When he came to the U.S., Lu Yi wanted to create a circus school that could be really famous, and he wanted everyone to know that it was created by Lu Yi. But it was different here and he couldn't do it. When I saw Lu Yi sick, I was really, really sad. Every time I talked about new shows or performers, he was so interested. He showed me he was doing push-ups. I said 'Nice!' Back in China, he was the boss. I lived with him more than my family. We traveled a lot and always lived together."

Alexis Cook (Greene): "I feel incredibly lucky to have been coached by Lu Yi when I was in high school—lucky to have learned hoop diving, pole, teeterboard, and the discipline of these traditions, to get swatted by his shoe, a tongue click and 'Uh, da girl' when it wasn't right, and his beaming sunny smile when it was. *Xièxiè* (thank you)."

Abigail Baird: "Lu Yi would call me out on my state of mind. He changed the voice of my inner monologue from constant critique, to a voice of understanding where I am in relationship to where I want to be. Lu Yi is always with me. I am a better student, teacher, and human because of the years I spent training with him."

Joel Baker: "My 50-year-old eyes are red and full of tears. I just woke up from a dream. Lu Yi came to say goodbye. I was sitting across from him, begging him for one last lesson before he left. His mouth, even though it was hard to move, managed one last master's smile of approval, the one he would give me when he was happy with my progress. He would often say to me, 'Good, for a clown.' In the dream, he was slowly standing to leave. I yelled, 'I love you, Lu Yi!' He said, 'Goodbye, I love you Joel Baker.' He slowly turned, and I woke up. Thank you, Master Lu Yi for starting me on this journey of passion, discipline, and love for circus that has become my daily life."

TIMELINE

10 BCE

• The tradition of Chinese acrobatics begins.

1768

• Phillip Astley and his wife Patty Jones create the first "western" circus.

1793

• John Bill Ricketts' circus opens in Philadelphia, credited as the first circus in the United States.

1850

• California joins the Union as a free, non-slavery state. The 31st American state.

1852

• The first Chinese troupe plays in San Francisco, offering "Magic, Necromancy, Juggling and Legerdemain."

1864

• Central Pacific Railroad begins hiring Chinese workers.

1870

• San Francisco passes the Cubic Air and the Stick ordinances.

1877

• Italian horseman Gaetano Ciniselli opens Russia's first circus.

1882

• The Chinese Exclusion Act is passed in America.

1917

• Russian Revolution; the new Soviet government gives circus the title "Art for the People."

1939

• Lu Yi is born in Jaingsu, China.

1943

• The U.S. Chinese Exclusion Act is repealed.

1947

• Lu Yi's family moves from Jiangsu Province to Shanghai.

1949

• People's Republic of China is established with Mao Zedong as the leader.

1956

• Lu Yi represents China on a trip to Soviet Bloc countries, and later to Africa.

1960s

• Flower Power in Haight/Ashbury.

Late 1960's

• Judy and Hovey go to see Lee Tang Wa Acrobatic Troupe.

1970

• Travel to Soviet Union OK'ed, Judy and Hovey tour Moscow Circus School.
• Lu Yi under "house arrest" during the Chinese Cultural Revolution.

1974

• Pickles Family Circus founded.

• Make*A*Circus comes to San Francisco from England.

• Lu Yi put in charge of Nanjing Municipal Acrobatic Troupe.

1979

• The United States recognizes the People's Republic of China.

1982

• Comprehensive Employment and Training Act (CETA) repealed; Pickles hit hard economically.

1983

• Lu Yi, Xia Ke Min and Lu Guang Rong lead workshops in Australia.

1984

• Pickle Family Circus School opens.

1986

• Switzerland's Circus Knie books Lu Yi's Nanjing Acrobatic Troupe.

1987

• Judy Finelli becomes Pickle Family Circus Artistic Director.

1989

• Lu Yi leads the Nanjing Acrobatic Troupe, including Xia Ke Min and Yang Xiao Di, to New York to work with the Big Apple Circus in *Big Apple Meets the Monkey King*.

• Judy Finelli and Lu Yi meet for the first time in Stony Brook, New York.

• Judy directs the circus play *Café des Artistes*.

1990

- Lu Yi arrives in San Francisco.
- Zhou Yue and Huang Zhen arrive.
- Lu Yue and Lu Na arrive; their mother, Wang Hong Zhu, arrives two years later.
- Lu Yi trains the cast of *La La Luna Sea* and starts the San Francisco Youth Circus.

1991

- Xia Ke Min, his wife Lin Qing, and their son Laurence arrive in San Francisco
- Director William Ball dies the day before joining the Pickles.
- Larry Pisoni returns to the Pickles to direct *Pickles on Parade*.

1992

- Tandy Beal and Lu Yi work together to create *Tossing and Turning*.

1993

- The Pickle Family Circus School becomes two schools: the San Francisco School of Circus Arts and Acrosports.
- Second Generation of the San Francisco Youth Circus.
- Pickle Family Circus declares bankruptcy and is purchased by Tandy Beal's Friends of Olympia Station. Name changed to the New Pickle Circus.
- The New Pickle Circus remounts *Tossing and Turning* for a second year.

1994

- Tandy Beal and Lu Yi create their second show together: *Jump Cuts! The Circus Goes to the Movies;* it also tours for two years.
- Lu Yi, representing his company "Spring Circus," directs the first Chinese acrobatics show in Branson, Missouri; a second attempt finally closes in 1996.

1997 - 2000

• New Pickle Circus continues to create shows with performers from China, the U.S., Russia and elsewhere under the direction of Tandy Beal.

1999

• Xiaohong Weng becomes Lu Yi's assistant at the San Francisco School of Circus Arts.

2000

• The Clown Conservatory opens at the San Francisco School of Circus Arts, with Xiaohong Weng as the acrobatic teacher.
• Trapeze Arts moves to Oakland CA; Lu Yi occasionally trains students there for the next decade.

2001

• San Francisco Circus Center is created from the San Francisco School of Circus Arts and the New Pickle Circus.

2004

• Professional Acrobatic and Aerial Programs start at San Francisco Circus Center.

2008

• Circus Center clowns first trip to Nanjing to teach 20 Chinese acrobats.

2009

• Circus Center clowns perform at Wuqiao Festival.

2010

• Sweet Can circus is created; many students of Lu Yi and Xiaohong Weng perform and direct with the organization.

2014

- Lu Yi and Xia Ke Min retire from San Francisco Circus Center.
- Lu Yi starts a two year stint training students at Acrosanct, an acrobatic studio in San Francisco.

2021

- *Dear San Francisco* opens at Club Fugazi in San Francisco's North Beach neighborhood; Lu Yi takes a bow.

2023

- Lu Yi's autobiography is released: *Training is Bitter* with Devin Holt.
- Work on this book begins.
- Lu Yi dies on October 25.

May 5, 2024

- This book is completed.

October 27, 2024

- The first chapter of this book is read on stage at Club Fugazi at a special event at *Dear, San Francisco*.

REFERENCES

Abdul-Jabbar, K. (2023, December 5). *Kareem Abdul-Jabbar Official Newsletter.*

Abdul-Jabbar, K. Obstfeld, R. (2017). *Becoming Kareem: growing up on and off the court.* Little Brown Books for Young Readers.

Ala-Rashi, M. (2022). *China's Bending Bodies.* (T. Wall, Ed.) Modern Vaudeville Press.

Albrecht E. (2009, Spring). Lu Yi. A tour of Chinese acrobatics. *Spectacle. A Quarterly Journal of the Circus Arts.* (12).

American Circus Educators. American Youth Circus Organization. (2022). *Circus Census 2022 Final Report.* Retrieved February 13, 2024, from https://www.americancircuseducators.org/wp-content/uploads/2022/10/ACE-AYCO-Survey-Final-Report.pdf.

Byamba, S. Serchmaa Byamba. Retrieved February 13, 2024, from https://www.mongoliancontortion.com/.

Carter. J. (2021, July 21). *Power of Symbolism: The swim that changed Chinese history.* The China Project.

Chen, K.B., Cortez, J. *Legacy of the Neighborhood Arts Program.* FoundSF. https://www.foundsf.org/index.php?title=Legacy_of_the_Neighborhood_Arts_Program

Chu, L. (2020). *Eat a Bowl of Tea.* University of Washington Press.

Circus Harmony. Retrieved February 13, 2024, from https://circusharmony.org/

Denworth, L. (2023, July 1). *Brain waves synchronize when people interact. The minds of social species are strikingly resonant.* The Scientific American.

Flocken, C. (1996, January 18). You Ought to be in Pickles: the circus goes to the movies, older audiences get reeled in. *Los Angeles Times.*

Foley, A. (2021). *The Editor Function: Literary Publishing in Postwar America.* University of Minnesota Press.

Gold chains. The hidden history of slavery in California. Retrieved February 6. 2024, from https://www.aclunc.org/sites/goldchains/

Gussow M. (1988, November 4). Big Apple is Back with Daredevils and Slippery Stars. *The New York Times.*

Honis, A (2023, July 6). An interview with Shana Carroll, member of the Order Arts and Letters of Quebec. *CircusTalk.* https://circustalk.com/news/shana-carroll-member-of-the-order-of-arts-and-letters-of-quebec

Huang, Y. (2023). *Daughter of the Dragon. Anna May Wong's rendezvous with American history.* Liveright.

Janiak, L.(2023, December 16) Review: 'Kaleidoscope' is an analog circus feast amid digital HQ of SoMa. *San Francisco Chronicle.*

Lanter, O. (1987). Fun getting pickled: The Pickle Family Circus offers as much to its performers as it does to its audience. There are no prima donnas. *Juggler's World,* 39 (1). http://www.juggling.org/jw/87/1/pickle.html

Lazarus E. (2002). "The New Colossus" In *Emma Lazarus: Selected poems and other writings.* Broadview Press.

Lei, D. (2003). The production and consumption of Chinese theatre in nineteenth-century California. *Theatre Research International.* 28(3), 289-302. https://doi.org/10.1017/S0307883303001147

Light A. (2023, November 3). Rock'n'Soul: The amazing story of Sly & the Family Stone. *The New York Times.*

Lorant, T. Carroll, J. (1986). *The Pickle Family Circus.* The Pickle Press.

Lu, Yi., Holt, D. (2023). *Training is Bitter.* Periodgraph Press.

Mykaltlewis1. (2015, May 17). Pickle Family Circus *"Pickles on Parade" Highlights.* [Video]. YouTube. https://www.youtube.com/watch?v=TuJboxja3O8

National Archives. *The Chinese Exclusion Act* (1882). https://www.archives.gov/milestone-documents/chinese-exclusion-act

Ngai M. (2023, December 11). Anti-Chinese Laws are on the Rise. We've Been Through This Before. *The New York. Times.*

Pierson, D. (2023, December 25). Mongolians are Circus Stars All Over the World, except at home. *The New York Times.*

Pierson, D. Swanson, A. Sanger, D. E. (2023, November 17). A Rare Opportunity to See China's Leader Up Close and (sort of) Personal. *The New York Times*.

Prescott Circus Theater. Retrieved February 13, 2024, from https://www.prescottcircus.org/about-us/our-work/.

Q with Tom Power. (2024, January 8). *Colman Domingo on his journey from circus performer to civil rights leader Bayard Rustin*. [Video]. YouTube. https://www.youtube.com/watch?v=qUgx0eGxwXk

Raz, J (2017). *The Secret Life of Clowns: a backstage tour of Cirque du Soleil and the Clown Conservatory*. Adams Court Press.

Raz, J. (2018). *The Snow Clown: cartwheels on borders from Alaska to Nebraska*. Adams Court Press.

Ryan, M., DeKornfeld, O., Yi, E. (2017, December 17). *Dancing in the Air with 9-foot Stilts* https://www.nytimes.com/video/style/100000005271902/dancing-trinidad-stilts.html.

Samels, M. (Executive Producer). (2018). *American experience: The Circus*. [TV miniseries] A Winter Pink Films Production; PBS. https://www.pbs.org/wgbh/americanexperience/films/circus/

San Francisco's Pickle Family Circus (1990, May). *La La Luna Sea*. [Program]. San Francisco, California.

Schechter J. (2001). *The Pickle Clowns: New American Circus Comedy*. Southern Illinois University Press.

Schiffman J. (1994, January). The Pickles Take Over the Circus. *American Theatre Magazine*.

Shepard, R.F. (1998, December 18). Monkey King Under the Big Top. *The New York Times*.

Soule, F. Gihon, J. Nisbet, J. Garcia H.E. (1998). *The Annals of San Francisco* Berkeley Hills Books.

Shirley D. (1992, October 21). Stage Reviews: Insomnia is Fun and Games for Pickle Circus. *Los Angeles Times*.

Taylor R. (1993, December 26). *Exuberant Pickle Acrobats Full of Juice*. Santa Rosa Press Democrat.

Tandy Beal & Company. Retrieved Retrieved February 13, 2024, from https://www.tandybeal.com/history

Tarnopolsky, M. (2023, November 16). American musicians are doing something profound in Beijing right now. *The New York Times*.

Qifeng, F. (1985). *Chinese Acrobatics Through the Ages* (Traditional Chinese arts and culture). China Books and Periodicals.

Wall, T. *(2019). Juggling - From Antiquity to the Middle Ages: the forgotten history of throwing and catching*. Modern Vaudeville Press.

Wasnak D. (2022, May 30). *Pino & Razz "Tossing & Turning" 1992 Pickle Family Circus*. [Video]. YouTube. https://www.youtube.com/watch?v=a5UbgwxV_ZA.

Winn, S. (1995, December 12). Pickle Circus Goes Off to the Movies. *San Francisco Chronicle*.

Winship, F.M. (1988, October 31). Big Apple Circus goes Oriental. *UPI*.

Wolff, C. (1989, August 9). 4 Chinese Acrobats Vanish as Interpreter Seeks Asylum. *The New York Times*.

Wu, C. Jenner, W.J.F. (2005). *Journey to the West*. (C. Fair, Ed.). Disruptive Pub.

Zhang, T.Y. (2016). Bending the Body for China: the uses of acrobatics in Sino-US diplomacy during the Cold War. *Int J Cultural Policy. (22), 123-146*. https://doi.org/10.1080/10286632.2014.956665.

Zhang, T. (2016). From China to the Big Top: Chinese acrobats and the politics of aesthetic labor, 1950 - 2010. *International Labor and Working-Class History*. (89), 40-63. https://doi.org/10.1017/S0147547915000332.

INTERVIEWS

These were conducted by Jeff Raz, Stephanie Greenspan, and Ori Doria-Quesada. Information quoted but not cited in the footnotes is from these sources. Dom Cruz also recorded an interview with his father answering our questions.

Y. Lu, personal communication, March 21, 2023

D. Cruz and D. Henderson, personal communication, April 7, 2023

Y. Lu, personal communication, April 9, 2023

M. Henderson and M. Kesselman, personal communication, April 14, 2023

Y. Lu and Y. Lu, personal communication, April 18, 2023

Y. Lu and Y. Lu, personal communication, May 1, 2023

D. Jando, personal communication, May 10, 2023

D. Wasnak, personal communication, May 10, 2023

D. Wasnak, personal communication, May 15, 2023

X. Weng, personal communication, May 18, 2023

N. Lu and Y. Lu, personal communication, May 21, 2023

O. Oppenheimer and R. Oppenheimer, personal communication, May 21, 2023

J. Finelli, personal communication, May 23, 2023

X. Weng, personal communication, May 24, 2023

J.Finelli, personal communication, May 28, 2023

J. Raz and S. Greenspan, personal communication, May 30, 2023

K. Quest, personal communication, June 1, 2023

J. Finelli, personal communication, June 1, 2023

X. Weng, personal communication, June 8, 2023

B. Henderson and S. Henderson, personal communication, June 9, 2023

W. Parkman, personal communication, June 20, 2023

F. Cruz and W. Underwood, personal communication, July 14, 2023

J. McKowan, personal communication, July 19, 2023

C. Orrick, personal communication, July 19, 2023

S. Carroll, personal communication, July 27, 2023

J. Vik, personal communication, July 29, 2023

H. Zhen, personal communication, July 31, 2023

J. Gilkey, personal communication, July 31, 2023

K. Sonkin, personal communication, August 1, 2023

J. Katz, personal communication, August 14, 2023

A. Munn, personal communication, August 31, 2023

D. McGee, personal communication, September 1, 2023

C. Kai Ku, personal communication, September 7, 2023

S. Greenspan, personal communication, September 7, 2023

O. Quesada, personal communication, September 8, 2023

G.R. Lu, personal communication, September 19, 2023

K.M. Xia, personal communication, September 23, 2023

S. Zenov, personal communication, October 8, 2023

D. Wyss, personal communication, October 16, 2023

A. Gavre, personal communication, October 31, 2023

P. Snider, personal communication, November 7, 2023

A. O'Shea, personal communication, November 12, 2023

F. Flanco, personal communication, November 25, 2023

L. Tipton, personal communication, November 25, 2023

T. Beal, personal communication, December 4, 2023

X. Weng, personal communication, December 6. 2023

F. Cruz, personal communication, December 10, 2023 (by Dom Cruz)

D. Wyss, personal communication, December 10, 2023

B. Forchion, personal communication, January 2, 2024

F. Hesed, personal communication, January 10, 2024

B. Belasco, personal communication, January 11, 2024

O. Quesada, personal communication, January 15, 2024

A. Moffitt, personal communication, February 26, 2024

B. Kibbe, personal communication, April 18, 2024

ACKNOWLEDGEMENTS

A huge thank you to all the people we interviewed. You invited us into your homes, met us at neighborhood coffee shops, sent us long emails and connected on Zoom from halfway around the world. You were vulnerable and open, you trusted us with your stories and you shared intimate, and sometimes challenging, moments in your lives and in your relationships with Lu Yi. Together, you gave us a vibrant picture of life in the circus arts. And, along with the writers we quoted, you gave us the historical facts, the emotions of the moment and the rich, surprising details that animate this book. This project would not have been possible without you.

A special thanks to Lu Yi and Judy Finelli, and the Lu and Xia families—Wang Hong Zhu, Lu Yue and Lu Na; Xia Ke Min, Lin Qing and Laurence Xia—who guided us from start, and to editor/publisher Thom Wall and writer/historian Mariam Ala-Rashi who guided us down the home stretch.

Thank you to San Francisco Circus Center for hosting Lu Yi's memorial, and Brad Post for organizing it, to Gypsy Snider, Shana Carroll and David Dower for honoring Lu Yi and his family's legacy in a show at Club Fugazi that featured guest appearances by many of the acrobats quoted in this book, to Tandy Beal and Diane Wasnak for fact checking the Pickle Circus cast lists, to the dear friends who gave feedback on early drafts—Johannes Mager, dede moyse, Peter Anderson, Gene Kahane and Zofia Burr—and to our families of birth and our families of choice for supporting us through this process.

Finally, we acknowledge and thank the hundreds of people who were part of the Nanjing/San Francisco affair between 1990 and 2010 who do not appear on these pages. This is not the last word, the full story or the complete history, and we hope this book inspires others to bring new points of view, new ideas and new stories to this rich and ongoing history.

ABOUT THE AUTHOR

JEFF RAZ has written twenty plays as well as three novels—*The Circus Trilogy*—inspired by his career performing in circuses (Pickle Family Circus, Cirque du Soleil, and more) and in theaters, including Shakespeare's Comedy of Errors on Broadway. He co-founded The Clown Conservatory at Circus Center San Francisco in 2000 and the Medical Clown Project in 2010.

Jeff continues to write, perform, direct, teach and work as communications and leadership consultant from his home in Alameda, California.

Other Books by Jeff Raz:

The Secret Life of Clowns: a Backstage Tour of Cirque du Soleil and The Clown Conservatory.
Adams Court Press, 2016.

The Snow Clown: Cartwheels on Borders from Alaska to Nebraska.
Adams Court Press, 2018.

Love Death Circus.
Adams Court Press, 2020.

Other Books by Devin Holt:

Training is Bitter: Reflections on Life, Effort and Acrobatics.
Periodgraph Press, 2023. (Written with Lu Yi.)

Performing Arts Research Publications by Dr. Stephanie Greenspan:

Preparation for flight: the physical profile of pre-professional
and professional circus artists in the United States.
International Journal of Sports Physical Therapy, 2024. (With Melanie Stuckey.)

Untangling risk factors including discipline-specific exposure for
pre-professional and professional circus artists in the USA.
BMJ Open Sport & Exercise Medicine, 2023. (With Melanie Stuckey.)

Circus-specific extension of the International Olympic Committee 2020 consensus
statement: methods for recording and reporting of epidemiological
data on injury and illness in sport.
BMJ Open Sport & Exercise Medicine, 2022. (With David Munro, Joanna Nicholas, Janine
Stubbe, Melanie Stuckey and Rogier Van Rijn.)

Injury patterns in subgroups of circus artists by circus discipline: a pilot study.
Orthopaedic Physical Therapy Practice, 2022.

Management of hypermobility in aesthetic performing artists: a review.
Orthopaedic Physical Therapy Practice, 2022. (With Aiko Callahan and Anna Squires.)

Amount and characteristics of injuries in adolescent and adult circus artists:
A prospective observational pilot study.
Medical Problems in Performing Artists, 2021.

OTHER BOOKS BY MODERN VAUDEVILLE PRESS

Juggling: What It Is and How to Do It

Thom Wall, et. al.
ISBN – 978-1-7339712-5-6
224 pages
MSRP: $25 USD

Juggling: What It Is and How to Do It teaches learners of all ages how to juggle – one of the world's oldest artforms. With a kind demeanor, humor, and enthusiasm, this authoritative manual explains the process of juggling through four different modalities, bolstered by the latest physical education research.

Juggling is an accessible primer that a middle-schooler can hit the ground running with, or that families can enjoy together. The result of six years of work by 2021 International Jugglers' Association *Excellence in Education* award winner and former Cirque du Soleil juggler Thom Wall and featuring guest chapters by some of today's juggling masters, *Juggling* provides great content for even the most serious adult learner.

Juggling: From Antiquity to the Middle Ages

Thom Wall
ISBN – 978-0578410845
129 pages
MSRP: $25 USD

As with dance, so with juggling—the moment that the performer finishes the routine, their act ceases to exist beyond the memory of the audience. There is no permanent record of what transpired, so studying the ancient roots of juggling is fraught with difficulty. Using the records that do exist, juggling appears to have emerged around the world in cultures independent of one another in the ancient past. Paintings in Egypt from 2000 BCE show jugglers engaged in performance. Stories from the island nation of Tonga place juggling's creation with their goddess of the underworld—a figure who has guarded a cave since time immemorial. Juggling games and rituals are pervasive in isolated Inuit cultures in northern Canada and Greenland. Though the earliest representation of juggling is 4,000 years old, the practice is surely much older—in the same way that humans were doubtlessly singing and dancing long before the first bone flute was created.

This book is an attempt to catalogue this tangible history of juggling in human culture. It is the story of juggling, represented in art and writing from around the world, across time. Although much has been written about modern jugglers–specific performers, their props, and their routines–little has been said about those who first developed the craft. As juggling enters a golden age in the internet era, *Juggling: From Antiquity to the Middle Ages* offers a look into the past—to the origins of our art form.

Artistes of Colour

Steve Ward, PhD
ISBN – 978-1-7339712-7-0
317 pages
MSRP: $25 USD

In a society that places an increasing value in ethnic diversity and cultural identity, the contribution that performers from a variety of ethnic backgrounds made to the development of the circus in the nineteenth century is often dismissed and largely forgotten. Using contemporary records and images, *Artistes of Colour* explores the wealth and depth of talented black and other performers of colour, and their contributions to the success of the nineteenth century circus. Ward draws iconic figures from the margins of history and gives them the recognition they deserve. Long-listed for the American Society for Theatre Research 2022 Book Award.

Body Talk: Basic Mime

Mario Diamond
ISBN – 978-1733971218
73 pages
MSRP: $15 USD

Body Talk: Basic Mime covers the fundamental skills of mime in an easily accessible workbook format. Diamond brings over 40 years of teaching and performance experience to *Body Talk*, which includes rich photography illustrating various mime techniques.

"[*Body Talk: Basic Mime*] should be required reading for any theater participant looking to incorporate elements of mime into their routines." - *Midwest Book Review*

Circus Games (v1.1)

Compiled by Lucy Little & the American Youth Circus Organization (AYCO)
ISBN – 9781733971225
124 pages
MSRP: $15 USD

With over 100 games organized for optimal use in cooperative movement based settings, this is a must have for every circus school, teaching artist, and arts education program! Games are organized by age, number of participants, energy level, and social/emotional learning outcome, and also includes special notes for working with a variety of populations that may require adaptation or modifications to each game. Find more info about the project here:
https://www.americancircuseducators.org/gamesproject/

The ABC Tour

Jon Udry
ISBN – 978-0578410852
MSRP: $25 USD

Ever felt like a challenge? For juggler and comedian, Jon Udry, the ABC Tour — 26 letters, 26 shows — seems the perfect way to shake things up.

What started as a silly idea he believed would take two to three months to complete, ended up being a mammoth three year project that included some of the toughest, most brutal and most enjoyable performances of his life.

From attempting to juggle while wearing roller skates and the unexpected discoveries of performing at a Naturist's Resort, to the challenges that came with working in rainforest conditions covered in ants or in snowy conditions at -10°C, Jon tells the full story from A to Z.

Circus Training Journal

Thom Wall & Rebecca Starr,
Consultant editor: Sarah Baker
ISBN – 978-1-7339712-9-4
9×6" paperback
380 pages
MSRP: $20 USD

What's measured is managed! The *Circus Training Journal* is the result of a year of collaboration between Thom Wall and Rebecca Starr, aerial coach. This undated journal, spanning three months of daily training, tracks workouts, nutrition, goal-setting, and more. Heavyweight paper optimized for ballpoint and pencil.

Juggling: Or How to Become a Juggler (annotated edition)

Rupert Ingalese, annotated by Thom Wall
ISBN – 978-1733971201
99 pages
MSRP: $15 USD

The fully annotated edition of Rupert Ingalese's 1921 "how to juggle" manual. This book covers basic juggling technique, tricks with hats and canes, practice methodology, and more. Ingalese's manuscript provides an interesting look at the state of juggling pedagogy in Britain's music hall era. Annotations by juggler and circus researcher Thom Wall bring insight and context to Ingalese's descriptions and instructions.

Pottery in Motion

Sam Veale
ISBN – 978-1733971232
71 pages
MSRP: $15 USD

British juggler Sam Veale's *Pottery in Motion* is the first of its kind - a straightforward book that provides aspiring plate spinners both the specifics of the props (such as plates, sticks, and rack) and comprehensive instruction on the skill of plate spinning itself. This small but detail-packed guide appeals to individuals looking to learn plate spinning and provides the knowledge to take it to a performance-ready level, just add practice.

Contortion and Practices of Body Flexibility in East Asia - Mongolia, China, Japan

Mariam Ala-Rashi
ISBN – 978-1-958604-04-5
MSRP: $25 USD

A collection of three monographs: *China's Bending Bodies: Contortionists and Politics in China; Mongolian Contortion: An Ethnographic Inquiry;* and *The Kakubei Jishi: The Rise, Fall, and Restoration of a Japanese Folk Performing Art.*

This compendium examines contortion and practices of body flexibility in East Asia. It explores the performance art forms Chinese contortion, Mongolian contortion and the Kakubei Jishi lion dance of the Niigata prefecture in Japan which utilizes body flexibility. It discusses the investigation of the history and genesis of these art forms and how they developed in various political and social dynamics. This work further offers vast knowledge about crucial elements such as the artist's training processes, their training environment, the development of aesthetics, symbolism in costuming and body movements, religious themes, mythology and natural phenomena, and costume designs. This compendium includes data from a wide range of literature, material evidence, oral history, current media reports, and considers recent work in anthropology, archaeology, and political history. It offers the interested reader, the scholar, the contortionist and contortion practitioner a substantial treatise about contortionism and practices of body flexibility.

The Contemporary Circus Handbook: A guide to creating, funding, producing, organizing and touring shows for the 21st century

Eric Bates
ISBN – 978-1-958604-03-8
MSRP: $25 USD

The Contemporary Circus Handbook contains interviews with more than 25 professionals, from Gypsy Snider of the celebrated contemporary circus company The Seven Fingers to Lydia Bouchard of La Resistance about their work in the performing arts world. Combining Eric Bates' (Cie Barcode, Cirque du Soleil, et. al.) hard won wisdom as well as tips and insights from his contemporaries, what emerges is an invaluable blueprint of how to progress from the seed of an idea for a show to the full touring timeline. The scope of the book is wide but deeply hands-on, diving into practical details on how to find an agent, start your own company, secure funding and build your niche brand. *The Contemporary Circus Handbook* truly is a unique offering to the circus world, full of insider tips and years of accumulated knowledge from industry insiders.

Opulence & Ostentation

Steve Ward, PhD
ISBN – 978-1-958604-02-1
MSRP: $25 USD

Since the foundation of the 'modern' circus in the eighteenth century, the circus has been presented in defined spaces. Initially, performances were given in the open air and, over a period of time, these spaces first became enclosed and then later roofed. In the nineteenth century, many permanent stone-built buildings were erected solely for the purpose of presenting circus. This phenomenon spread from the UK across Europe and beyond, creating a style of circus architecture that has never been repeated. The purpose of this book is to examine what caused these buildings to be constructed and their design and architecture. Examples of key structures will be explored in detail, some of them still surviving today and still being used for circus performances. The book will also look at the developments of contemporary circus architecture and raise questions as to the future of the circus building.

Cleverer Than God

CLEVERER
THAN
GOD

ERIK ÅBERG

Erik Åberg
ISBN – 978-1958604113
MSRP: $25 USD

Cleverer Than God is a book that tells the story of Paul Cinquevalli, a juggler who rose from the Circus circuit of the 1880s, to attain celebrity status in the British Music Hall and American vaudeville stages until the outbreak of WWI. Through quotes by Cinquevalli himself, woven together with excerpts from journalists and writers of his era, the book tells his story as poignant fragments, capturing the essence of Cinquevalli's triumphs, defining moments, and heart-rending tragedies.

BADGE BOOK

Youth Juggling Academy

The Juggler's Badge Book

Author: Benjamin Domask-Ruh
Editors: Thayer Slichter, Afton Benson
Illustrators: Thayer Slichter and Louis Skaradek
ISBN – 978-1-958604-19-9
MSRP: $25 USD

Introducing *The Juggler's Badge Book*, the ultimate companion for aspiring jugglers! Track your progress, unlock achievements, and earn badges as you learn the art of juggling. With its engaging format and rewarding sticker system, *The Juggler's Badge Book* makes learning to juggle an exciting and fulfilling adventure. Whether you're a beginner or a seasoned juggler, let *The Juggler's Badge Book* be your guide to skillful juggling and a collection of well-earned accomplishments. Start achieving your juggling journey today with this activity book from the Youth Juggling Academy, a program of the International Jugglers' Association!

Published in collaboration between the
International Jugglers' Association and Modern Vaudeville Press.

Coming Soon:

Captain George

Amelia Osterud with Fritz Grobe
MSRP: $25 USD
Coming in 2024!

He appeared out of the blue in Vienna, covered from head to toe in Burmese tattoos. Then, as the Golden Age of American circus began, P. T. Barnum made him the most famous tattooed performer of all time. He said he had been a pirate and a patriot, a rebel and a slave. He claimed he had been tortured by an evil Tatar despot, tattooed by a vengeful sailor in Kashgar, or inked by a princess in Turkistan. Captain George Costentenus told so many outrageous and conflicting tales – what is the truth?

By Royal Command: Barnum in Europe

Steve Ward, PhD
Edited by Thom Wall
MSRP: $25 USD
Projected Release: Winter 2024

Everybody seems to have heard of the name Phineas T Barnum. He is, without a doubt, a world-wide celebrity known for being an entrepreneur, a showman, and the 'king of humbug'. But Barnum was a complex character, driven by the ambition to be the best. He was a self-promoter and when he toured Europe with his protégé Tom Thumb, he sought royal approval, both in England and in Europe. By Royal Command charts the progress of this tour with all its ups and downs, its triumphs and disasters, that would enshrine Barnum as being the most well-known and wealthiest showman of the age.

The Century's Juggler

Reinhold Batburger, translated by
Kathrin Wagner, edited by Thom Wall
MSRP: $25 USD
Projected release: Winter 2024

He throws a ball in the air and makes millions. And millions of people watch – and did for more than fifty years.

His performance takes seven minutes, and that's his life. Reinhold Batberger tells a family story – the story of a world career, the story of the life and art of juggler Francis Brunn (1922-2004).

MVP Mission

Modern Vaudeville Press is a mission-driven, artist-owned independent publishing company. We strive to build a platform for unique nonfiction titles in juggling, circus, vaudeville, and related fields. MVP aims to drive the conversation about circus forward by increasing accessibility to high-quality titles about the history and instruction of circus arts.

Our award-winning books are carried in shops on four continents, as well as by many large online retailers.

Oleg Popov Bookplate. G. Kravtzov. 1968.